IN FROM THE COLD

THE REPORT *of the* TWENTIETH CENTURY FUND TASK FORCE ON THE FUTURE OF U.S. INTELLIGENCE

IN FROM THE COLD

Background Papers by

Allan E. Goodman ◆ *Gregory F. Treverton* ◆ *Philip Zelikow*

1996 ◆ The Twentieth Century Fund Press ◆ New York

The Twentieth Century Fund sponsors and supervises timely analyses of economic policy, foreign affairs, and domestic political issues. Not-for-profit and nonpartisan, the Fund was founded in 1919 and endowed by Edward A. Filene.

Library of Congress Cataloging-in-Publication Data

Twentieth Century Fund. Task Force on the Future of U.S. Intelligence.
    In from the cold : the report of the Twentieth Century Fund Task Force on the Future of U.S. Intelligence / with background papers by Allan E. Goodman, Gregory F. Treverton, Philip Zelikow.
        p. cm.
    Includes index.
    ISBN 0-87078-392-0
    1. Intelligence service--United States. I. Goodman, Allan E., 1944- . II. Treverton, Gregory F. III. Zelikow, Philip, 1954- .
    IV. Title.
    JK468.I6T94 1996
    327.1273--dc20   96-24244
                                                                                  CIP

Cover design and illustration: Claude Goodwin
Manufactured in the United States of America.

❚ Foreword

I t would be remarkable if the arrangements that were put in place for intelligence gathering and analysis during the decades of the cold war matched our needs today. Instead, it is likely that the perception of American interests that has been evolving since 1989 will result in significant changes in the missions, structures, and budgets of all the key elements that comprise America's national security organization.

The post-cold war shifts have already resulted in a number of major studies of the intelligence community, including those by the Presidential Commission on the Roles and Responsibilities of the U.S. Intelligence Community, the House Permanent Subcommittee on Intelligence, and the Council on Foreign Relations. Taken together, these reports provide a substantial base of information and impressive menu of possible reforms. Still, informed opinion overwhelmingly holds that many of the important questions about the intelligence agencies have yet to be addressed. The reasons for this view are complex, but they certainly include the popular impression that the intelligence community is mismanaged, ripe for budget cuts, and only of limited usefulness to policymakers.

These criticisms of the intelligence community are in large part a result of newsworthy events over the past few years—the failure to foresee the collapse of the Soviet Union, the Aldrich Ames debacle, the disappearance of several billion dollars in the National Security Agency budget, and other embarrassments. Those developments were important and deserve remedial responses. But the Twentieth Century Fund created its Task Force on the Future of U.S. Intelligence to answer more fundamental, if less sensational, questions about the intelligence community: How has the mission changed? How good a job is it doing? How well does the present structure work? What will be required to meet the changing needs of the nation and its leaders?

Our group was modest about its ability to answer fully any of these important inquiries, especially because it had no access to classified information. Still, building on the experience and knowledge of a diverse, bipartisan membership, it was able to reach several important conclusions. As a first step, the Task Force reached consensus on the continuing need for a first-rate intelligence operation—and one that is not dramatically dissimilar from what we have today. In this context, the Task Force also felt that much of the public focus on clandestine operations, covert action, and accountability had already improved conditions somewhat and could be expected to do so to a greater extent in the foreseeable future.

But the Task Force also discerned basic problems that merit far greater attention. Foremost among them is the intelligence community's increasing preoccupation with military priorities since the Soviet Union's collapse, which has coincided with a decline in the usefulness of intelligence to civilian policymakers. To help strike a more equitable balance between the military and civilian needs of the government, the Task Force proposes specific recommendations for strengthening what it perceives to be four pervasive shortcomings: 1) the atrophying analytic capabilities of the intelligence community and U.S. foreign policy agencies; 2) the lack of productive and effective interactions between the intelligence community and civilian officials who make foreign policy decisions; 3) a clandestine service whose costs have too often exceeded its benefits; and 4) poorly organized, unfocused, and often mediocre economic intelligence efforts.

The Task Force, which was ably chaired by Ambassador Stephen Bosworth, benefited from the work of the three authors of the background papers that appear in this volume: Allan E. Goodman, associate dean of Georgetown University's School of Foreign Service; Gregory F. Treverton, director of the International Security and Defense Policy Center at RAND; and Philip Zelikow, associate professor of public policy at the John F. Kennedy School of Government at Harvard University. Allan Goodman's paper lays out the main issues that the intelligence community faces in the wake of the cold war. Greg Treverton's work examines how and why military concerns have increasingly dominated the intelligence agenda while exploring in depth the role of technological resources for collecting information. Philip Zelikow's paper presents the first extensive analysis of how economic intelligence has evolved, incorporating case studies that illustrate past successes and failures in order to glean lessons for the future from those experiences. All three authors also helped to draft the Report of the Task Force. The Fund is grateful for their efforts.

The Twentieth Century Fund has supported a number of works in the area of intelligence and national security affairs, including Morton Halperin and Daniel Hoffman's *Top Secret: National Security and the Right to Know*, Richard Morgan's *Domestic Intelligence: Monitoring Dissent in America*, Walter Laqueur's *A World of Secrets: The Uses and Limitations of Intelligence*, and most recently, *The Need to Know: The Report of the Twentieth Century Fund Task Force on Covert Action and American Democracy*.

One problem is intrinsic to the very nature of many intelligence activities: they are secret. That simple fact opens a permanent gulf between the intelligence community and the rest of the nation. The width of that gulf, however, can vary from time to time, depending both on the unanimity of public support for intelligence activities (at its highest, obviously, in war time) and the shifting standards of public disclosure and accountability (which are probably more extensive than they have ever been right now). We believe that this Task Force Report will add considerably to the public's understanding of how intelligence ought to serve U.S. national security interests.

RICHARD C. LEONE, PRESIDENT
The Twentieth Century Fund
June 1996

Contents

MEMBERS OF THE TASK FORCE

Ambassador Stephen W. Bosworth, *Task Force Chair*
Executive Director, Korean Peninsula Energy
Development Organization

Mort Abramowitz
President, Carnegie Endowment for International Peace

Christopher Andrew
Professor, Corpus Christi College, Cambridge University

Henry S. Bienen
President, Northwestern University

Brewster C. Denny
Professor and Dean Emeritus, University of Washington

I. M. Destler
Professor, School of Public Affairs
Director, Center for International and Security Studies, University of
Maryland

Rita E. Hauser
International Lawyer, President, The Hauser Foundation

Jane Holl
Executive Director, Carnegie Commission on Preventing Deadly Conflict

Richard J. Kerr
Former Deputy Director, Central Intelligence Agency

David McCurdy
Chairman, The McCurdy Group
Former U.S. Congressman and Chairman of the House Intelligence Committee

Matthew Nimetz
Partner, Paul, Weiss, Rifkind, Wharton & Garrison

Janne Nolan
Senior Fellow, Brookings Institution

Lieutenant General Harry E. Soyster
Vice President, International Operations, Military Professional Resources, Inc.
Former Director, Defense Intelligence Agency

Gregory F. Treverton, *Background Paper Author*
Director, International Security and Defense Policy Center, RAND Corporation

Clifton R. Wharton, Jr.
Former Deputy Secretary of State, U.S. Department of State

Philip Zelikow, *Background Paper Author*
Associate Professor of Public Policy, John F. Kennedy School of Government, Harvard University

Robert Zoellick
Executive Vice President and General Counsel, Federal National Mortgage Association

Mortimer B. Zuckerman
Chairman, Boston Properties

Allan E. Goodman, *Task Force Executive Director and Background Paper Author*
Associate Dean, School of Foreign Service, Georgetown University

REPORT OF THE TASK FORCE

The Soviet Union's collapse eliminated the central organizing principle of American foreign policy—and the preoccupation of U.S. intelligence since World War II. More than five years later, fundamental questions remain unanswered. What are the nation's foreign policy priorities? What do senior government officials most need from the intelligence community? How can intelligence help lead to better decisionmaking?

The cold war may be over, but in many ways the world remains dangerous. Weapons of mass destruction—nuclear, biological, and chemical—are spreading, as well as their kin, deadly conventional weaponry. Terrorism respects no boundaries. Nor do organized crime and drug trafficking. Ethnic groups come more frequently into conflict in places with potentially important but unfamiliar implications for U.S. interests. Global economics are taking the world onto unexplored terrain, creating new opportunities but also new hazards that need to be understood. The United States would be ill-equipped to address these challenges without intelligence, including information provided by secret sources.

Our nation's intelligence community was organized to gather an amazing amount of secret data—from satellites and spies—mostly about the Soviet Union. We protected that data. We counted it. We stored it. Now, much less of the world is denied to us, and a torrent of information has become available to anyone with a computer. Today,

3

organizing and correctly understanding that information has become at least as important as collecting it.

In this new world, as in the days of the cold war, the president of the United States and the secretary of state must bear the responsibility for ensuring that intelligence effectively serves American interests. They set the nation's foreign policy goals and priorities. A lack of clarity about those goals and priorities at the top directly reduces the value of intelligence efforts that are supposed to support our foreign policy aims. If the priorities of policymakers are unclear, the intelligence community will be uncertain about what it is expected to deliver and will exert its energies toward efforts that may be ignored. Indeed, that too often has been the case in recent years.

For all these reasons, the Twentieth Century Fund convened a Task Force on the Future of U.S. Intelligence. Its central conclusion: the intelligence community is not fulfilling its mission. America's leaders often do not get the information they want, and what they do get is all too frequently not very helpful. Even when they get the right information, it may be without the context or insight that would make it useful to decisionmakers. At the same time, the policymakers who receive intelligence are failing to communicate effectively their needs to the community and generally make poor use of the intelligence resources available to them.

The recently released report of the Presidential Commission on the Roles and Capabilities of the U.S. Intelligence Community, under the chairmanship of Harold Brown, and the Report of the House Permanent Subcommittee on Intelligence, chaired by Representative Larry Combest of Texas, contained some useful recommendations. But those reports and other recent studies, in our view, posed questions too narrowly. Reshaping intelligence is not a task just for the director of central intelligence (DCI) and the intelligence community. At issue, rather, are America's eyes and ears for detecting, and its mind for comprehending, U.S. interests in an uncertain world. The president, in partnership most especially with the secretary of state, must ensure that the intelligence community serves what he defines to be the nation's foreign policy priorities. And the agencies that develop and carry out foreign policy—the Departments of State, Defense, Treasury, and Commerce; the Office of the U.S. Trade Representative; and the National Security Council and the National Economic Council—must be fully engaged in efforts to make the best use of all possible sources of knowledge available through intelligence but not confined to it.

Other studies have not paid enough attention to the most important structural feature of America's intelligence community now that the cold war is over: the increasing dominance of military needs in the intelligence process. Technical intelligence collection is almost entirely controlled by the Defense Department, and the civilian Central Intelligence Agency devotes more and more of its resources to supporting military operations. While much lip service is paid to meeting the needs of civilian policymakers who focus on international political, economic, and social questions, few steps have been taken to address their needs better. The value of what policymakers actually receive may have even declined in recent years.

The Task Force believes that, first and foremost, a more equitable balance must be struck between military and civilian needs. That fundamental shift should be pursued in conjunction with four essential changes that would strengthen the nation's intelligence community and our government's knowledge about questions vital to our national interest:

▲   **The atrophying analytic capabilities of the intelligence community and foreign policy agencies must be reinvigorated.** Satellites and eavesdroppers cannot answer all the questions, including some of the most portentous ones, for example: What course would a new Russian president pursue? Will China become more aggressive militarily? Analyzing a wide assortment of public and secret information is essential to guiding policymakers about the necessary context within which to formulate policy.

▲   **The interactions between the intelligence community and officials who make foreign policy decisions need to be vastly more productive and effective.** A variety of efforts must be made to ensure that senior officials, civilian and military, receive the information and analysis they need, when they need it. Reversing the long decline of the State Department and better integrating intelligence into the policymaking process are essential steps.

▲   **The clandestine service, the source of the CIA's long stream of publicized embarrassments but an essential national security**

resource, must be significantly improved and streamlined. Plagued by a string of failures that put its credibility at risk, the CIA's Directorate of Operations requires a fundamental review to decide more precisely what secrets it needs to collect and how, as well as ways to enhance the quality of personnel.

▲ **Economic intelligence needs to be upgraded and focused more sharply on those questions where it is most likely to add value.** Economic intelligence is poorly understood. Usually equated with industrial espionage or with trade negotiations, economic intelligence judgments cover a far broader array of questions that are critical to almost every national security problem, from Libyan chemical weapons to the future of China to the stability of world currency markets to money laundering of drug traffickers. The issue is not whether the CIA spies on foreign companies to help America's own corporations. It does not and should not. What is at issue is how well the government understands the economic forces at work around the world, how such forces influence and are influenced by political and social developments, and how those interactions affect threats, opportunities, and priorities in other nations.

STRENGTHENING ANALYSIS

The cold war legacy for the intelligence community is the concentration of more than 90 percent of its budget—reportedly $29 billion in fiscal year 1996—on the collection of information. Most of that money pays for satellites and other costly technology that detect electronic signals and images. The Defense Department operates most of those systems, and priority is given to answering questions about battlefields or potential foes, including the location of enemy troops, weapons stockpiles, and other possible targets.

This concentration on the support of military operations is not sinister. The technical collection systems were in place when the Soviet Union collapsed; finding a new purpose for them was only logical. And technology had advanced to make support for military activities possible and increasingly useful. For example, ten years ago satellites could not pinpoint the location of an Iraqi tank column in time to be of help to a U.S. commander trying to strike it. Now they can. Moreover, unlike the heads of civilian agencies, defense leaders have actively sought to bend intelligence efforts to their purposes. It is only natural that the community would respond.

But the focus on gathering information for immediate, tactical military purposes neglects the needs of civilian officials. Penetrating analyses, based on both secret and public information, can be enormously valuable in helping policymakers reach wise decisions as they negotiate agreements, assess the stability of other nations, or evaluate political forces elsewhere.

Unfortunately, government officials outside the Defense Department today do not much value the analysis they receive. Although some of the analytic work currently conducted is of high quality, policymakers too often consider intelligence analysis to be unreliable, unhelpful, or irrelevant. Intelligence competes with a plethora of other sources of information—from policymakers' own colleagues and contacts to CNN and the *New York Times* to think tanks and advocacy groups. And it often loses out in the competition. An inadequate analytic capability is hardly the CIA's problem alone. It afflicts not just intelligence agencies but the analytical functions of the Treasury and State Departments as well. The problem with analysis has become so pervasive that it will take many years to correct.

Specifically, the Task Force recommends:

▲ **Budgets for intelligence analysis should be doubled or more, even if a corresponding reduction in allocations for intelligence collection is required.** The Task Force lacked access to classified information about intelligence spending, but it is convinced that more resources for analysis are needed. The current mindset heavily favoring collection over analysis must be changed. In the information age, when masses of data are openly available, collecting more should be less of a priority than selecting which information to rely on and making sense of what is already known or knowable. The new era requires a much stronger analytic capability than we now support. We need more analysts and we need better analysts. Analysts are inexpensive compared to the costs of collection, so doubling our analytic capabilities and improving the quality of analysts, while not cheap—on the order, say, of several hundred million dollars a year—would be sensible and affordable.

▲   **The long decline of the State Department's Foreign Service capabilities must be reversed.** The diminution of the State Department, which once produced first-rate political reporting abroad and analysis at home, must at long last be turned around. Leaders of both the State Department and Congress, which holds the purse strings, need to take active steps to rekindle the Department's vital Foreign Service reporting and analytic functions. At present, they continue to weaken them.

▲   **Career incentives that currently encourage flexibility over depth and managerial experience over analytic prowess should be changed.** At the heart of the challenge of improving the quality of analysts and their analysis are career patterns and incentives. The best analysts inside government need to share in the professional status of their peers outside. They thus need to be permitted to become real experts, fluent in the languages and steeped in the cultures of other nations, with the opportunity to specialize over long periods of time, to mix easily with outside colleagues, and to publish their findings openly. To facilitate that process, the intelligence community—and the CIA in particular— needs to open itself to greater interaction with experts in other government agencies and with private scholars. Direct contacts that could be productive are too infrequent.

▲   **The National Intelligence Council (NIC), or another, similar body, should take the lead in assembling experts and interacting with outsiders.** The NIC, which works for the director of central intelligence in producing National Intelligence Estimates, already attracts some of the best analysts from both inside intelligence and outside government. It interacts with outsiders in a range of ways, from informal discussions to joint seminars. Moved to downtown Washington to be nearer its policymaking clients, given more resources and a broader mandate, and perhaps renamed, the NIC could better enable its insiders to share ideas and learn from the best minds outside government—in academia, think tanks, business, and, importantly in today's world, nongovernmental organizations.

▲   **As a long-term goal, if and when the political weather permits, a new institution based on the model of the Defense Department's**

federally funded research and development centers should be created to engage academic and private-sector analysts in intelligence analysis. Managed by the DCI for the benefit of the policy agencies that need a wider base of analytic support (like State and Treasury), the institution would take the lead in assembling networks of outside experts, commissioning them as appropriate to expand the reservoir of knowledge at hand for policymakers. These networks, including an Intelligence Reserve Officer Corps, would be especially useful for insights about countries or issues not now on the front burner that may suddenly become more important. Because the intelligence community cannot afford to commit its own scarce resources so broadly, such an institution would provide a depth of understanding about situations where the United States may face agonizing choices about committing its authority or its soldiers in places or for purposes that nobody imagined yesterday.

For the best minds outside government, the "taint" of working with intelligence has faded somewhat but still remains. So have the formidable administrative annoyances of security clearances, insistence on polygraphs, and commitments to have academic publications reviewed lest secrets inadvertently seep out. A new institution would be one step further removed from secret operations, and its work would be mostly open, diminishing whatever negative associations outsiders might have toward working on intelligence matters.

▲ **Greater sharing of analyses with foreign counterparts should be encouraged.** During the cold war, U.S. intelligence emphasized keeping secrets, not sharing them. Procedures and mindsets developed accordingly. As a result, intelligence sharing was limited, regarded as part of service-to-service relationships, mostly with fellow English speakers. Now, though, times have changed, and so should practices. The United States should take a more strategic view of intelligence sharing. Information is a powerful tool of American foreign policy and should receive the kind of attention we give to more traditional instruments of influence. Reciprocal understandings may solidify new "intelligence coalitions" on various subjects. In all probability, greater intelligence-sharing efforts will enable us to learn something from a far larger set of countries than those with which we have cooperated closely in the past.

IMPROVING THE CONNECTION BETWEEN INTELLIGENCE AND POLICY

By the test of the market, intelligence is in trouble. Policy officials, at least those outside the military, often do not value the intelligence they receive. Simply exhorting them to pay more attention will not suffice. While experienced policymakers often come to appreciate and make effective use of the intelligence community, many senior officials—political appointees but often experts themselves—come to their jobs with scant understanding of what intelligence is or what it can do. And they rarely stay in office long enough to find out.

Thus, the onus of responsibility for improving the connection will be on the intelligence community. Offering better analysis is the first necessity. But the intelligence community also needs to develop a variety of ways to make it easier for policymakers to use what intelligence has to offer.

Congress plays a critical part in the connection between intelligence and policy. In a very real sense, the intelligence agencies work for Congress because it provides the money that enables them to function. Yet for much of the cold war, the intelligence community—especially the CIA—considered itself to be a servant of the executive. Now, Congress is welcomed as a new consumer of intelligence, but the relationship is often problematic because the intelligence community knows those congressional consumers are not disinterested: they have agendas and biases of their own that often conflict with those of the executive branch. Most of the time, the executive branch and Congress tug the community in differing directions without pulling so hard that it can no longer function. But it is often difficult for intelligence to offer frank, unvarnished advice to administration officials when it knows that sooner rather than later it will have to speak to Congress on the same issues. At the same time, the executive branch may become unwilling to bring intelligence into the most sensitive deliberations since it cannot count on confidentiality.

Specifically, the Task Force recommends:

▲ **The State Department's policymaking capabilities, which have been undermined by severe budget cuts, must be rebuilt**. Reduced budgets have diminished the ability of State Department policymakers to provide direction to the intelligence community. During the most recent political season, good arguments about the need to reshape the department were hijacked by those who wanted to slash, not reform, it. The State Department was funded at only 40 percent of recent cold war-era budgets, while defense and intelligence budgets were at 80 percent of their previous levels. Few secretaries of state within memory have paid much attention to the department's capacity as an institution. And because the department lacked the money even to open embassies in the newly independent states of central Asia, it had to depend on intelligence community resources. Diplomacy thus became the tail of intelligence—just the reverse of wise foreign policy.

The Task Force recognizes that Congress is not now likely to shift money from intelligence to the State Department. But it is the Task Force's view that nothing would be as cost-effective in improving our nation's intelligence in foreign affairs, conceived broadly, as a better staffed, open diplomatic presence around the world and an enhanced policymaking and analytic capability in Washington. Parallel strengthening of other departments would also bring substantial benefits.

▲ **Policy processes should be designed with intelligence in mind.** Intelligence needs to know and understand better what is afoot on the policy agenda, the specific shape of the issues, and deadlines. Regular access and interaction would limit these problems. On occasion, ad hoc processes will be unavoidable and will necessarily leave intelligence in the dark. But to the extent senior officials want to be served well by their intelligence analysts, they and their staffs need to think about sharing their agendas, schedules, and presumptions with intelligence counterparts.

▲ **The bright white line separating intelligence from policy in the American tradition—a line designed to keep intelligence from being "politicized" by the stakes of policy—should become a less rigid barrier.** Britain's experience with its joint intelligence committee is instructive. It functions somewhat like the U.S. National Intelligence Council but integrates policy officials at each stage of the process of writing and approving intelligence analysis. Politicization of intelligence is a risk, to be sure, but that potential drawback is more than offset by increased relevance; intelligence analysts hear firsthand what is on the policymaking agenda.

What policymakers can really add to the intelligence process are the value judgments and the sense of priorities that should drive final decisions. Intelligence producers must add depth to their policymaking clients' comprehension of reality, their calculations about hypothetical moves, and the formulation of questions requiring analysis. Policy-relevant intelligence is inseparable, both intellectually and operationally, from good policy analysis. The cure for politicization is the same as for any judgment that might be biased by a hidden agenda: a transparent presentation of the evidence and the reasoning underlying the conclusion.

▲   **CIA and other intelligence officers should serve on rotations in policy agencies.** Officials involved should serve as regular staffers rather than liaison officers so that they can gain a more intimate understanding of how the policy process works. Their links back to intelligence are natural; what is important in making the connection is that they fall into the pace and shape of the policy agenda.

▲   **Formal mechanisms, like the Brown Commission's recommendation of a National Security Council "Committee on Foreign Intelligence," should be pursued to serve as a catalyst for determining intelligence priorities and suggest intelligence collection assignments.** The Task Force recognizes that as a practical matter no senior NSC committee will be able to devote much attention to intelligence. Still, such a committee could provide greater guidance than now exists.

IMPROVING AND STREAMLINING THE CLANDESTINE SERVICE

The CIA's efforts through its Directorate of Operations (DO) to gather secret information about other countries through the use of spies and paid informants can yield important, useful information. When bungled, though, these clandestine activities have proved to be costly not only in financial and human terms but also with respect to the nation's public image. The Aldrich Ames debacle is the most damaging in a long string of embarrassments attributable to clandestine activities.

The Task Force does not believe that clandestine operations should be abolished. Indeed, the members of the Task Force think the nation needs a first-class clandestine capability. But we do not now have one. A comprehensive review of the scope, scale, and purpose of clandestine efforts is needed to assess their benefits relative to a broad measure of their costs. The secretive environment in which intelligence officers work has perpetuated a culture ill-suited to interagency cooperation.

The starting point for change is distinguishing among the DO's activities. While those efforts are kindred, they are also separable: liaison, espionage, and covert action. Liaison means sharing information and working with foreign intelligence and police services. It is not without risk, depending on the country, for it associates the CIA with the actions of those foreign services. But it is in a different category from espionage—persuading foreigners with money, ideology, or other inducements to provide information, secretly, on their country's politics and institutions.

Covert action is the opposite of espionage. While both depend on secret links to foreigners, for espionage those relationships are patient, passive, and quiet; their purpose is to gather information. Covert action, by contrast, seeks to influence events in foreign countries. The foreign connection is asked to act, and the risk increases that the secret connection to the CIA and to the United States will be revealed.

Specifically, the Task Force recommends:

▲ **The scope of clandestine efforts should be narrowed to focus on potential foes proximate to deployed U.S. troops, the governments of a small number of potentially destabilizing rogue states, groups that threaten to engage in terrorist activities against the United States, and countries with nuclear capabilities.** In the post-cold war world, far-flung clandestine activities throughout the globe with a large standby capability can no longer be justified. The cost and riskiness of clandestine operations warrants their judicious use only when the information obtained covertly would be likely to enhance significantly U.S. national security. According to studies conducted for the Brown Commission, 80 to 90 percent of the information collected by the clandestine services arises from open sources. Even if that figure is high, it is wasteful for clandestine collectors to gather so much publicly available information. A streamlined clandestine service should yield a greater payoff for the government.

This implies that the CIA would no longer have stations all around the globe. The Task Force recognizes that there is merit to the counterargument—that tomorrow's untidy world makes it impossible to predict where the United States will want to act, and so some infrastructure for spying should be sustained almost everywhere. On balance, though, the Task Force believes that the costs of such a comprehensive presence are simply too high relative to the benefits.

▲ **Accordingly, the clandestine service should be assigned tasks separate from, and more narrow than, the rest of the intelligence community.** It should focus only on those high-value secrets that cannot be collected another way. The value, to be sure, can be assessed only in light of what is available openly. But the task for the clandestine service is obtaining the critical secrets.

▲ **Periodic reviews of ongoing collection operations, both within the executive branch and with congressional overseers, should be conducted.** The Task Force explored the idea of reciprocal understandings to limit spying in countries friendly to us. In the end, those seemed unworkable. But periodic reviews outside the DO would impose a broader standard of risk and cost. Does the information gained really justify the potential risk, conceived broadly?

▲ **Covert action should be undertaken only as a last resort.** The Twentieth Century Fund's Task Force on Covert Action released its report in 1991. There is neither need nor space to restate all of its conclusions here. But the members of this Task Force support its basic recommendations, although not all of the members endorse its detailed prescriptions:

   ◆ **that covert action should never be deemed routine.** It should be undertaken only in support of publicly articulated policy and only when overt means are unavailable, insufficient, or judged too costly in terms of human life.

♦ **that review procedures, within both the executive
   and Congress, be strengthened in a variety of ways,
   including, critically, periodic reviews of ongoing
   actions.** The ban on assassinating foreign leaders
   should be enacted in law.

♦ **that routine cold war propaganda operations
   be terminated.**

IMPROVING ECONOMIC INTELLIGENCE

Contrary to widespread perceptions, economic intelligence has little
to do with espionage against commercial adversaries in world trade. A
wide array of foreign policy questions requires a deep understanding of
economic forces, including the economic strengths and vulnerabilities
of particular countries, the status of global resources that are vital to
America's prosperity, the ebbs and flows of the international financial
system, and the condition of American trade and competitiveness in
world markets. The Mexican peso crisis of 1994 is a vivid example of
how a flawed economic intelligence process contributed to a financial
mess that might otherwise have been contained.

The growing availability of economic information from the private sector, international organizations, and international financial
institutions raises the question of whether the U.S. government
should be engaging in economic intelligence at all. The Task Force
believes that the intelligence community should take full advantage
of the more extensive, sophisticated flow of economic information
available from private sources and avoid replicating tasks already performed adequately by others. Intelligence need not and should not
duplicate the data gathering carried out by State, Commerce, and
Treasury. Nor should intelligence reproduce what is done better in
the private sector—for instance, developing macroeconomic models
of major trading partners. But in some instances intelligence has
unique responsibilities in the collection and preparation of economic information.

Several traditional roles of intelligence in the economic realm
remain important, and several new ones have acquired urgency. The
fundamental responsibility is to fill gaps and make connections that

other agencies or the private sector do not address and to make use of the government's special capabilities. Those priorities should include:

Understanding the intersection of economics and politics (including relationships within governmental bureaucracies) in major nations. This has been a traditional role of intelligence but one that has not always been done well. Nonetheless, the challenge is all the more imperative because of economic globalization.

Supporting U.S. economic negotiators, just as intelligence supports negotiators in arms control or other issues. Here, the government can use its unique resources, including eavesdropping and espionage. These endeavors are hardly without risk, but government officials generally value economic intelligence gathered by such means, even if the flashes of insight gained are unpredictable or episodic.

Monitoring the movements of technology and resources used in the construction of weapons of mass destruction. Such transactions, which constitute multinational commercial activity, often occur secretly and pertain to U.S. national interests.

Understanding the economic dynamics of countries or markets that exclude U.S. business. For instance, the state of the North Korean economy matters to the U.S. government, but the private sector has little interest because it is excluded from activity in that country. The export efforts of the Ukrainian arms industry and the finances of the Cali cocaine cartel are other examples where economic intelligence can be helpful.

Assessing the impact of sanctions where, by definition, open information will not suffice. This has been a major role of intelligence during the Balkans conflict.

Monitoring foreign exchange flows to detect speculative pressure on the dollar as well as the currencies of countries important to U.S. policy.

Investigating possible bribes or side payments offered by trade competitors to win contracts in other countries. Again, nations or companies seldom advertise their bribes openly.

Assessing important raw material supplies. The intelligence role in these cases is justified by the government's special collection resources and by concerns about bias in open information. For example, the oil industry may not be an objective source about whether the United States needs to enlarge its petroleum reserves.

Specifically, the Task Force recommends:

▲ **Economic analysis should be of better quality and given higher priority within the intelligence community**. As a special part of improving analysis, particular attention needs to be devoted to economic topics. The intelligence community should recruit greater numbers of highly qualified economists.

▲ **The executive and Congress, through its intelligence committees, need to shape a better understanding of the value of economic intelligence.** Congress is ambivalent about economic intelligence, alternating between uncertainty about why intelligence is involved in economics at all and wonder at why it is not doing a better job of it. The public often mistakenly equates economic intelligence with spying for American companies. Those misguided perceptions need to changed through an open, ongoing discussion about the scope and limits of economic intelligence.

One critical component of that dialogue is the scope of spying and eavesdropping on friends. The Task Force does not oppose such collection efforts under every conceivable circumstance but does worry about the extent to which they are used. Recent disclosures have underscored the costs of such operations when they fail. There would be less temptation to rely on covert sources if the State and Treasury Departments were equipped to do a better job of reporting on economics—on the economic institutions of major economic powers and on international financial institutions.

▲ **Compartmentalization of economic analysis should be broken down.** Time and again studies show how neither economic nor political nor sociological analysis alone can yield vital conclusions. Only the interaction of their arguments can illuminate the choices that must be made by foreign governments. Analysts in these different disciplines are not trained to work with each other in academia. Government must overcome this liability of over-specialization.

▲   **Gaps in interdepartmental analysis should be closed.** In the period preceding the Mexico crisis, Federal Reserve, Treasury, and CIA analysts all detected pieces of the potential problem but rarely compared notes. Washington thus experienced the same kind of intelligence policy failure that had occurred only two years earlier in London during the European financial crisis. Both the National Economic Council and the National Intelligence Council can accept responsibility for closing these gaps.

                              *   *   *

The clarity of purpose that defined the work of the intelligence community for decades has vanished. But spies who have come in from their cold war assignments, and intelligence generally, remain valuable assets to U.S. foreign policy. The challenge is to make the most of them. The recommendations of this Task Force, and those proposed in other reports, will make relatively little difference if the nation's foreign policy goals and priorities remain uncertain. Where missions are clearly defined, however, the Task Force believes the ideas proposed here would improve the effectiveness of both the intelligence community and the government agencies that develop and implement foreign policy.

DISSENT AND COMMENTS

DISSENT

Richard J. Kerr

It is fashionable to beat up on the clandestine service and this Report follows that trend by overdramatizing its problems and misunderstanding its contribution. Much has been done to improve the performance of the service and to ensure it focuses on what others cannot do. There is room for further improvement, and a debate on the role of clandestine operations is worthwhile.

Two conclusions in the Report, however, deserve comment: the assertion that a worldwide presence is no longer justified and the judgment that covert action should be undertaken only as a last resort.

PRESENCE: The cost of maintaining a worldwide presence is small in comparison to technical collection or maintaining the military. The benefits of such a presence are significant. It is important for the United States to have regular and formal contact with foreign governments outside of diplomatic channels. Knowledge of the local government and direct and frequent contact with counterpart intelligence services, senior officials, and the elite in a country are necessary inputs to the policy process. Often the last to leave a country in crisis, case officers and communicators are much more than just agent recruiters. This Report indicates that the Brown Commission said that 80 to 90 percent of the information collected by the clandestine collectors was publicly available. That figure is questionable, but it also is important to note that publicly available information in a foreign country is not

21

valuable until it is identified, organized, and combined with other information and then made available to policymakers.

COVERT ACTION: The United States should consider covert action as one of its instruments of foreign policy. We have become conditioned to accept the use of military force to change situations that are unacceptable to us. Why should we be so reluctant to use political action or clandestine military support to affect change if our policy is clearly defined and our interest fully identified? Supporting a political group that is trying to change its country's government or policies or is trying to replace a bad leader is in our interests. Using information—or, if you wish, propaganda—to change the behavior of a government while concealing the hand of the United States is a better option than sending in F-16s or the Marines. Obviously, covert action requires special attention from the policymaker and must be part of an overall policy. It should not be a last resort after all else has failed; without being part of a larger policy, covert action will not work. It also requires careful oversight from the executive and from the Congress.

COMMENT

Gregory F. Treverton

I wholeheartedly endorse this Report. It speaks eloquently to the major issues confronting American intelligence. I would only like to add a comment on one issue—the future of the clandestine service, the CIA's Directorate of Operations (DO). The DO was not the Task Force's principal focus. Nor is it an easy institution for outsiders to address. Yet if war is too important to be left to the generals, so also is spying too sensitive to be left to the spymasters.

I do not claim to be an expert, though I have investigated the clandestine service from Capitol Hill, studied it from the outside, and had the opportunity to serve with its officers inside the government. The discussions of the Task Force sharpened my thinking. I found Richard Kerr particularly thoughtful on the subject, though he draws conclusions that are very nearly the opposite of mine.

For me, the essential dilemma is this: those attributes that have enabled the DO to be effective and creative are, alas, precisely the opposite of accountability in the American system of governance. The dilemma runs through all of government but is painfully pointed for the DO. When the clandestine service is creative, it is so because junior officers are cut a wide swath of discretion and encouraged to react quickly to changing circumstances. Their dedication to duty is legendary. They are rewarded for acting, for solving problems, not referring them to superiors. The action is abroad, in the DO's stations, whose chiefs often effectively outrank their Washington division chiefs.

Exactly these attributes, however, frustrate accountability in the American government which, for better or worse, seeks to narrow discretion downward while it pushes accountability upward. The DO is a more disciplined and bureaucratic structure than it was when I first encountered it seriously two decades ago. It is probably also less dynamic. Yet its very success, I think, depends on traits that are the obverse of accountability. The same attributes that produced a Bob Ames, the DO's legendary Middle East hand and penetrator of the PLO, also resulted in an Aldrich Ames.

The Task Force's recommendations for shrinking and targeting the clandestine service surely go in the right direction. The United States at this point in history has neither need nor place for a large, far-flung clandestine service. If America is to spy, it should concentrate on penetrating its real enemies.

Yet the dilemma can only be limited, not made to go away. Spying is the world's second oldest profession (some might say the first), and so there is force to the argument that it cannot be made to go away. The Task Force has, I believe, only opened the debate about how much spying the United States's security requires and how much its institutions of government can afford. That is a debate for another time and place.

COMMENT

Brewster C. Denny

I commend the Report's distinctive recognition that what we need to know about the rest of the world does not come only—or even principally—from the intelligence community. Even during the cold war, some of our best and most useful appraisals of the closed societies of the Soviet bloc came from outside the intelligence community. Of course, as long as there are any closed societies, or potential aggressors, there will still be a need for the kind of intelligence, mostly military, the intelligence community collected and analyzed in great volume and with great success during the cold war. But this need has been substantially reduced with the collapse of the Soviet Union and now can be met at considerably reduced cost, freeing resources for meeting the dramatically increased need for staffing and supporting our foreign service capacity to learn about the world ahead.

Accordingly, the Task Force calls for a substantial buildup in the size and quality of all our foreign services. The number of well-trained people seeking careers in foreign service is substantially down. We twice have skipped the annual Foreign Service exam, and sharply reduced the number of persons appointed. Many of our embassies and consulates are understaffed. The best trained and most experienced professionals often don't work on the most important tasks or in the countries of their greatest knowledge.

Unfortunately, further severe cuts in staffing and training are planned. One of the most dangerous areas in which severe cuts are planned is in government support for in-depth area and language training in universities and in the various foreign and intelligence services, especially since the number of countries vital to our interests has multiplied. There is a critical need for a substantial increase in area and language training, always a great deficiency in our country—a deficiency now worsening rapidly. It is in our urgent national interest to reverse this trend, even though doing so will require an enormous effort.

The Task Force wisely recommends sharp curtailment and reevaluation of clandestine collection and covert action programs and the reduction—I would favor elimination—of CIA stations in U.S. embassies. I would go even further. The time has come to get out of the covert action business and restrict our other clandestine activities to those absolutely essential to counterespionage, counterterrorism, and preventing proliferation of nuclear and other instruments of mass destruction. The systems of executive and congressional oversight adopted in response to various scandals have totally failed to prevent unconstitutional, illegal, shameful, foolish, and unsuccessful operations. We can, therefore, no longer leave in place the temptation, the resources, or the standby capability for such activities.

The Task Force recommends that we use eavesdropping and spying to meet the demand for economic intelligence. Given the multinational nature of business activity, such eavesdropping and spying could, however inadvertently, entail spying on American citizens and those of friendly countries. We must explicitly prohibit the use of these intelligence assets for spying on American citizens or the citizens of friendly countries.

Would curtailment of clandestine and covert activities hinder the government from doing everything it sincerely believes we ought to do in our interests? Of course it would. It is the kind of hindrance a great democracy should wear as a badge of honor. Only one thing is worse than to stay in the covert action business and to continue to do it badly and at great cost to our capacity to understand the rest of the world, to our reputation, and to our precious liberties. That would be to stay in it and do it well. For, in the powerful words of Hodding Carter's dissent to the Report of the Twentieth Century Fund Task Force on Covert Action and American Democracy: "To continue covert action now is to admit that we have become what we fought."

BACKGROUND PAPERS

Intelligence in the Post-Cold War Era

Allan E. Goodman

I Overview

The end of more than forty years of confrontation between two superpowers has necessitated a fundamental reevaluation of the structure of the U.S. national security establishment. Seeking to maintain its leadership in a dramatically changed world, Washington has had to adjust the way it conducts security affairs across the board; as part of this process, officials have begun to look hard at the government's information needs and to ask what the mission of intelligence should be in the 1990s. With old dangers having receded, the key question raised by Congress in its oversight role is whether the intelligence community is prepared—in terms of organization, training, and bureaucratic culture—even to recognize the new generation of security threats, much less contribute meaningfully to averting them.

The CIA, searching to justify its budget allowance, has encouraged a multitude of agencies, many of which are not directly involved in the formulation of security policy, to become avid users of intelligence today. Less than a decade ago, there would have been only half as many governmental "consumers" of the work of intelligence agencies. With a wider audience and with new challenges to face, intelligence is now not only more expensive to provide but also more difficult to get right and deliver to the appropriate government offices where it can make a difference.

The director of central intelligence and the policymakers who assign responsibilities to the intelligence community must decide whether to emphasize global threat monitoring and assessment or to stick to issues and areas in which intelligence commands unique resources and expertise. One way to redesign the mandate for intelligence is first to delineate the manifest threats to American national security and then to aim at providing the best possible strategic intelligence. Even that mission conception would require the collection and analysis of vast amounts of data needed to support U.S. operational military commanders and policymakers engaged in a wide variety of pursuits from arms control to foreign espionage to global warming and other possible perils to the environment.

Although Congress has passed legislation to streamline the nation's information gathering and analysis functions, there is room enough for further centralization. The intelligence "community" is still composed of autonomous agencies and specialized bureaus within cabinet departments. Each of these bodies tends to guard its turf fiercely, and rivalry rather than cooperation between them is the behavioral norm. As a result, there is considerable, costly duplication of effort in some realms of knowledge even as critical issues in others remain neglected. Moreover, the intelligence bureaucracy collectively cannot be proud of its history of frequent failure to give sufficient warning of danger signs so that government could prepare to respond. The community needs new paradigms to guide its analyses, as well as more effective command and control, with the role of the chief intelligence officer and the relationships between agencies more precisely defined and oversight arrangements made transparent. Additionally, Congress must further clarify what types of clandestine activity are beyond the bounds of legality and public tolerance.

Central to the discussion of the nation's intelligence structure are several public policy questions, namely those concerning the working relationship of the intelligence community to the president and National Security Council; the desirability of forming a congressional joint select committee on intelligence in the interest of more expert review of operations and assessment of results; the centralization of budgets, operations, and formulation of policy under a single head, as well as the unification of specialized collection efforts such as aerial and satellite imagery now dispersed through several agencies; how to obtain the most out of research and analysis—making sure it is sharper and more relevant; and whether a mutually beneficial liaison with foreign intelligence services can be established to allow resources to stretch further and to assure new ideas and fresh perspectives.

What emerges from the debate over intelligence reorganization and reform is that the intelligence agencies have their work cut out for them in terms of repairing an overwhelmingly negative public image, restoring the trust of their congressional overseers, and adapting to a greatly altered global security climate. In fact, though unflattering revelations about the intelligence services have surfaced since the cold war concluded, many of the issues of purpose and reorganization now in discussion predate the political and military transformations that have occurred. Such issues cannot be resolved without also examining the role of intelligence in the entire U.S. national security establishment, particularly the information gathering and assessment that takes place under the secretaries of State, Treasury, Energy, and Commerce and the heads of agencies like USAID, EPA, FAA, FEMA, and the NRC.

The intelligence agencies will continue to keep an eye not only on potential threats but also opportunities to further American security and strategic interests. Many of the threats of today tend not to be identified with any particular nation state; rather they are amorphous, spilling across national boundaries to link up ethnic or religious cohorts or involving shadowy terror groups or criminal organizations. The new opportunities concern private-sector trade and investment more often than political influence or strategic alliances. To cope with the radically changed expectations and demands on its resources will require all the ingenuity and imagination the intelligence community can muster. Conducting business as it was during the height of the superpower rivalry is no longer an option; the only alternative to proving how and why intelligence is vital is a slow fade into irrelevance.

Chapter 1

INTELLIGENCE AND THE EMERGING STRUCTURE OF WORLD POLITICS

The end of the Cold War increases our security in many ways. . . . But, even now, this new world remains dangerous and, in many ways, more complex and more difficult to fathom.

—President Clinton
address at CIA headquarters, January 4, 1994

SCOPE OF THE STUDY

The world is a less dangerous place today than it was a decade ago. The central adversary confronting the U.S. conception of world order no longer exists. Even though the Soviet target actually came to command less attention from the intelligence community in the 1980s—dropping from a high of nearly 60 percent of its overall budget resources in 1980 to 50 percent by fiscal year 1990—the existence of communism helped to determine the importance of many other targets, which came to be evaluated in terms of anticipating and containing the projection of the primary adversary's military and political power.[1] Currently, about a third of the total intelligence budget and less than 15 percent of the CIA's budget supports collection and analysis programs that focus on the former Soviet Union.[2] As the Soviet threat receded and then disappeared, no comparable menace developed to replace it as far as the intelligence community was concerned.[3] Threats judged to be of lesser seriousness during the cold war (for example, ethnic and tribal conflicts) are taking on greater importance, while entirely new threats (such as the ability of hackers and international criminals to invade, manipulate, and even paralyze the information transmission systems on which governments, economies, and industries depend) are coming into view. As they do, the intelligence community is finding that it is getting harder to provide timely and accurate intelligence because of unfamiliarity with their dynamics and the tendency of policymakers to put off setting priorities for the intelligence agenda. The result is that most politicians discover what they had hoped intelligence would provide them, as one former assistant to the president for national security affairs put it, "only when they see it on CNN."

In response to the great geopolitical shifts of recent times, which have necessitated a review of the kind and quality of information fed to the government's defense and foreign policymakers, the national security establishment of the United States is in the process of an overhaul. The proper mission for intelligence in the late 1990s and beyond is the subject of much debate. Supporters as well as critics of the intelligence community organization question how good the product is in light of past and persistent intelligence failures (especially in such areas as forecasting foreign leaderships' intentions to use force, violate human rights, abuse covert aid from the United States, acquire weapons of mass destruction, and project power). Priorities at home also demand a reallocation of government resources generally that is reducing the national intelligence budget by at least 10—and perhaps as much as 20—percent over the next several years.

One recent director of central intelligence has compared the challenges the intelligence community faces today to that of a hunter operating in a jungle filled no longer with dragons but with snakes. While the threat of nuclear confrontation with the Soviet Union has clearly receded, there are nonetheless numerous deadly threats for which the United States must be prepared and forewarned by timely and accurate intelligence. The end of the cold war has meant the obsolescence of first principles about what constitutes a threat to U.S.

security as well as a breakup of the strategic consensus over which global, regional, and even local developments necessitate a U.S. response. The complexity of today's threats, coupled to the conceptual uncertainty accompanying the redefinition and appropriate framing of U.S. foreign policy responses, has led many policy officials to respond to intelligence agency surveys asking about their needs by saying that they require as much information from as many different sources as possible about all the things that could go wrong or precipitate crises that might involve the United States. Such a response is entirely understandable given the disorder and disorientation associated with the end of the cold war. However, for the intelligence community to try to provide all that has been asked of it would—at a minimum—result in the proliferation of redundant reports. Probably it would also prove to be a questionable use of increasingly stretched information-gathering assets as well as of analytical resources, particularly so long as these lack the conceptual and practical bases for working effectively across the entire range of new problems that have surfaced as national security threats and concerns.[4]

Overview of the New Intelligence Challenge

In adopting a time frame focused on the remainder of this decade as well as the first decade of the next century, this paper has chosen to look further ahead than interagency studies designed to identify and prioritize strategic intelligence needs and potential targets conducted by both the Bush and Clinton administrations. Such reviews are driven by the need to determine budgets and therefore concentrate on problems as they will manifest themselves during the next several fiscal years. The broader question examined here is what types of information the U.S. government will need about the general environment and range of situations that could pose grave threats to American national security. Also of interest is a discussion assessing the issues for which the intelligence community is perhaps uniquely placed to collect information.

Intelligence, according to the CIA's official *Consumer's Guide*, is "knowledge and foreknowledge of the world around us . . . that helps consumers, either civilian leaders or military commanders, to consider alternative options and outcomes."[5] It is provided by an intelligence community consisting of the following agencies and departmental units: the Central Intelligence Agency, the National Security Agency (NSA), the Defense Intelligence Agency (DIA), the Central Imagery Office (CIO), the National Reconnaissance Office (NRO), the Federal Bureau of Investigation (FBI), and the intelligence bureaus and offices in the Departments of State, Treasury, and Energy. Not every member of the community has as its primary mission the collection of intelligence, nor does the work of all the members encompass the entire range of "finished intelligence": current situation reports, estimates of how situations will unfold, warnings about situations where policy actions will urgently need to be taken, basic and operational research, and scientific and technical studies of foreign weapons and other military-related systems. There is no statutory charter for the intelligence community as such today. The National Security Act of 1947 (as amended) establishes the director of central intelligence as the president's and the NSC's primary adviser on national foreign intelligence matters, that is, "information relating to the capabilities, intentions, or activities of foreign governments or elements thereof, foreign organizations, or foreign persons . . . which pertains to the interests of more than one department or agency of the Government . . ." (Sec. 3 [50 U.S.C. 401a], paragraphs 2 and 5 [a]). An executive order (no. 12333) drafted in the Reagan administration and issued on December 4, 1981, specifies the goals and components of the intelligence community and is the most comprehensive statement to date of the mission of intelligence in providing for U.S. national security. There is, however, some doubt about whether this order can and should serve as the charter for intelligence activities in the post-cold war era. There is no doubt that we are in an age of transition to security, economic, and political orders (or chaos) quite unlike any known previously, uncharted territory where outcomes will be tough to predict because socioeconomic and political structures and concepts will be newly unfamiliar.[6] The post-cold war global environment consists of "a system in which transnational, regional, nation-state, and local, even tribal, structures compete and coexist."[7] The arrival of a "new world order" has affected every phase of the intelligence process: priority setting, information gathering, data processing, analysis, writing and disseminating reports. During the cold war, by contrast, when there was a need for change or reform it was limited to a few targets or parts of the intelligence apparatus.

The intelligence community is already anticipating operations in a much more complex world. According to James Woolsey, who recently resigned as director of central intelligence (DCI), the guidebook quoted above was prepared because "in today's challenging international environment, the range of consumers of intelligence is growing rapidly, including many who have never before used intelligence products."[8] An annex to the publication lists the following "Major Consumers of Intelligence":

▲ the White House;

▲ the Departments of State, Defense, Treasury, Justice, Commerce, Agriculture, Energy, Labor, and Transportation;

▲ the Congress;

▲ the agencies dealing with development assistance, arms control, drug enforcement, the dissemination of public information about the United States abroad, emergency management;

▲ the FBI, United States Marshals Service, the Federal Aviation Administration; and

▲ the Office of Management and Budget, Federal Reserve, United States Trade Representative, National Aeronautics and Space Administration, Federal Communications Commission, and Nuclear Regulatory Commission.

A few years back, there would have been only half as many clients for intelligence, threat perceptions were more narrowly focused, and the CIA, NSA, and NRO would not be routinely sharing vast amounts of information that their collection systems intercepted. While many of the agencies listed above do not have high priority intelligence needs (or are not directly involved in setting national security policy), they are avid consumers of intelligence today. The CIA, in particular, has encouraged them to become so in its search for customers to demonstrate demand for its products in order to justify maintaining cold war-era budgets. The greatly expanded role of Congress in foreign affairs and national security policy has also brought considerable pressure for more extensive CIA collection and analysis. According to some professionals, the Agency spends as much time providing informational support to Congress as to the president.

While serving more consumers on a ever-widening range of topics, the intelligence community must operate in a fiscal environment where resources are scarce and likely to remain so. According to a recent chair of the House Permanent Select Committee on Intelligence, "it is no longer possible to automatically assume that intelligence budgets of yesterday, or even last year, are tolerable given the fiscal realities this country faces." For any resources at all to be allocated for intelligence will require the executive and legislative branches to justify "the community's genuine value in a world that is growing increasingly impatient with secrecy and clandestine activities."[9] For these reasons, the task of producing intelligence and disseminating it properly is becoming tougher. For the first time in its history, the U.S. intelligence community is facing the conjunction of deep challenges over what it should be focusing on, for whom, at what cost, and with what allowance for secrecy and the inevitable compromise of American democratic values and governmental procedures that the pursuit entails. If one accepts that many familiar forms of organization and behavior in international relations will change as a result of the end of the cold war and the emergence of new patterns of projecting power—especially taking into consideration that knowledge (including that derived from fundamentalist religious beliefs and values) and information are becoming the prime sources of influence over political, economic, and military conduct—the intelligence community is doubly challenged. Not only does the operational environment require that it serve new consumers with a broader range of needs but also that it be prepared to deal with and comprehend entirely new phenomena and organizations. Conventional labels and paradigms no longer apply. The focus of intelligence collection and analysis is also likely to shift to subjects currently receiving only marginal attention. This prospect is not good news for intelligence agencies that have specialized in comprehending and predicting the behavior of a limited number of states and organizations that seem to be receding in importance.

Strikingly, a good deal of the information that the U.S. government needs to know about the threats ahead will come from open sources. The figure most frequently mentioned by analysts is 80 percent. This represents coming full cycle, since it was to make more effective use of such library resources that the analysis section of the Office of Strategic Studies (OSS, later the CIA) was born and the efforts were housed initially at the Library of Congress.

Information in today's world is being generated at a rate equivalent to millions of bits of data per day, according to some estimates, and by the end of the decade perhaps as many as 100 million persons will have access to such data via the information superhighway.[10] In just five years, traffic on the Internet has risen from a little over two billion data "packets" per month to more than 70 billion[11] and there are now more than seven thousand computerized data bases to which a user can have access. Facts about countries, people, and financial transactions flow freely across most borders; even the remaining authoritarian regimes are having increasing difficulty keeping word about their policies and activities from leaking out. And the advent of remote sensing technologies makes it possible for data about many situations to be gathered for public use, data that a decade ago would have been available only to those with the highest U.S. government security clearances. Consequently, the intelligence community needs to determine whether a set of operational organizations, primarily designed to collect and analyze information that was either stolen, tightly controlled, or obtained in ways that an adversary would not expect possible can and should now devote a major part of its manpower and technology to acquiring and handling open sources and whether such open sources can make a genuine difference to classified analyses.[12]

This might mean that the value the intelligence community adds to the government's decisionmaking processes could come not from penetrating the inner circles of another government but from collecting, organizing, summarizing, and evaluating the sheer volume of public information that already exists and that is being created at a staggering rate. Currently, the CIA maintains a hundred-page catalog of publications and maps released to the public. The analytic material covers nearly fifty countries and every region, and ranges from leadership directories to ruling family profiles, bureaucratic histories, humanitarian and peacekeeping operations reviews, macroeconomic trend studies, appraisals of trade and development prospects, and global statistical handbooks.[13] A review of such material immediately raises the question of just how many of the various products advertised are unique to intelligence analysis or the resources at the community's disposal, as well as the deeper question of whether doing such basic research (regardless of whether or not it is made public) contributes to and improves the process of intelligence analysis. Peter Sharfman offers the following assessment of the proliferation of open-source material and the electronic dissemination of all the types of information used by intelligence analysts:

> Today, bureaucratic and political power in the intelligence arena is frequently derived from being in a position to know things that others do not know, or at least to know them first. . . . The world of electronic dissemination will still have some of this, but relative to today's environment there will be much more equality of access to information, and especially of access to information upon which judgments and estimates were based.
>
> One predictable effect will be to flatten organizations, just as the proliferation of computers and communications has tended to flatten business organizations in the last few years. The people at the top of hierarchies will be able to get direct access to the information produced by the people at the bottom, and those in the middle will have much less opportunity to contribute to the process. It becomes the case . . . that [when] a senior policy-maker or military commander exchanges E-mail directly with the analyst who is the acknowledged expert on the issue at hand, what is the function of that expert's boss, or of the boss's boss? From the perspective of the analyst, direct access on matters of substance to the user will increase the opportunities to present his or her best judgment, independently of the "corporate view" of the organization which employs the analyst.
>
> Indeed, corporate views of intelligence agencies may tend to wither away. . . . In an age of electronic dissemination . . . there will certainly be ambiguities, uncertainties, and disputes regarding the facts, and ideally there will also be competing analyses, but the competing perspectives will have to compete on their own merits, rather than on the political weight of the organizations that espouse them.[14]

The greater use of open-source data might also help to assure that inbred conventional wisdom and assumptions received greater scrutiny and challenge. However, the DCI has yet to make the case for doing such research as a means to improving the accuracy and accountability of intelligence work. Rather, open-source collection and analysis is supported largely because the material "is there," can reduce the burden on clandestine activities, and does not require supplemental resources: "CIA has the people and computers to process it." In many cases, intelligence consumers have either requested open-source collection and analysis or expressed appreciation for its value in helping policymakers to manage and prioritize the growing volume of information in their specialized field.

As the environment in which intelligence functions as an instrument of government changes, so also may the culture inside the agencies and among their major consumers. For at least a decade, there has been growing intolerance by the public for keeping much of what the government does secret. Almost daily, major U.S. newspapers contain statements by senior White House, State Department, or Defense Department officials that openly and explicitly refer to intelligence information in order to persuade attentive publics that particular policies or responses to crises are justified or otherwise prudent. And much of what has come to light about such alleged intelligence failures as those associated with the collapse of communism in the Soviet Union and Eastern Europe or the Iraqi invasion of Kuwait suggests that the very secrecy with which intelligence judgments were held and information collected and used led to faulty analysis rooted in unexamined—and often critically flawed—assumptions. Several DCIs, in fact, have called for greater openness about what the intelligence community does, the use of outside expert review panels to evaluate particularly the national intelligence estimates that are regularly prepared, and the exposure of analysts to academic specialists—all in the effort to assure that the culture surrounding intelligence analysis does not blind those who work within it to aberrant facts, countervailing trends, and unconventional interpretations that could prove vital to assessing a situation correctly. A recent deputy director for intelligence (DDI), moreover, has called attention to the fact that fundamental changes in "analytic tradecraft . . . have been needed for some time. . . . It has taken the events generated by the end of the Cold War to make clear that not making these changes ultimately would entail even higher costs than making them. In sum, the need for change has existed for some time, but the end of the Cold War clearly generated force for change and provided the occasion and conditions for implementing change."[15]

The issues of mind-set and bureaucratic culture have also begun to call attention to the potential of the clandestine service to attract the highest-quality personnel. Career planning and placement officers in academia note that it is becoming more difficult to find young people, especially those with area expertise, who have an interest in pursuing careers in intelligence as field operatives. The complaints and grievances that have surfaced publicly about the intelligence community's low level of commitment to affirmative action and diversity in the workforce, moreover, also have had a dampening effect on recruitment of employees who can work effectively in many of the cultures of the developing world. Serious breaches of security—aggravated by the length of time traitors, double agents, and persons demonstrating patterns of mental instability have apparently had to continue their subversive dealings and try to cover their tracks—have also raised questions about the culture of machismo, fraternalism, and compartmentalization surrounding those who work as case officers. Recent exposés of renegade operatives and the discovery that a career officer (Aldrich Ames) was able to function for some time as a double agent for a foreign intelligence service also indicate that a complacency exists within the bureaucratic culture of intelligence that invites security lapses. The endorsement by the DCI of internal studies calling for "changes . . . in the way we do business at the C.I.A.—and in the culture of the C.I.A. itself"[16] strikes many considering careers in intelligence as a limp response to deeply entrenched patterns of discrimination and mismanagement.

It should come as no surprise that because of such problems and scandals, some critics of CIA performance have recommended that the Agency be disestablished and the intelligence community thoroughly overhauled.[17] After every war the United States has fought, the nation's intelligence establishment has been deconstructed, in part because of the realization that the processes and qualities involved in wartime intelligence operations were not well adapted to peacetime conditions and requirements. There is also a persistent and fundamental unwillingness in American government to suffer for very long the compromises that secrecy requires of democracy except when the nation is at war or faces a threat that is the moral equivalent to fighting one.[18] Despite the dramatic revelations surrounding the Ames case and of the bureaucratic culture of the Directorate of Operations, the importance of intelligence gathering and analysis to governing wisely is still generally acknowledged. The coming struggle over the size of the intelligence budget will require the intelligence community to seek the broadest possible array of customers, and many will come to its defense. Unfortunately, one effect will probably also be to postpone the hard decisions involved in narrowing the scope of intelligence missions.

Nevertheless, there is growing consensus among professional intelligence officers that in order to provide timely and accurate intelligence in the period ahead, the following will be required:

▲ changing collection priorities and the paradigms of analysis to reflect more cost-effective and focused responses to the broad range of issues now considered as appropriate intelligence targets and subjects and

▲ breaking down the barriers between and especially within the organizations that collect, process, and use the product.

As long as defense and security-related budgets are shrinking, however, intelligence will probably have to do less in order to do well. For purposes of discussion, the mission for intelligence under such constraints can be redefined by concentrating on strategic intelligence directed against the most credible dangers to American security. This would necessitate the gathering and scrutiny of information related to the warning of war or technological or commercial assaults against U.S. and allied interests, monitoring international arms control agreements and developments relating to nuclear, conventional, chemical, and biological weapons and the means to deliver them, assessing developments that could destabilize remote regions where there are no other reliable sources of information, and reporting on foreign espionage, sabotage, organized crime links, and assassination plans and activities. The problem for the DCI will be to know how to strike a balance between such global threat monitoring and assessment (just to be sure that nothing escapes notice) and the traditional activities of intelligence, areas where it can claim unparalleled strengths and expertise.

Chapter 2

CONCEPTUAL CHALLENGES AND INTELLIGENCE REQUIREMENTS OF THE POST-COLD WAR ERA

There is as yet no definitive portrait of the emerging structure of international relations or accurate catalog of strategic threats to the United States in the post-cold war era. In fact, the literature is far better on what the period ahead does not portend. Henry Kissinger, for example, in his latest book puts the present situation succinctly (but in terms that many international affairs scholars and statesmen have used): "In the post-Cold War world, there is no overriding ideological challenge or . . . single geo-strategic confrontation. Almost every situation is a special case." The result, he argues, is "ambiguities of choice" about threats which would require an American response (as well as what tools of foreign policy will be the most effective) and the conundrum that foreign policy will inevitably involve winning domestic political support for "a vision of a future that cannot be demonstrated when it is put forward. . . ."[1] Nowhere is the demonstration of such vision more important or more difficult than in the case of framing U.S. intelligence requirements to pass the scrutiny of the budgetmakers. Certainties are needed precisely because reliable intelligence capabilities (collection and analysis) cannot be developed quickly. Furthermore, the funds that once provided for experimentation and afforded the cushion for following all leads and investigating all possibilities no longer exist within the budgets of either the Department of Defense or the various intelligence agencies. Finally, a vision of what the future holds for security—as well as how intelligence can best contribute—is essential because the threats to U.S. welfare are no longer limited to a few primary sources or generated by forces with which intelligence professionals have had much experience.

Even the sharpest critics of the performance of and rationale for maintaining the present structure and system do not doubt that the government will continue to need intelligence. But they are surely right in suggesting that doing intelligence in the same way and with the same mission and focus as prevailed during the cold war makes little sense now. As the former chairman of the House Permanent Select Committee on Intelligence, Representative Dan Glickman of Kansas, observed:

> Because of the rapidly changing nature of threats to American interests . . . the need for timely and reliable intelligence is greater when our military forces are being withdrawn from overseas deployments and reduced in size. Early warning of hostile intentions or of the development of dangerous situations is critical if policy makers are to have the opportunity to consider a full range of responses. Intelligence provides that warning. It gives us notice of terrorism against U.S. interests at home and abroad; awareness of narcotics trafficking; understanding of regional and ethnic hostilities; and knowledge of economic threats against American interests. It also keeps an eye on the rapidly changing political atmosphere in the former Soviet Union.[2]

The implication for intelligence operations, then-Congressman Glickman continued, is that "we need to maintain sharply honed, flexible capabilities against selective targets, rapier-like blades as opposed to sledge hammers, capabilities that can deny a drug trafficker his profit, interdict a missile shipment, identify a would-be proliferator before he can produce weapons of mass destruction, and alert policy makers to a foreign government's political or economic policy intentions."[3]

The behavior of nation states and those who lead them, in fact, is likely to play a decreasing role as some of the gravest menaces to U.S.

security are mounted by transnational terrorist and criminal forces, cur-rency speculators, drug dealers, and ethnic, tribal, and religious leaders seeking to achieve regional and even global aims that are anathema to American policies and values. As for many countries that were U.S. adversaries or periodic sources of concern during the cold war, sources and methods of analysis need to be developed to comprehend the impli-cations for regional stability of two entirely new phenomena:

▲ the "postmodernist" identity crisis of states undergoing what Vaclav Havel recently called "a mixing and blending of cultures and a plurality or parallelism of intellectual and spiritual worlds," result-ing in "periods when all consistent value systems collapse," increas-ing the potential for cultural conflicts "and making them more dangerous . . . than at any other time in history,"[4] and

▲ the upheavals involved in the transitions of former and still-committed socialist countries from centrally planned economic and authoritarian political systems to societies with free markets, pluralistic political systems, and greater recognition and protec-tion of individual human rights.

Intelligence professionals of every nation are practicing their craft in an age of intellectual, strategic, and political uncertainty. They find themselves having to focus increasingly on threats and phenomena that have none of the predictability or familiar characteristics of those prevalent during the cold war. And they are having to provide their reports and analyses to a growing body of national and international consumers, ranging from traditional international organizations like the UN and NATO that are now taking on new roles and members to multinational military commands engaged in peacemaking as well as peacekeeping operations. Intelligence networks worldwide have responded by changing at the margins and only very slowly since the shape of the post-cold war era and the magnitude of the threats it poses have not yet come into sharper view. In the United States, there is growing pressure to do more than this even before the contours of the new strategic landscape are clear. As the most recent report of the House Permanent Select Committee on Intelligence argues, the end of the cold war and other geopolitical changes "have not eliminated the need for effective intelligence. In some ways they have increased it. It does not necessarily follow, however, that effective intelligence can only be produced by an intelligence community of a size, in terms of either budgetary dollars or personnel, which approximates its Cold War predecessor. Nor should it be assumed that the means by which intelligence agencies conducted their activities during the Cold War are necessarily well-suited to the challenges they will face in the future."[5] But in the debate over the future of intelligence, few are ready to say precisely what it should and should not do.

At least initially, the collapse of the bipolar standoff has unleashed new conditions in world politics that presage more conflict between states but especially within them. Leaders of most states now perceive they can operate without reference to the overarching goals of stability and balance to which both the United States and the USSR subscribed in order to prevent nuclear war between them. And while many insurgent groups may have less external support to make their "revolution" or achieve "liberation," they also have much less constraint on determining how they should try to fulfill such aims. Ethnic conflicts, moreover, are about religions/confessions, tribal relations, and geographical and cultural boundaries that no longer (if they ever did) lend themselves to subordination to systemwide goals and values. In fact, most wars to be fought in the last half-decade of this century will not be about the struggle to create a new world order, nor will they be resolved in the name of its principles.

Regional security systems are also in the process of fundamental transformation from alliances and dynamics based on the US-USSR rivalry to a completely new set of power relationships. We do not know yet what these will be. The emerging international system defies labels. It includes actors and problems that are not states or the artifacts of national policy at all (for example, fiercely separatist ethnic groups, subnational but very internationally open and linked trade zones, multinational corporations, holes in ozone layers) but have a tremendous impact on modern diplomacy and foreign policy. As a result, the issues considered appropriate or potential subjects for intelligence are growing in number and complexity. So also is the difficulty in making choices about which issues are best left to other agencies of government to analyze, or are worthwhile studying at all. As the cold war-era military alliances break down or change their orientation, the intelligence sharing that was a by-product of alliance relations is also likely to diminish.

Nevertheless, Saddam Hussein and the successors to Kim Il Sung are not the last of the autocrats who possess significant armies; the end of the cold war has not meant that the global trade in arms will wind down in the near future; and the processes of self-determination and democratization now occurring broadly appear to be neither trouble-free nor irreversible. If indeed there is a total of two hundred members of the United Nations by the year 2000, many countries will have been created from the chaos associated with the breakup of empires (especially the Soviet system), and others will have emerged from the divisions caused by long-repressed ethnic and religious strife. On the sidelines, extremists and terrorists will probably resort increasingly to ever more powerful weapons in order to obtain settlements on terms they judge to be favorable. They will undoubtedly apply pressure, and perhaps resort to private armies, in the quest for a legitimate political role.

On the other hand, the next century could be one in which many of the traditional incentives and capabilities that enabled nations to go to war will have been altered. The expanding communications, cultural, and economic ties between countries and regions will likely promote such a high degree of interaction, collaboration, and mutual reliance that the momentary gains of using force will rarely, if ever, appear worth the significant risk to the system. Many social and ethnic groups already will have achieved self-determination or autonomy within federal structures, moreover; even the civil wars dominating our headlines today will eventually be settled or played out. The trend toward interdependence will continue, as ethnic conflicts or other circumstances result in the creation of new, smaller countries that will find economic and security cooperation essential to their ultimate survival. Finally, the industrialized as well as developing countries will be full partners in a global collective security system whose roots were probably secured during Desert Storm. All of these developments will require new paradigms in intelligence work not only to study threats to U.S. security but also to anticipate those conditions and forces that could undermine interdependence and create disharmony.

While by some accounts American intelligence personnel and budgets are stretched very thin by all that the organizations have to do, only this country has the public and private resources available to generate information about, and analyze the consequences of, global security threats, whether narrowly or broadly conceived. In Washington, D.C., alone, in addition to the Library of Congress and the libraries of ten universities and colleges, there are more than two hundred specialized libraries and research collections, many of which deal with international affairs, foreign policy, and national security issues. Within a ten-mile radius of the Washington Monument, more than five hundred think tanks, federally funded research and development centers, and consulting firms do work that is very similar to that done by the Directorate of Intelligence at the CIA, many units within the DIA, and some components of the NSA. The U.S. government has a Foreign Service, Foreign Commercial Service, Foreign Agricultural Advisory Service, and a worldwide system of cultural, economic, scientific, and defense attachés. Each of the federal departments has specialized intelligence and research units that collect, process, and disseminate information and analysis, as one former DCI put it, "just like the C.I.A." Because these resources all exist independently of the formal intelligence agencies, and because many have been toiling on issues and problems that until recently were not considered intelligence targets, there has never been a comprehensive review of how their work might relieve the pressure on the intelligence community. But their presence will have to be taken into account when considering the question of how much the intelligence community should realistically aim to do in the post-cold war era.

Chapter 3

THE STRATEGIC CONTRIBUTION OF INTELLIGENCE

We have the greatest obligation and opportunity that a nation ever had . . .
we are called to put the world in order again.

—Allen Dulles
letter from the American embassy, Bern, September 1918

Critics of the growth and cost of the intelligence agencies question why the U.S. government still needs specialized and secretive organizations to collect information, especially given the nature of many of the topics of rising concern, now that the cold war is over. They argue that a growing proportion of the information provided by intelligence organizations can be provided by "line" outfits such as the military services or State Department, or by the private sector. The counterarguments to this position need to be stated explicitly because they not only make the case for why the U.S. government continues to need a separate intelligence community, but also suggest general guidelines for institutionalizing intelligence activities in the post-cold war era. What follows is a summary of the contributions intelligence has made in the past to national security decisionmaking and a brief explanation of why it is still reasonable to continue pursuing strategic information:

▲   *Providing independent analyses and assessments beyond what ordinary government departments are capable of providing.* Presidents and the Congress have thought it useful to have a source of expertise other than the armed services or the State, Treasury, and Commerce departments. Such agencies will always be suspected, validly or not, of parochialism. The existence of a centralized clearinghouse for information collection and analysis, in addition to the benefits of timeliness and efficiency, increases the chances that U.S. decisionmakers will act on the basis of information that is not derived from sources that have a direct political or budgetary stake in the outcome.

▲   *Producing information that is economically infeasible for other organizations.* At some price the private media could build reconnaissance satellites to detect North Korean troop movements, send investigators to register Chinese military radar parameters, or retain stringers to report on nuclear projects in Iran or biological weapons research in Iraq, but to this point they have not found it profitable or safe to do so. The government must thus provide such resources for itself.

▲   *Taking advantage of economies of scale, coordinating the joint use of common resources, and making hard choices about competing priorities.* Every policymaking department head would apparently like to have his or her own dedicated space-based reconnaissance program, spy network, and all-purpose analytic organization. However, efficiency and affordability require centralized, common-use intelligence programs, just as there is a centralized, common-use General Services Administration to provide for the logistical and maintenance needs of the government as a whole.

If the U.S. government did not have a centralized intelligence service, Congress would soon find it necessary to create one.

CURRENT AND PROJECTED MISSIONS: POLITICAL AND MILITARY INTELLIGENCE

Noting that "the dangers we face today are more diverse" than those of the cold war, the White House's latest public statement concerning national security strategy highlights the following as the major and relatively new threats with which the United States must contend:

▲ the spread of ethnic conflict;

▲ the ability of "rogue states" to destabilize entire regions;

▲ the proliferation of weapons of mass destruction; and,

▲ "large scale environmental degradation, exacerbated by rapid population growth," which "threaten[s] to undermine political stability in many countries and regions."[1]

While the first three of these topics are traditional subjects for intelligence, it is important to point out that many so-called new agenda environmental issues as well are already an established feature of intelligence support to policymakers. As Director of Central Intelligence (DCI) Robert Gates testified (in the first-ever field hearing of the Senate Select Committee on Intelligence),

> Since the late 1980s, the Intelligence Community has been contributing to US government efforts to work with other countries to protect the global environment from a host of threats:
>
> ◆ Ozone depletion. . . . The Intelligence Community has been following this problem for several years and is starting work on a program to determine whether we can monitor emissions of CFCs [chlorofluorocarbons].
>
> ◆ Tropical deforestation. . . . CIA analysts have done work on these issues, using satellite imagery and other tools, to support US policymakers in their multi-year efforts to secure an international treaty on forest protection.
>
> ◆ Possible climate change and measures adopted by governments, and measures adopted by governments to reduce greenhouse gas emissions in an effort to avert it. . . . As US negotiators worked at length to forge the international agreement on this important issue . . . CIA analysts

provided them, over the course of a three-year period, with a comprehensive series of reports. . . .

Other similar issues that are the subject of ongoing work include: ocean dumping of hazardous substances; water scarcity and degradation; the environmental consequences of narcotics cultivation; the impact of earthquakes and other natural disasters; food shortages and agricultural resource decline; and the pressures faced by developing and industrialized countries alike as they grapple with the costs of environmental protection. While some of these projects have been started within the past several years, many go back a long way.[2]

The report of this field hearing expands on this list and adds to it problems labeled "troubling uncertainties and clear threats" that have been of substantial concern for some time:

▲   the "wrenching economic and political transitions" in the countries of the former Soviet Union and Central and Eastern Europe;

▲   the assumption by China of "a more important economic and political role in global affairs";

▲   the threats posed to peace processes by "violent extremists";

▲   the "resurgence of militant nationalism";

▲   "transnational phenomena such as terrorism, narcotics trafficking, . . . and refugee flows."

Newer areas of activity also encompass the following traditional intelligence missions applied to current concerns:

▲   the need for gathering information on and in "denied areas" such as Iran, Iraq, North Korea;

▲   monitoring of arms control (especially the problems posed by the need to dispose safely of more than a hundred tons of weapons-grade plutonium)[3] and other international treaties such as those relating to resource conservation and environmental protection[4] as well as "nontraditional" arms control treaties such as the 1992

Open Skies Treaty that do not involve the usual types of system limits or behavioral prohibitions with which the intelligence community has largely been concerned.[5] Additionally, advising U.S. treaty negotiators;

▲ support to operational military commanders engaged in regional conflict resolution and peacekeeping operations;[6] and,

▲ counterintelligence.

Combining the two sets of threats, it becomes apparent that

> intelligence [needs to] address a much wider range of threats and dangers. . . . Intelligence will . . . be critical for directing new efforts against regional conflicts, proliferation of WMD [weapons of mass destruction], counterintelligence, terrorism and narcotics trafficking. In order to adequately forecast dangers to democracy and to U.S. economic well-being, the intelligence community must track political, economic, social and military developments in those parts of the world where U.S. interests are most heavily engaged and where overt collection of information from open sources is inadequate. Finally, to enhance the study and support of worldwide environmental, humanitarian, and disaster relief activities, technical intelligence assets (principally imagery) must be directed to a greater degree towards collection of data on these subjects.[7]

As this work is done, managers of intelligence will have to help policymakers appraise which threats are likely to increase as well as determine where the counteractions will require far more warning than present analyses and forecasting methods can provide.

In a January 1994 hearing by the Senate Select Committee on "Current and Projected National Security Threats," then-DCI James Woolsey offered one of the most comprehensive and public reviews of current missions responding to regional, political, and military threats, and of the types of support that the intelligence community is providing to policymakers. An outline of his comments is offered here:

▲ North Korea: assessment of the regime's nuclear capability, analytical support to U.S. diplomats dealing with the North Koreans and with

U.S. allies in the region, current intelligence supplied to the U.S. military commander in Korea, monitoring of "what North Korea calls its war preparations program, including both improvements in military capabilities and continuing efforts to bring their economy and society to a heightened state of military readiness."

▲   China: "We are focussing our efforts on the political, economic, and military evolution in China."

▲   Russia and the former Soviet Union: "First, we are providing critical—and sometimes unique—political and economic analysis to policymakers to warn them of potential risks facing Russia's uncertain future and to help them sort out the myriad confusing and conflicting aspects of the Russian economy. . . . Second, we continue to monitor the disposition and status of Russia's 27,000 or so nuclear warheads, as well as the strategic systems still deployed to deliver these weapons. . . . Third, the intelligence community continues to monitor the state of Russia's general purpose forces. . . . Fourth, we are closely monitoring Russia's relations with its newly independent neighbors [as well as political, military, and economic developments within these countries]."

▲   The Middle East: "First, we are providing daily, intense intelligence support to our negotiators involved in the peace process. Second, we are continuing our liaison efforts with intelligence services throughout the region to help nurture an atmosphere of confidence and trust. Third, as we have for twenty years, we are continuing to use our unique intelligence capabilities to monitor existing peace agreements in the Sinai and Golan. . . . Fourth, we are continuing vigorous counter-terrorism intelligence efforts to help keep the opponents of the peace process at bay." Regarding Iran and Iraq, there is a continuing effort to monitor and defeat those nations' weapons acquisitions programs and thwart their support of terrorism, as well as to assist U.S. diplomats in persuading European and Asian allies of the threats posed.

▲   Regional conflicts: "technical support to U.S. forces . . . [and analysis and monitoring of] attempts to circumvent [embargoes] . . . and watching closely for any indication of an immanent [sic] exodus [of refugees]."

Acknowledging that "local strife" is a major threat to regional stability, DCI Woolsey recalled that monitoring "these types of conflicts [is] not new to U.S. intelligence: half of the stars etched into the marble wall at CIA are dedicated to those officers who lost their lives to such conflicts" since the agency was created in 1947.[8] What is new is that intelligence missions may be conducted as part of the process of supporting UN military commanders and multinational forces deployed in such conflicts. New ways will have to be found to protect intelligence sources and methods when information is circulated well beyond the small circle of countries with which the United States has developed intelligence-sharing relationships.

A review of recent congressional hearings and statements by members of the select committees on intelligence,[9] as well as of the academic literature, only adds targets and functions to the already substantial list of current and projected missions. First, the role that intelligence services generally play in the post-cold war era is to verify that onetime adversaries are genuinely committed to peaceful relations. This may explain why the Russian intelligence service kept Aldrich Ames on as a paid agent and why, conceivably, his reports may have been of interest to President Yeltsin despite the risks that disclosure might be thought to have for the future of U.S.-Russian cooperation. As Thomas Powers observed recently, "Intelligence Services touch, watch and listen to each other at a thousand points." During the cold war, "the intimate knowledge revealed by the wrestler's embrace freed both sides from the ignorance, rumor, and the outbreaks of panicky fear that spark big wars no one wants."[10] Such tacit surety will continue to be as important and serve as a rationale for intelligence activities that pose inevitable risks to critical diplomatic relationships.

Second, the need for a wide range of very specialized military intelligence continues to grow and cannot be effectively filled by greater reliance on open sources. Information about such things as radar parameters, weapons systems performance characteristics, C3I (command, control, communication, and intelligence) hardening, and the state of readiness of certain military and paramilitary forces is central to national security planning and decisionmaking. These are not the usual subjects of inquiry for dissertation writers or contributors to academic journals, nor is the press very skilled at (or interested in) conducting detailed military assessments and maintaining the databases to do so.

Third, intelligence is responsible for protecting the integrity of communications, for gauging and defeating foreign threats to penetrate secure U.S. government networks or to alter commercial channels (for such purposes as manipulating stock markets or laundering drug money transactions) and data exchanged via the Internet system.[11] Fourth, there is still some need for the covert action capabilities of the intelligence community to provide the president with options for situations where it would be desirable to influence foreign leaders, political parties, or situations without revealing the direct role played by the U.S. government.[12] Fifth, there is growing concern that Russian organized crime has developed in such a way and to an extent that it represents a challenge to government and civil society. The Russian "mafiya" threatens political stability inside the country but also throughout the region and even globally because of its suspected involvement in the illicit arms trade, especially as it encompasses weapons of mass destruction. At present, the DCI estimates that there are "200 large, sophisticated criminal groups engaged in criminal activity throughout the former Soviet Union and in 29 other countries, including the United States."[13] The growth and influence of these organizations—and the need for police intelligence services to exchange information about them—led in part to the opening of a "branch office" of the FBI in Moscow earlier this year.[14]

Sixth, intelligence has served to drive the U.S. research and development community to and beyond the edge of known technological capabilities. As Director Woolsey explains, "Our intelligence has promoted U.S. competitiveness and has created new jobs. For decades the special requirements of the intelligence community have stimulated technological innovation, especially with regard to aerospace, electronics, sensors, and information processing. . . . The products and technologies derived from intelligence requirement include, for instance, high efficiency solar cells and batteries, high speed computer networks, digital image processing algorithms, and advanced optical and magnetic recording systems."[15] Sometimes intelligence gathering requires systems at the absolute limits of known technology (or even the willingness to risk going a little beyond). Without the intelligence community to fund programs pushing the edge, private industry would go no further than what is commercially feasible.

The current and projected missions highlighted here are not, of course, the exclusive concern or preserve of intelligence. All of the subjects mentioned (except for counterintelligence) are considered foreign policy challenges as well as national security problems, and information is collected about them and analysis performed by U.S. government departments and agencies that are not members of the intelligence community. Intelligence agencies have developed special sources and methods to analyze dynamics and anticipate threats. But they are not always right, or listened to when they are, or even among the first to know when adverse developments occur. In addition, policymakers want a range of views on most subjects and have varying degrees of experience in using, as well as varied levels of confidence in, intelligence assessments.

Managing all these missions—and providing accurate and timely intelligence about the targets and phenomena involved to all the consumers who claim a need to know—has already begun to change the way intelligence is done as well as modify the very organizations that provide it. The White House acknowledges that any national security strategy designed to meet the challenges of the new era requires "that we take steps to reinforce current intelligence capabilities and overt foreign service reporting . . . and . . . to enhance coordination of clandestine and overt collection."[16] But the Clinton administration, like its predecessor, has not taken many initiatives toward reorganization. Despite the need for assessments of many new problems and the preference for diversity of analytical sources, moreover, by the beginning of 1990 the portion of departmental budgets devoted to the study of most of these subjects had substantially eroded. That of the intelligence community had declined in dollar terms compared to 1980.[17] And by 1997, according to Woolsey, the CIA will cut "down to the same number of analysts as we had in 1977, yet we will have twice as many subjects to follow."[18]

ECONOMIC INTELLIGENCE

In addition to the traditional focus on strategic questions and problems, the White House has suggested that there is another role for intelligence: namely, that of identifying "opportunity for advancing our interests," especially when it can serve to enhance American international economic competitiveness.[19] According to this viewpoint, intelligence collection can support U.S. trade negotiators and help level the economic playing field by identifying threats to U.S. companies from unfair trading practices and those abroad who would steal secrets.

The question facing the intelligence community in commerce is not whether the U.S. government needs to know more about international economic transactions but whether the collection of such information by intelligence agencies is inherently better and more cost-effective than relying on other sources. While the top management of the intelligence community has consistently affirmed that economic intelligence is an appropriate target, recent DCIs have taken different positions on just how far the CIA and NSA should go in gathering, assessing, and disseminating the data. William Webster, for example, was not skeptical of the importance of knowing what is happening in the world of high finance and foreign trade but cautious about the value that could be added by intelligence in an international financial environment where "traditional distinctions have been blurred between domestic and international markets, between the different kinds of financial transactions, and even between who is a market participant and who is not."[20] Admiral Stansfield Turner, in contrast, argued the case for "redefining 'national security' by assigning economic strength greater prominence" and refocusing intelligence resources on warning of "such worldwide developments as technological breakthroughs, new mercantilism strategies, sudden shortages of raw materials or unfair or illegal economic practices that disadvantage the country."[21]

Director Woolsey noted in his nomination hearing the need to conduct, in conjunction with the National Economic Council, "a thorough review . . . of the whole field of economic intelligence and come up with a systematic policy" for the collection and sharing of economic and commercial intelligence within the U.S. government and with American industry.[22] A year later, Woolsey told the Senate Select Committee that "the intelligence community is being asked to provide a strong supporting role in this new international economic arena," and summarized the assistance currently provided in the following terms:

> First, we are providing policymakers analytical support on world economic trends and on key international trade issues. This support includes evaluating the economic plans, intentions and strategies of foreign governments and their impact on U.S. interests and initiatives. It also includes analytical to American negotiators involved in foreign trade discussions. . . . Second, we are providing analytical road maps on how well or poorly the nations in the former Soviet Union and in Eastern and Central Europe are faring with their economic reform efforts. . . . Third, we are providing our expertise in trade, finance and energy to help the Administration thwart efforts by countries such as Iraq, Libya, and Serbia from circumventing [sic] United Nations sanctions. Fourth, we are assessing how some governments violate the rules of the game in international trade. . . . We are paying

careful attention to those countries or businesses who are spying on our firms, to the disadvantage of American businesses and American workers, and to those governments and foreign companies that try to bribe their way into obtaining contracts that they cannot win on the merits.[23]

According to intelligence community surveys, Treasury and Commerce Department and U.S. Trade Representative officials are highly appreciative of such general economic intelligence support. Neither these officials nor U.S. businesspeople are suggesting that the intelligence community get into the field of commercial or competitor intelligence, however.[24] No one disputes that it would be good to know more about international trading practices or that the gaps in present systems developed by the U.S. government for reporting and tracking capital flows and transactions should be eliminated.[25] But many professional intelligence officers remain skeptical that devoting intelligence resources to commercial topics is worthwhile or that energy and manpower should be spent tackling what is already the subject of sophisticated and well-developed private-sector analytical organizations and companies.[26]

All governments collect data about the economies and leading businesses of their neighbors and adversaries, and governmental leaders today recognize the overwhelming importance of the economic dimensions of national security. In some systems of government, there is, moreover, no tension or dispute arising from the collection of such information and its selective dissemination to the private sector in order to enhance the prospects and balance sheets of specific companies. Because such tensions arise much more readily in the American democratic system, the U.S. government has always shied away from the public release of clandestine economic information, especially when it involved proprietary information and data concerning particular firms. In fact, the United States now probably lags well behind the efforts made by the economics and trade ministries, to say nothing of the intelligence services, of such countries as France, Japan, and Germany. Without an established ethic or methods of collection, the use of the intelligence agencies to gather competitiveness-enhancing intelligence becomes doubly problematic. American intelligence also lacks the experience that other countries' services have gained over many decades in collecting and distributing specific information that clearly helps business. To do so—even if Washington were good at it—would involve government officials in such conundrums as what constitutes an American company, how many such entities should be privy to the material collected, and whether companies' use of the information provided would reveal sources and methods of collection that would jeopardize future operations.

Few if any business leaders today use the unclassified data and current forecasts made by the intelligence community. When information and projections of rivals' behavior or conditions ahead are needed, U.S. firms do the work in-house or retain the services of specialized consultants.[27] Even the macroeconomic trends reported on by other government agencies and bureaus are of limited use in making business decisions.

Recently, however, intelligence has been cited for two services that business cannot entirely perform by itself. First, U.S. intelligence agencies apparently have the ability to recognize when the clandestine services of other countries have targeted specific U.S. firms in order to steal industrial secrets and can warn such firms to upgrade security and take other countermeasures. Second, there is no doubt that the signals capabilities of the intelligence community (SIGINT)—intercepting official foreign closed-door communications—make it possible to read negotiating instructions and listen in on the discussion within the decisionmaking circles of capitals abroad about how particular companies can be helped to win contracts. For U.S. trade and commerce officials, knowing when foreign governments are prepared to intervene behind the scenes in favor of their own companies allows for a chance to expose the scheme, protest the measures being used, and perhaps assure that the playing field remains level for a particular deal or project. Using such information, of course, is problematic. It almost certainly risks revealing to particular governments that the United States has penetrated sensitive communication systems, resulting in diplomatic rancor as well as a tightening of communications security, making the next piece of information much harder to get. Using SIGINT more widely also risks exposing the capabilities of the source itself.

This kind of economic intelligence is provided to top policymakers on a daily basis. Congressional oversight teams report that it is extremely well received and represents a concrete example of how intelligence can provide something of unique value. Intelligence officers responsible for protecting the systems that yield such information, however, think its more frequent use will result in countermeasures and disinformation that will be very hard to defeat or discern.

WHAT NEW MISSIONS IMPLY ABOUT THE NEED FOR A FRESH APPROACH

By now, it should be clear that to conduct intelligence effectively—and to anticipate the security environment and threats likely to be manifest by the next century—agencies and analysts will need to be thinking about new paradigms and collecting and processing information in ways that reflect adaptation to changed circumstances.[28] With the United States evolving into a knowledge-based society and economy, for example, intelligence will have to shift its focus away from threats against territory to those that affect the generation and transmission of information domestically and internationally. This does not mean simply staying ahead of computer hackers or the eavesdropping capabilities of others but rather anticipating and countering entirely new threats for which today's organizations and methods are unprepared. In addition, the world of the next century will contain (as it does now) a number of countries that are in the midst of socioeconomic transition. Currently, attention within the intelligence communities is focused on how such countries as China and Russia can create effective and self-sustaining market economies, and the implications for American economic security if they succeed or fail. A decade from now, the most critical issue may well be how the political developments unleashed by the transition in these countries will affect such issues as the commitment to the disposal of nuclear arms, nonproliferation, regional arms trade, and prospects for the negotiation and peaceful resolution of separatist claims and ethnic conflict. These are not new topics for intelligence analysis. What will be new is comprehending that threats to American policies and national security could be posed by adverse developments arising from the dynamics of processes we understand poorly if at all and from political forces that are, as yet, not even formed.

All of this will change the ways intelligence professionals are recruited, work, and think, as well as the nature of the intelligence cycle itself. According to James Woolsey, "We have to understand the revolutionary developments that can, in ways different from during the Cold War, undermine US security."[29] Even in cases where the pace of change is not rapid or the seriousness of the danger readily perceived, in practical terms it may be necessary, as Jessica Matthews recently argued, to develop "new tools to deal with . . . slow-motion security threats" stemming from "a varying mix of too many people, environmental shortages and acute poverty." As is increasingly apparent after the interventions in Somalia, Haiti, Rwanda, such threats are "capable of dismembering nations as thoroughly as any external attack, and of metasticizing [sic] to neighboring states through ethnic tensions and floods of refugees. . . . We have to learn how to decipher what the future holds in their earliest stages. We need some kind of early intervention mechanism with a low political threshold that can act long before inaction becomes intolerable . . . and before population, economic and environmental imbalances spiral into irreversible or nearly irreversible decline."[30]

In the closely related field of political intelligence, to take another example, intelligence officers are finding themselves involved in collecting information in ways departing from the past and making different judgments as a result. David Boren, former chairman of the Senate Select Committee on Intelligence, said, "American intelligence, long aimed at penetrating leadership and command groups, must now develop a greater ability to predict popular attitudes and actions. It requires a different kind of ability to read the mood of the people on the streets of Moscow, Baghdad, or Panama City than to interpret the way in which a military commander fits into a preconceived order of battle. . . . In addition, American leadership will rely more upon collective action and intelligence must therefore provide policymakers with more information about the tools of persuasion."[31] Stansfield Turner pointed out that "CIA case officers are trained in recruiting agents, planting bugs and photographing documents. To ask them to go out and sense public attitudes is almost like asking a fighter pilot to leave his supersonic jet and become a crop duster in a propeller-driven biplane."[32] Other U.S. government officials may already be better suited to collecting and analyzing information of this type, such as those in the foreign service. But there is professional as well as departmental reluctance to do too much that would be perceived as intelligence work out of concern that the activity would jeopardize the functioning of the embassy or the relationship that must be maintained between the staff and the host government.[33]

The importance of comprehending the democratization process, as yet another example, may also require that the intelligence community enter virgin territory—or persuade policymakers that it would be unwise to do so and that other parts of the government are equipped to do better work. DCI Woolsey made the latter case recently when he told the

Senate Select Committee that "we are not really in the election esti-mating business. Outcomes of elections in which free voters can make their choice in a ballot booth, which is—was [sic] now, really for the first time in a long time, the case in Russia, are in the categories of mys-teries rather than secrets. . . . How people are going to vote in a free election is something that we have our hunches on, but they are not necessarily going to be any better than that of a good university faculty or the newsroom of a good newspaper."[34] Thus far, U.S. officials in charge of initiatives to promote democratization abroad note that the bias of those in intelligence toward collecting and relying on clandes-tine sources of information has not proved helpful to the task of deter-mining what is going on in situations where America seeks to support those forces independent of established governments.

Developing information of the type highlighted above and basing judgments on it will also require much greater openness and exchange of perceptions between intelligence officers and academic experts. This will be especially true if intelligence agencies increasingly focus on eco-nomic and commercial issues—fields where their professionals have little experience.

Treaty monitoring functions will probably also require the devel-opment of new procedures and new standards, as well as greater toler-ance for error. When Woolsey testified in support of ratification of the new global chemical weapons ban treaty, in fact, he signaled that "the chemical weapons problem is so difficult from an intelligence perspec-tive that I cannot state that we have high confidence in our ability to detect noncompliance, especially on a small scale."[35] The shift in arms development and manufacturing from single-country, sole producers to collaborative, multifirm, and multinational enterprises will require new ways of thinking about how to track, measure, and anticipate develop-ments that could undermine existing treaties or bilateral understandings or increase the proliferation of weapons that destabilize countries and regions of geopolitical importance to U.S. security.[36]

On the analytic side, the arrival of what Dave McCurdy, former chairman of the House Permanent Select Committee on Intelligence, has called the "CNN era" has placed tremendous demands on intelli-gence. The product "must now be more rapid and thorough than ever before to allow decision-makers to respond speedily, and it must be accurate enough to allow public officials to correct the truncated, sound-bite version of events so often provided by television news."[37] As if this pressure were not enough, the expanding definition of national security requires that the shrinking corps of analysts be spread much more thinly over a broader range of topics. As a result, according to deputy director of intelligence (DDI), "dramatic changes in national priorities and the resulting funding reductions require a reexamination of the fundamental purposes and processes of intelligence analysis. We need to go back to the basic questions of what we do and what is the best way to do it."[38] Improved performance will have to come from deeper understanding of the means by which intelligence is collected, analyzed, and used, as well as of the nature and dynamics of the emerging structure of world politics. This will involve intensive exploration of those recent national intelligence estimates that proved correct and the all too many in the past that turned out wrong, to see whether any useful lessons can be drawn.

The Directorate of Intelligence will have to take the lead in developing not only more transparent analyses shared extensively and vetted by a wide group of experts but also different methods of analysis that identify more readily what the DDI calls sources, the "linchpins" or "drivers" of the judgments being made about the subjects under study, and that sort out the relationships between sources and conclusions.

This approach to analytic tradecraft—facts and findings, and linchpins—forces systemic attention to the range of and relationships among the factors at play in a given situation. Laying out the linchpins encourages testing of the key subordinate judgments that hold estimate conclusions together. . . . Finally, this approach helps to focus ongoing collection and analysis: what indicators or patterns of development could emerge to signal that the linchpins were unreliable? What triggers or dramatic internal and external events could reverse the expected momentum?[39]

In order to implement the new approach, the Directorate has established a training board to reengineer guidance and professional education for all levels in the analytical service. But much more needs to be done. As congressional and academic critics of intelligence performance argue, the same agencies that failed to provide timely and accurate forecasts of the end of the cold war, the collapse of the Soviet Union, the onset of every regional war in which the United States has become involved since 1950, and most of the dramatic military, political, and economic events that have transformed the world over the past four years will not necessarily do any better by generating new professional courses and mid-management educational programs.

To function effectively, the intelligence community generally—and the CIA especially—must constantly improve the relevance and integrity of analysis. Ideally, the distance between analyst and con-sumer should be as short as possible, and the DCI should be able to select and plan the most efficient mix of information-gathering tools or procedures for the requirements at hand. Yet, as one might expect, in the U.S. government the reality and ideal often do not match. Currently, intelligence collection systems are coordinated and assigned responsibilities through the DCI's Community Management Staff, which assesses requirements based on feedback from intelligence con-sumers and helps to plan technical collection programs. There is good reason to believe that this arrangement will not be able to keep up with demand any better than it did during the cold war. Though the formal requirements process is centralized, the intelligence community itself remains a patchwork that the DCI struggles to control. The collection and analysis organizations have remained within their parent organi-zations (for example, the National Security Agency and other major intelligence collection organizations are still housed in the Pentagon, the Bureau for Intelligence and Research in the State Department, etc.), where their day-to-day operations are often beyond the effective control of the DCI and their budgets are ultimately controlled by their parent organizations. Ironically, what drives the process least is policy-makers' needs, even when these are known to all and well established.

The integrity of analysis was a public policy issue long before charges and countercharges surfaced so visibly in the confirmation hearings of Robert Gates for director of central intelligence in September 1991, or before the results of a survey partly released by Gates himself in March 1992 indicated that "forcing a product to con-form to a view thought to be held by a manager higher up the chain of command occurs often enough to be of concern" and was profession-ally "disturbing."[40] One reason why the issue is continually raised is that it is genuinely hard to detect when politicization materially affects intelligence, harder to design review systems to rule it out, and even harder still to demonstrate that they work. Also, politicization can take many forms: analysts can be intimidated by subtle (or not so sub-tle) feedback from their superiors; alternatively, analysts can impose their own self-censorship and cease writing judgments that they think might be unwelcome. There are also built-in disincentives for indi-viduals or the CIA itself to deliver bad news, or news that is inconsis-tent with the beliefs and preferences of the agency's consumers. Moreover, it is hard to determine whether politicization in one area affects analysis in other areas.

It is impossible to protect completely against the threat of politicization, but experience so far suggests that taking the following steps (as is now being done at CIA) can help foster integrity in analysis:

▲ reviewing intelligence estimates and forecasts regularly to determine both the degree of accuracy achieved and the sources that most influenced the judgments reached;

▲ providing analysts with regular opportunities to speak out about the review process and its value as well its effect on the intelligence product;

▲ asking analysts to document the sources used in intelligence analyses and indicate the weight they assigned to each of the sources they used in reaching their judgments;

▲ evaluating feedback from consumers to make improvements while at the same time guarding against the possibility that praise might breed complacency or promote conventional thinking.

None of these steps, by themselves, will assure that intelligence judgments will always be right or timely. But they are bound to help nowadays when there is so little of which even the most diligent analyst can be certain and in a bureaucratic culture that apparently lends itself to political and other distortions of the facts and logical reasoning.

Finally, the need for new technical and linguistic skills has led some in Congress to question whether the present personnel and the human resource strategies of the intelligence agencies are up to the task. Congress has already supported enhanced early retirement programs to spur attrition and allow new skills to be recruited. Nevertheless, legislators are clearly concerned that this step does not go far enough toward rejuvenation. The House Permanent Select Committee on Intelligence has concluded in its latest report that "it is uncertain how much success the community will have in retraining a workforce, whose average age will only increase through the decade, in highly demanding skill areas, both technical and linguistic." The committee is also concerned "that the performance evaluation system currently in place in the intelligence community fails to provide managers with a frank appraisal of the quality of its workforce. . . ." The gap between what is going to be needed and the abilities of those currently on the job is so great that the committee members have called for "serious consideration of selective, involuntary separations."[41]

As part of the process of rethinking what analysts do and for whom, managers and analysts alike will need to gain a better understanding of the role of intelligence in the policy process. Analysts especially need to have more direct exposure to the workings of the national security decisionmaking process and to see how policymakers use as well as abuse intelligence products. More direct contact with policymakers through expanding the practice of rotational assignments in policy agencies would help analysts learn how to produce reports with greater relevance and more precise descriptions of the degree of confidence they have in their assessment.

In sum, the intelligence profession is at a watershed in its intellectual history. For nearly a hundred years, the focus of intelligence operations had remained unchanged. The categories of information required for country outlook assessment and the analysis of military capabilities and intentions were largely the same in 1909 and in 1989. In the twenty-first century, intelligence work promises to be fundamentally different. If so, then an evolutionary approach toward the training of intelligence personnel and the development and organization of collection methods and systems—even toward the process of analysis itself—will no longer suffice to assure timely and accurate intelligence about the threats ahead.

Chapter 4

POLICY, ORGANIZATIONAL, AND MANAGEMENT CHOICES AHEAD

The future of Intelligence is hard. In the past war, the nature of the weapons, the brilliance of our sources and the mistakes of our enemies all weighed in the balance in our favour. It may well not remain so in the future.

—R. V. Jones
"Scientific Intelligence" lecture to the Royal
United Services Institution, February 19, 1947

While there are many voices calling for intelligence reform,[1] most agree that the collection and analysis of information by intelligence agencies is still needed to fill in the contours and context of the strategic picture with data that is not available from other sources or analytic methodologies. While acknowledging repeatedly the need for a thoroughgoing review and overhaul of the intelligence community as called for by many inside the profession and on Capitol Hill, as well as in the report by a special task force of the Carnegie Endowment for International Peace that received considerable attention during the presidential transition phase, the Clinton administration did not launch such a process.[2] As pressure to do so mounted, the administration resisted to the point where the House Permanent Select Committee on Intelligence in its June 1994 report openly criticized the CIA for failing to develop a strategic plan that "defines essential roles and missions, maps a course for organizational restructuring and streamlining, and allocates scarce resources."[3] And in September, the House and Senate oversight committees mandated the establishment of a presidential commission to study the future role and organization of the intelligence community as part of the fiscal year 1995 authorization act.

Throughout both the 102d and 103d Congresses there were calls for such a commission. Legislation was actually introduced to reorganize the intelligence community even before the findings of any commission study would have been available. A summary of the provisions of the House and Senate bills (H.R. 4165 and S. 2198) are contained in the Appendix to this paper. The legislation would have resulted in the writing of a new charter for the nation's intelligence agencies and for their management by a director of national intelligence. As such, it constitutes the most detailed statement yet of what a post-cold war intelligence community might look like and how it could be managed.

The need for organizational change stemmed not only from the challenges of the new era but also from an assessment of how and why, over the postwar years, the relationship between intelligence and policy and between the DCI and the other intelligence chiefs broke down in ways that indicated systemic problems and shortcomings. In the more than five hundred pages of public hearings about the 1992 legislation (and many more in closed session), these were the central issues reviewed and debated:

▲   What is the proper and effective relationship between the president, the National Security Council decisionmaking process, and the intelligence community? Currently "there is no provision in law for the Director of Central Intelligence to have a role in the National Security Council process. Nor is there a structure in law or Executive Order for translating the objectives and priorities of a particular President into requirements and priorities for the Intelligence Community. . . . Nor is there any organizational structure at the White House, apart from the President's Foreign Intelligence Advisory Board . . . to hold the Intelligence Community accountable for its performance."[4]

▲ What would it take to provide the DCI (or any equivalent successor position) with the legitimacy and authority needed to draw up and manage the budgets, operations, and organizational priority setting for the intelligence community as a whole? In practical terms, this is a question of providing the head of the intelligence community with the same degree of command and control that the DCI presently has only over the CIA. Congress has been uneasy about this issue of concentrating authority in a single pair of hands ever since it was first raised by the Church Committee investigating CIA activities in the 1970s.

▲ How centralized should the intelligence community be? Right now, as the *New York Times* recently editorialized, "Rival agencies do almost everything the C.I.A. does. The State and Defense Departments collect and assess intelligence. The armed services run covert operations. The F.B.I. has expanded its role in counterintelligence. Other agencies operate spy satellites and process what they photograph and overhear."[5] This raises the issues of how much diversity of opinion is desirable, what the division or duplication of labor accomplishes versus what it costs, and the impact on foreign policy and national security decisionmaking when signals get mixed.

▲ Who should determine and monitor defense intelligence activities, as well as intelligence support to tactical and operational military commanders? Is this activity better performed by an intelligence agency or by a unit within the Department of Defense?

▲ Where and how will the intelligence community get the best analysis? Would relocating analysts from the individual agencies into a single organization produce sharper and more focused research, as well as more illuminating answers to the questions that lead so many intelligence reports and analyses to be characterized by either "mushiness" or so many conflicting interpretations of international events and developments as to suggest that the internal bureaucratic politics of the intelligence community is at fault rather than the difficulty of the problem being discussed?[6] So far, there has been some success with creating task-oriented analytical centers within the CIA to deal with such issues as nuclear proliferation, narcotics, and terrorism. How applicable is this model to other agencies and other types of problems? Should only the CIA be the host to such centers? The fallout from the Aldrich Ames case—and from the controversy over the DCI's handling of it—have also produced a suggestion from one former DCI that the CIA ought to be divided into two organizations in order to separate analysts from the ill effects of the long-dominant clandestine services.[7]

▲   Should and can human intelligence be managed for the intelligence community as a whole? This transcends the customary debate over the emphasis that should be placed on human source collection versus more technical means. As Senator Boren has noted: "Under the existing framework, CIA is charged with coordinating clandestine collection using human sources or agents. This has historically meant making sure other agencies' operations do not conflict with or jeopardize those of CIA. CIA has not, however, seen its role as questioning the need for other agencies' collection activities. . . ."[8] The issue now is that if the Agency did so, and human intelligence were to be centralized, would accuracy as well as cost-effectiveness increase?

▲   Are other parts of the U.S. government now better suited and equipped to conduct the kind of intelligence operations and do the type of analysis required by the nature of today's global problems and emerging issues? Should in any case nonintelligence agencies and services (such as the Foreign Service, Foreign Commercial Service, and Foreign Agricultural Advisory Service) be designated as "national security agencies," expected to contribute more to intelligence collection and be at the table when intelligence responsibilities are dealt out?[9]

▲   Should a unified system for the collection, processing, and dissemination of imagery data be created, as has been done in the field of signals intelligence?

▲   How can the process of intelligence best be overseen by Congress? Would a Joint Select Committee assure both increased security and greater staff professionalism in the review of intelligence operations and performance? The experience of the past several years suggests that the intelligence community is still not prepared for extensive oversight or ready to deal with the current criticism of its work and

its approaches that emanates from Capitol Hill. Intelligence officials work well with congresspeople who understand and appreciate their product. But they are unused to those who are critics or
skeptics, and they still tend to brief Congress in ways that obscure
operational details and costs, as the recent episode involving the
National Reconnaissance Office's extravagant new headquarters in
Virginia illustrates, making credibility gaps almost a certainty.
Suspicions are mutual; there is a widespread feeling among intelligence professionals that oversight has been too intrusive and that
the congressional intelligence committees have sought involvement in the actual approval process for operations.

▲ What should be the relationship between the intelligence community and foreign intelligence services? In an increasingly open and
   interdependent world, can U.S. intelligence resources go further
   and penetrate difficult problems more deeply through intelligence
   sharing? What level of risk does intelligence sharing represent to
   special sources and methods or to the American private sector when
   foreign intelligence services also engage in commercial espionage?

These issues should serve at least as initial focal points for discussion by
any commission reviewing intelligence.

Many of these questions predate the contemporary political and
military transformations. While they are central to the agenda of any
commission charged with reorienting U.S. intelligence, they may not be
answerable without also considering the role and effectiveness of the
entire U.S. national security establishment, including the contributions of the information-gathering and -assessing organizations under
the control of the secretaries of state, Treasury, and commerce as well as
the heads of such agencies as USAID, EPA, FAA, FEMA, and the
NRC. The role of the nation's Foreign Service (as well as the Foreign
Agricultural Advisory Service and the Foreign Commercial Service),
USAID missions, and the diplomatic reporting they provide should
also be examined since they, too, are undergoing fundamental change.
As the demand for political and economic intelligence increases, it
may well turn out that this can be better done by a better-trained
Foreign Service and Foreign Commercial Service than by increasing
intelligence community resources devoted to human intelligence.

Whatever the outcome of present and future reviews, the central
purpose of intelligence in the U.S. system will remain that of warning

the president and the National Security Council of manifest threats to—as well as opportunities to advance—American security and strategic interests.[10] However, it is not easy to agree on what actually constitutes a manifest threat to the security of the United States today. Most threats are more subtle than they were in the cold war era when the projection of Communist power in virtually any location and in any form was a matter of grave strategic concern. Increasingly, threats the intelligence community is involved in monitoring stem from the actions of groups and forces that are identified with no particular sovereign state and that promise to be even more transnational in character tomorrow.

For the past ten years, U.S. intelligence has operated under a code of conduct drawn up by President Ronald Reagan and the late William Casey. Known as "Executive Order 12333," it has served as a charter for all intelligence activities, including, unhappily, those that led to the Iran-contra affair and "Iraqgate." If there is any clear lesson for the intelligence community growing out of its missed forecasts and the persistent failure to curb abuses of its operations from within, it is that intelligence needs a compelling vision of its strengths and role, not simply a burgeoning laundry list of rules of conduct. Despite recent legislation to foster greater coherence and centralization, the position of DCI has too little authority to pursue this vision, and the intelligence "community" remains a collection of powerful agencies and bureaus whose managers still behave as if they were working solely for the heads of their host departments. Expensive data collection efforts are duplicated, yet numerous gaps remain in coverage of critical problems, and the track record of delivering timely warnings is poor. What is now needed is a straightforward statement of who's in charge, what agencies are included, what kind of clearinghouse is to be set up at the center, the executive and legislative oversight arrangements to which all must adhere, and the activities and operations that are illegal. To continue to manage the intelligence community the way it was during the cold war is the clearest recipe for irrelevance as well as failure.

❚ Appendix

Summary and Comparison of Major Reorganization Provisions of Intelligence Community Legislation

<table>
<tr><td>

S. 2198
Intelligence Reorganization Act of 1992

</td><td>

H.R. 4165
National Security Act of 1992

</td></tr>
<tr><td>

Official Title: A bill to amend the National Security Act of 1947 to reorganize the United States Intelligence Community to provide for the improved management and execution of United States Intelligence activities, and for other purposes.

</td><td>

Official Title: A bill to reorganize the United States Intelligence Community, and for other purposes.

</td></tr>
<tr><td>

Title I

</td><td>

Title I

</td></tr>
<tr><td>

Amends the 1947 Act to authorize a "Director of National Intelligence" to attend and participate (but not vote) in NSC meetings.

Establishes within the NSC a Committee on Foreign Intelligence (CFI).

The CFI establishes the overall requirements and priorities for the Intelligence Community (IC) and conducts regular assessments of IC effectiveness.

</td><td>

Redesignates the office of the DCI as DNI and empowers the DNI to serve as the principal intelligence adviser to the President and the NSC. [NSC role for DNI specified in Title II].

Requires intelligence to be timely and objective and defines the components of the Intelligence Community, including a new National Imagery Agency and Reconnaissance Support Activity.

Directs the President to include in the annual budget for the National Foreign Intelligence Program an unclassified statement of the aggregate budget. Considers any amount appropriated to the Program appropriated to the DNI for allocation within the IC.

Establishes Deputies for Intelligence Community Functions, Warning and Crisis Support, Estimates and Analysis. Places current intelligence under Estimates and Analysis and establishes

</td></tr>
</table>

S. 2198	H.R. 4165
	an Office of Open-Source Information to prepare, manage, and execute a single, open-source program and budget, coordinate, and disseminate all such openly available information, and serve as the sole agent within the IC for the procurement of open-source material.
	Requires the DNI to establish evaluation board.
TITLE II	TITLE II
New Leadership: Creates the position of DNI, and deputies for the IC and for Estimates and Analysis.	Establishes within the NSC the Committee on Foreign Intelligence.
Responsibilities: Makes the DNI responsible for providing timely, objective intelligence to the President, appropriate heads of executive departments and agencies, the Chairman of the JCS, senior military commanders, and Congress. DNI also responsible for preparing and presenting an annual budget, managing the collection capability of the IC to assure the satisfaction of national requirements, eliminating waste and unnecessary duplication, providing guidance, direction, and approval for procurement and operation of overhead reconnaissance systems, and protecting intelligence sources and methods.	[See Title I.]
Estimative Intelligence: Establishes a National Intelligence Council (NIC) to produce national intelligence estimates.	[See Title I.]
Current Intelligence: To be provided by an Office of Intelligence Analysis comprised of analysts assigned to agencies within the IC.	[See Title I; places Current Intelligence under the Deputy for Estimative Intelligence.]

TITLE II cont.	TITLE II cont.
Warning Intelligence: To be provided by an Office of Warning and Crisis Support under the Deputy DNI/IC. Office to be responsible for identifying on a regular and continuing basis any immediate threat to national security or any area or circumstances where U.S. intervention or involvement is, or may become, necessary or desirable and providing to the President and senior officials options pertaining to such intervention.	[See Title I; position elevated to the Deputy level.]
Evaluation: Requires the DNI to establish an independent, full-time evaluation board.	[See Title I.]
CIA: Makes the Director of the CIA subordinate to the DNI and responsible for collecting human source intelligence, providing overall direction for human source collection throughout the IC, performing such services of common concern to the IC that the DNI determines can be accomplished more efficiently by centralization, and, when directed, conducting covert action operations. Within CIA, creates an Assistant Deputy Director for Operations for Military Support to serve as the principal liaison between the Agency and the Department of Defense.	
Intelligence sharing: Requires each component of the IC to provide access to the DNI to any intelligence related to national security.	

S. 2198

TITLE II cont.

Fiscal management: Makes the DNI responsible for the allocation, obligation, and expenditure of funds within the National Foreign Intelligence Program and specifies that no funds may be reprogrammed by any component of the IC without the prior approval of the DNI. Authorizes the DNI to reprogram funds.

Collection: Authorizes the DNI to direct that use of any collection capability within the IC to satisfy a priority intelligence requirement.

Personnel: Requires the DNI to institute policies and procedures to provide for the rotation of personnel within the IC and to consolidate personnel, administrative, and security programs to reduce overall costs.

Budget: President must include in any future budget request an aggregate amount for the National Intelligence Program. DNI is to obligate, expend, and allocate funds authorized to be appropriated for the Program.

TITLE III

Makes Secretary of Defense responsible for ensuring the implementation of policies and resource decisions of the DNI by elements of the DOD within the National Intelligence Program and ensuring that the tactical intelligence activities of DOD complement and are compatible with the intelligence activities funded within the Program.

H.R. 4165

TITLE II cont.

[Provides the DNI with essentially the same authority in collection, personnel, and budget matters as S. 2198.]

TITLE III

Essentially the same as in S. 2198.

TITLE III cont.

Tactical Intelligence: Requires the Secretary to indicate to Congress those tactical intelligence activities that produce positive intelligence in peacetime and interface directly with national intelligence systems.

NSA: Requires the Agency to operate subject to the authorities and guidance of the DNI and for the purpose of creating a unified organization within the IC for signals intelligence.

Imagery: Creates a National Imagery Agency to operate a unified organization within the IC for imagery intelligence collection and analysis.

DIA: Allows the director to have access to any intelligence within the IC and to direct that military intelligence requirements be satisfied when appropriate by alternative means in order to avoid unnecessary duplication.

TITLE IV

Oversight: Amends S. 400 to allow the Senate Select Committee on Intelligence jurisdiction over tactical intelligence activities.

TITLE III cont.

Establishes a Reconnaissance Support Activity within the Department of Defense to be solely responsible for the conduct of research, development, testing, evaluation, procurement, launch, operation, and final disposition of overhead reconnaissance systems as may be required to satisfy intelligence requirements of the IC.

Source: U.S. Congress, Legislative Digests, 102d Cong.

| Notes

Chapter 1

1. When he was DCI, James Woolsey estimated that the "something between two-thirds and three-quarters of the major problems we looked at during the Cold War derived in one way or the other from Moscow. . . ." Statement of R. James Woolsey, U.S. Congress, House, hearing before the Permanent Select Committee on Intelligence, 103d Cong., 1st sess., March 9, 1993, p. 16.

2. Testimony by Robert Gates, U.S. Congress, *To Reorganize the United States Intelligence Community*, S. 2198 and S. 421, joint hearing before the Select Committee on Intelligence of the United States Senate and Permanent Select Committee on Intelligence of the House of Representatives, 102d Cong., 2d sess., April 1, 1992, p. 19.

3. Ernest May, "Intelligence: Backing into the Future," *Foreign Affairs* 71, no. 3 (Summer 1992): 63. For a somewhat less sanguine view about whether a Soviet-type threat has truly disappeared, see Georgi Arbatov, "A New Cold War?" *Foreign Policy*, no. 95 (Summer 1994): 90–104.

4. See U.S. Congress, House, *Intelligence Authorization Act for Fiscal Year 1995*, report of the Permanent Select Committee on Intelligence, 103d Cong., 2d sess., June 9, 1994, pp. 29–32. Considerable duplication already exists for many of the "new agenda" targets such as nuclear proliferation. A recent internal study by the Arms Control and Disarmament Agency found that the organization was receiving intelligence assessments and reports from eighty different units and offices within the intelligence community.

5. Central Intelligence Agency, Office of Public Affairs, *A Consumer's Guide to Intelligence* (Washington, D.C.: Central Intelligence Agency, February 1994), p. vii.

6. See, for example, the prognoses in Peter F. Drucker, *Post-Capitalist Society* (New York: Harper Business, 1993); Allan E. Goodman, *A Brief History of the Future* (Boulder, Colo.: Westview Press, 1993); and Joseph S. Nye, Jr., "Peering into the Future," *Foreign Affairs* 73, no. 4 (July–August 1994): 82–93.

7. Drucker, *Post-Capitalist Society*, p. 4.

8. Central Intelligence Agency, *A Consumer's Guide to Intelligence*, p. iii.

9. Dan Glickman, U.S. Congress, House, hearing before the Permanent Select Committee on Intelligence, 103d Cong., 1st sess., March 9, 1993, p. 2.

10. Robert K. Heldman, *Information Telecommunications: Networks, Products, and Services* (New York: McGraw-Hill, 1993).

11. Peter H. Lewis, "U.S. Begins Privatizing Internet's Operations," *New York Times*, October 24, 1994, p. D1.

12. The third international symposium of the "Open Source Solutions" association focused on "National Security and National Competitiveness" and featured presentations on implications deriving from the use of open-source information in the war on drugs for national intelligence generally, the impact of open-source exploitation on U.S. relations with other governments, the role such information can play in low-intensity conflict operations, and an address by Senator John Warner on "Open Source Solutions for National Security and National Competitiveness."

13. Central Intelligence Agency, Office of Public Affairs, *C.I.A. Maps and Publications Released to the Public* (Washington, D.C.: Central Intelligence Agency, April 1994).

14. Peter Sharfman, "Intelligence Analysis in an Age of Electronic Dissemination," paper prepared for the Conference on Intelligence Analysis and Assessment, Canadian Association for Security and Intelligence Studies, Ottawa, October 27–29, 1994, pp. 16–17.

15. Douglas J. MacEachin, deputy director for intelligence at the Central Intelligence Agency, "The Tradecraft of Analysis: Challenge and Change in CIA's Directorate of Intelligence," unpublished manuscript, August 1, 1994, pp. 2–3.

16. R. James Woolsey, quoted in "Spy Case Prompts C.I.A. Chief to Vow Overhaul of Agency," *New York Times*, July 19, 1994, p. A16.

17. See, for example, Daniel Patrick Moynihan, "Our Stupid but Permanent CIA," *Washington Post*, July 24, 1994, p. C3.

18. See Stansfield Turner, *Secrecy and Democracy* (Boston: Houghton Mifflin, 1985).

Chapter 2

1. Henry A. Kissinger, *Diplomacy* (New York: Simon and Schuster, 1994), pp. 803, 833–35.

2. Dan Glickman, U.S. Congress, House, hearing before the Permanent Select Committee on Intelligence, 103d Cong., 1st sess., March 9, 1993, p. 2.

3. Ibid., p. 3.

4. "The New Measure of Man," *New York Times*, July 8, 1994, p. A27.

5. U.S. Congress, House, *Intelligence Authorization Act for Fiscal Year 1995*, report of the Permanent Select Committee on Intelligence, 103d Cong., 2d sess., June 9, 1994, p. 19.

CHAPTER 3

1. The White House, "A National Security Strategy of Engagement and Enlargement," Government Printing Office, July 1994, p. 1.

2. Quoted in U.S. Congress, Senate, *Radioactive and Other Environmental Threats to the United States and the Arctic Resulting from Past Soviet Activities*, hearing before the Select Committee on Intelligence, 102d Cong., 2d sess., August 15, 1992, pp. 125–26.

3. The internal politics and military developments in the nuclear-capable states of Russia, Ukraine, Belarus, and Kazakhstan, for example, will remain sources of continuing national security concern and require watching by intelligence sources. What all these states do with the nuclear weapons they possess as well as with the nuclear material taken out of weapons that are dismantled due to arms control is a valid inquiry for intelligence to pursue. The Russian Federation has committed itself to an ambitious, ten-to-fifteen-year R&D program for weapons systems that will require monitoring as well. The myriad conflicts (ethnic, political, military, and criminal) taking place within these societies, the parallel governments, ideologies, and subcultures they are creating, and the impact such developments have on political evolution and future national security doctrine have been subjects for intelligence community analysis and forecasting but are also covered by other agencies and departmental bureaus that deal with intelligence.

4. See, for example, the discussion of the sixteen major treaties on natural resources and environmental protection discussed in Susan Cutter, "Exploiting, Conserving, and Preserving Natural Resources," in George J. Demko and William B. Wood, eds., *Reordering the World: Geopolitical Perspectives on the Twenty-first Century* (Boulder, Colo.: Westview Press, 1994), pp. 123–40.

5. U.S. Congress, Senate, *Intelligence and Security Implications of the Treaty on Open Skies*, report of the Select Committee on Intelligence, 103d Cong., 1st sess., May 19, 1993.

6. In its report on the FY 1994 intelligence appropriations, the Senate Select Committee noted that "the job of the Intelligence Community is to anticipate where such deployments might occur and maintain an information base

capable of supporting such contingencies. This function entails not only identifying the capabilities and vulnerabilities of opposing military or paramilitary
forces, but also gathering information to be used in planning U.S. operations,
targeting data to guide U.S. 'smart' weapons, data to counter enemy radars and
sensors which otherwise might threaten U.S. aircraft, and other military support functions." U.S. Congress, Senate, *Authorizing Appropriations for Fiscal
Year 1994 for Intelligence Activities of the U.S. Government and the Central
Intelligence Agency Retirement and Disability System and for Other Purposes*,
S.Rpt. 103–115, 103d Cong., 1st sess., July 28, 1993, p. 5. UN secretary-general Boutros Boutros-Ghali identified the nature of today's peacekeeping operations in the following terms: "Peacekeepers have been sent to areas where
there are no agreements, where consent to a U.N. presence is sporadic and
where governments do not exist or have limited effective authority. And
peacekeeping is more than just keeping apart the warring parties. It may be
aimed at protecting vulnerable populations, delivering humanitarian relief
or responding to the collapse of a state. It may entail restoring democracy or
building a foundation for national recovery." Cited in "Beleaguered Are the
Peacemakers," *New York Times*, October 30, 1994, section IV, p. 15. The
intelligence required to support such operations will require the sharing of
information between governments that may not have a tradition or any experience of doing so, as well as the collection of data about entirely new targets,
as turned out to be the case even for the U.S. Defense Intelligence Agency in
Somalia. See the testimony of Lt. Gen. James R. Clapper, in U.S. Congress,
Senate, *Current and Projected National Security Threats to the United States and
Its Interests Abroad*, hearing before the Select Committee on Intelligence,
103d Cong., 2d sess., January 25, 1994, pp. 26–29.

7. The White House, "A National Security Strategy of Engagement and
Enlargement," p. 14.

8. U.S. Congress, *Current and Projected National Security Threats to the United
States*, pp. 5–11.

9. The supplemental material in the Senate Select Committee hearing on
Current and Projected National Security Threats to the United States contains two
letters (dated February 10, 1994) from the chairman to the director of central
intelligence and the director of the Defense Intelligence Agency with more
than one hundred questions reflecting current intelligence interests of Senate
members. The material also contains the CIA and DIA unclassified responses to these questions. See also U.S. Congress, Senate, *Nomination of R. James
Woolsey*, hearing before the Select Committee on Intelligence, 103rd Cong.,
1st sess., February 2–3, 1993; U.S. Congress, House, hearing before the
Permanent Select Committee on Intelligence, 103d Cong., 1st sess., March 9,
1993; U.S. Congress, Senate, Select Committee on Intelligence, *Report [to
accompany S. 2082] Authorizing Appropriations for Fiscal Year 1995 for the
Intelligence Activities of the U.S. Government*, S.Rpt. 103–256, 103d Cong., 2d

sess., May 5, 1994; and U.S. Congress, House, *Intelligence Authorization Act for Fiscal Year 1995*, report of the Permanent Select Committee on Intelligence, 103d Cong., 2d sess., June 9, 1994.

10. Thomas Powers, "The Truth about the CIA," *New York Review of Books*, May 13, 1993, p. 55.

11. See, for example, the U.S. government officials' views reported in Peter H. Lewis, "Computer Snoopers Imperil Pentagon Files, Experts Say," *New York Times*, July 21, 1994, pp. A1, B4.

12. For a discussion of potential threats for which such an option would be useful, see *The Need to Know: Report of the Twentieth Century Fund Task Force on Covert Action and American Democracy* (New York: Twentieth Century Fund Press, 1992).

13. U.S. Congress, House, Foreign Affairs Committee, Remarks by R. James Woolsey before the International Organizations, International Security and Human Rights Subcommittee, 103d Cong., 2d sess., June 27, 1994, p. 7.

14. Reported in Steven Erlanger, "Old Enemies Now Allied against Crime," *New York Times*, July 6, 1994, p. A3.

15. Statement of R. James Woolsey, U.S. Congress, House, Hearing before the Permanent Select Committee on Intelligence, 103d Cong., 1st sess., March 9, 1993, p. 8.

16. Ibid.

17. See statement of Robert Gates, U.S. Congress, Joint hearing before the Select Committee on Intelligence of the Senate and Permanent Select Committee on Intelligence of the House of Representatives, *To Reorganize the United States Intelligence Community*, S. 2198 and S. 421, 102d Cong., 2d sess., April 1, 1992, pp. 19–20.

18. R. James Woolsey, "National Security and the Future Direction of the Central Intelligence Agency," address delivered at the Center for Strategic and International Studies, Washington, D.C., July 18, 1994, p. 19.

19. The White House, "A National Security Strategy of Engagement and Enlargement," p. 14.

20. William Webster, remarks to the Los Angeles World Affairs Council, September 19, 1989.

21. Stansfield Turner, "Intelligence for a New World Order," *Foreign Affairs* 70, no. 4 (Fall 1991): 151.

22. U.S. Congress, *Nomination of R. James Woolsey*, p. 88.

23. Statement by R. James Woolsey, U.S. Congress, p. 11.

24. See the testimony and conclusions reported in U.S. Congress, Senate, *Economic Intelligence*, hearing before the Select Committee on Intelligence, 103d Cong., 1st sess., August 5, 1993.

25. The specific shortcomings are well summarized in the companion background paper for the Task Force developed by Philip Zelikow, "American Intelligence and the World Economy." See especially chapter 4 and the advance look it provides of the findings of the National Research Council of

the National Academy of Sciences on the adequacy of existing data collection methods and systems.

26. See the analysis and view presented in Mark Burton, "Government Spying for Commercial Gain," *Studies in Intelligence* 37, no. 5 (1994): 17–23. Burton is an analyst with the Department of Defense.

27. See William Johnson, *Who's Stealing Your Business? How to Identify and Prevent Business Espionage* (New York: AMACOM, 1988); John J. McGonagle, Jr., and Carolyn M. Vella, *Outsmarting the Corporation: Practical Approaches to Finding and Using Competitive Information* (Naperville, Ill.: Sourcebooks, 1990); and George S. Roukis, Hugh Conway, and Brian Charnov, eds., *Global Corporate Intelligence: Opportunities, Technologies, and Threats in the 1990s* (New York: Quorum Books, 1990). The track record for such business intelligence is probably no better than that of the intelligence community, and in some areas may be a good deal worse. In one study of stock market forecasting over the past twenty-five years, the author found that most professional investment advisers' judgments about whether a bull or a bear market lay ahead turned out to be wrong nearly all of the time. See Martin Zweig, *Winning on Wall Street* (New York: Warner Books, 1986). Economic forecasting generally has proved only a little more accurate. See William Ascher, *Forecasting: An Appraisal for Policy-Makers and Planners* (Baltimore: Johns Hopkins University Press, 1979). Even leading social scientists have far from accurate track records, as suggested in Charles Wolf, Jr., "The Fine Art of the False Alarm," *Wall Street Journal*, November 1, 1994, p. A20.

28. Intelligence professionals and agencies are not the only persons and organizations facing an overhaul of their conceptual framework; see, for example, the case made for new thinking among academics focusing on international affairs and issues by Stanley J. Heginbotham, "Shifting the Focus of International Programs," *Chronicle of Higher Education*, October 19, 1994, p. A68.

29. R. James Woolsey, "U.S. National Security and the Future of Intelligence," address to the World Affairs Council of Boston, May 13, 1994, p. 3.

30. "The New Security Puzzles," *Washington Post*, July 24, 1994, p. C7.

31. David L. Boren, "The Winds of Change at the CIA," *Yale Law Journal* 101, no. 4 (January 1992): 855. CIA studies of national and other leaders have also been questioned, and their methods are currently under review. For an assessment, see Thomas Omestad, "Psychology and the CIA: Leaders on the Couch," *Foreign Policy*, no. 95 (Summer 1994): 105–22 and a letter in reaction to it by the founder of the agency's center for the study of political behavior, Jerrold Post, in *Foreign Policy*, no. 96 (Fall 1994): 194–97.

32. Turner, "Intelligence for a New World Order," p. 157.

33. See Robert Hopkins Miller, *Inside an Embassy: The Political Role of Diplomats Abroad* (Washington, D.C.: Congressional Quarterly Books, 1992), especially the discussion of "Reporting and Analysis," pp. 26–32.

34. Quoted in U.S. Congress, *Current and Projected National Security Threats*, p. 29.

35. Reported in Michael R. Gordon, "C.I.A. Backs Arms Treaty on Chemicals," *New York Times*, June 24, 1994, p. A9.

36. See the forecast and analysis in Richard A. Bitzinger, "The Globalization of the Arms Industry: The Next Proliferation Challenge," *International Security* 19, no. 2 (Fall 1994): 170–98.

37. Dave McCurdy, "Glasnost for the CIA," *Foreign Affairs* 73, no. 1 (January/February 1994): 127.

38. Douglas J. MacEachin, deputy director for intelligence at the Central Intelligence Agency, "The Tradecraft of Analysis: Challenge and Change in CIA's Directorate of Intelligence," unpublished manuscript, August 1, 1994.

39. Ibid., pp. 11–12.

40. Quoted in Elaine Sciolino, "C.I.A. Chief Is Upset over 'Politicization' Seen within Agency," *New York Times*, March 28, 1992, p. 1.

41. U.S. Congress, *Intelligence Authorization Act for Fiscal Year 1995*, p. 24.

CHAPTER 4

1. For a sampling, see Bruce D. Berkowitz and Allan E. Goodman, "Intelligence without the Cold War," *Intelligence and National Security* 9, no. 2 (April 1994): 301–19; Edmund C. Blash, "Strategic Intelligence Analysis and National Decisionmaking: A Systems Management Approach," *International Journal of Intelligence and Counterintelligence* 9, no. 4 (Winter 1993): 55–68; David Boren, "The Winds of Change at the CIA," *Yale Law Journal* 101, no. 4 (January 1992): 853–65; David Boren, "The Intelligence Community: How Crucial?" *Foreign Affairs* 71, no. 3 (Summer 1992): 52–62; Russell J. Bruemmer, "Intelligence Community Reorganization: Declining the Invitation to Struggle," *Yale Law Journal* 101, no. 4 (January 1992): 867–91; Angelo Codevilla, *Informing Statecraft: Intelligence for a New Century* (New York: Free Press, 1992); interview with William E. Colby, *Omni*, February/March 1993, pp. 75–76, 78, 89–92; David D. Dabelko and Geoffrey D. Dabelko, "The International Environment and the U.S. Intelligence Community," *International Journal of Intelligence and Counterintelligence* 7, no. 1 (Spring 1993): 21–41; Don Edwards, "Reordering the Priorities of the FBI in Light of the End of the Cold War," *St. John's Law Review* 65 (Winter 1991): 59–84; Loch Johnson, "On Drawing a Bright Line for Covert Operations," *American Journal of International Law* 86, no. 2 (April 1992): 284–309; Dave McCurdy, "Glasnost for the CIA," *Foreign Affairs* 73, no. 1 (January/February 1994): 125–40; Frank McNeil, "Post-Cold War Intelligence: Meeting the Need for Reform," *Foreign Service Journal* 69, no. 2 (February 1992): 20–23; Marvin Ott, "Shaking Up the CIA," *Foreign Policy*, no. 93 (Winter 1993–94): 132–51; Paula L. Scalingi, "U.S. Intelligence in an Age of Uncertainty: Refocusing to Meet the Challenge," *Washington Quarterly* 15, no. 1 (Winter 1992), pp. 147–56; *The*

Need to Know: The Report of the Twentieth Century Fund Task Force on Covert Action and American Democracy (New York: Twentieth Century Fund Press, 1992); Stansfield Turner, "Intelligence for a New World Order," *Foreign Affairs* 70, no. 4 (Fall 1991): 150–66; U.S. Congress, Senate, *To Reorganize the United States Intelligence Community*, hearings before the Select Committee on Intelligence, S. 2198 and S. 421, 102d Cong., 2d sess., April 1, 1992; and U.S. Congress, Joint hearing before the Select Committee on Intelligence of the Senate and Permanent Select Committee on Intelligence of the House of Representatives, 102d Cong., 2d sess., April 1, 1992.

2. See the views reported in Walter Pincus, "White House Labors to Redefine Role of Intelligence Community," *Washington Post*, June 13, 1994, p. A8.

3. U.S. Congress, House, *Intelligence Authorization Act for Fiscal Year 1995*, report of the Permanent Select Committee on Intelligence, 103 Cong., 2d sess., June 9, 1994, p. 20.

4. Prepared statement of Senator David L. Boren, in U.S. Congress, *To Reorganize the United States Intelligence Community*, February 20, 1992, p. 167.

5. "The C.I.A. Club Needs a Cleanup," *New York Times*, September 30, 1994, p. A30.

6. The case for this is made in Allan E. Goodman, "Fixing the Intelligence Mess," *Foreign Policy*, no. 57 (Winter 1984–85): 160–79.

7. Stansfield Turner, "For Smarter Intelligence: Separate Spies from Analysts," *Washington Post*, July 24, 1994, p. C3. See also Melvin A. Goodman, "We Need Two C.I.A.'s," *New York Times*, July 21, 1994, p. A23.

8. U.S. Congress, *To Reorganize the United States Intelligence Community*, p. 170.

9. See the case for this made, for example, in Institute for the Study of Diplomacy, *The Foreign Service in 2001* (Washington, D.C.: School of Foreign Service, Georgetown University, August 1992).

10. The White House, "A National Security Strategy of Engagement and Enlargement," Government Printing Office, July 1994, p. 14.

Bibliography of Additional Studies Consulted

Adams, James. *The New Spies: Exploring the Frontiers of Espionage*. London: Hutchinson, 1994.

Alright, D. E. *Threats to U.S. Security in a Postcontainment World*. Maxwell A.F.B., Ala.: Center for Aerospace Doctrine, Research and Education, 1992.

Branscomb, Ann Wells. *Who Owns Information? From Privacy to Public Access*. New York: Basic Books, 1994.

Brugioni, Dino A. *From Balloons to Blackbird: Reconnaissance, Surveillance, and Imagery Intelligence*. McLean, Va.: Association of Former Intelligence Officers, 1993.

Charters, David A., ed. *Peacekeeping and the Challenge of Civil Conflict Resolution*. Fredericton, N.B.: Center for Conflict Studies, University of New Brunswick, 1994.

Computer Crime: Citations from the Information Services for the Physics and Engineering Communities Database. Tolland, Conn.: NERAC Inc., 1993.

Conner, William E. *Intelligence Oversight: The Controversy Behind the FY 1991 Intelligence Authorization Act*. McLean, Va.: Association of Former Intelligence Officers, 1993.

Davis, Jack, and L. Keith Gardiner. *Analytic Support for Peace Talks*. Washington, D.C.: Center for the Study of Intelligence, 1992.

Ford, Harold P. *Estimative Intelligence: The Purposes and Problems of National Intelligence Estimating*, rev. ed. Washington, D.C.: Defense Intelligence College, 1993.

Frost, Mike (as told to Michel Gratton). *Spyworld: Inside the Canadian and American Intelligence Establishments*. Toronto: Doubleday Canada, 1994.

Grose, Peter. *Gentleman Spy: The Life of Allen Dulles.* Boston: Houghton Mifflin, 1994.

Hamel, Gary, and C. K. Prahalad. *Competing for the Future.* Boston: Harvard Business School Press, 1994.

Harkavy, Robert E., and Stephanie G. Neuman, eds. *The Arms Trade: Problems and Prospects in the Post-Cold War World.* A special edition of *Annals of the American Academy of Political and Social Science* 535 (September 1994).

Hastedt, Glenn P., ed. *Controlling Intelligence.* London: Frank Cass, 1991.

Holt, Pat M. *Secret Intelligence and Public Policy: A Dilemma of Democracy.* Washington, D.C.: Congressional Quarterly Books, 1994.

Kay, David. *Denial and Deception: Iraq and Beyond.* Washington, D.C.: Consortium for the Study of Intelligence, 1994.

Kober, Stanley. *The CIA as Economic Spy: The Misuse of U.S. Intelligence after the Cold War.* Washington, D.C.: Cato Institute, 1992.

Morel, Benoit, and Kyle Olson, eds. *Shadows and Substance: The Chemical Weapons Convention.* Boulder, Colo.: Westview Press, 1993.

Mussington, David. "Understanding Contemporary International Arms Transfers." Adelphi Paper no. 291, International Institute for Strategic Studies, London, September 1994.

Paschall, Rod. *LIC 2010.* Washington, D.C.: Brasseys, 1990.

Preston, Richard. *The Hot Zone.* New York: Random House, 1994.

Riebling, Mark. *Wedge: The Secret War between the FBI and CIA.* New York: Alfred A. Knopf, 1994.

Rich, Ben R., and Leo Janos. *Skunk Works: A Personal Memoir of My Years at Lockheed.* Boston: Little, Brown and Company, 1994.

Schweizer, Peter. *Friendly Spies: How America's Allies Are Using Economic Espionage to Steal Our Secrets.* New York: Atlantic Monthly Press, 1993.

Sterling, Claire. *Thieves' World: The Threat of the New Global Network of Organized Crime.* New York: Simon and Schuster, 1994.

U.S. Congress, House. *Intelligence Successes and Failures in Operation Desert Shield/Desert Storm.* Hearings before the Committee on Armed Services, 103d Cong., 1st sess., August 1993.

_____ ,Permanent Select Committee on Intelligence. *Compilation of Intelligence Laws and Related Laws and Executive Orders of Interest to the National Intelligence Community as Amended through June 8, 1993.* Washington, D.C.: Government Printing Office, July 1993.

U.S. Congress, Senate. *To Improve U.S. Counterintelligence Measures,* S. 2726. Hearings before the Select Committee on Intelligence, 101st Cong., 2d sess., May 23 and July 12, 1990.

_____ , *Special Report: Committee Activities of the Select Committee on Intelligence, January 3, 1991, to October 8, 1992.* Washington, D.C.: Government Printing Office, 1993.

U.S. Department of Defense. *Centralized Management of Department of Defense Human Intelligence (HUMINT) Operations.* Washington, D.C.: Assistant Secretary of Defense, Command, Control, Communications, and Intelligence, 1992.

U.S. Department of State. *Patterns of Global Terrorism, 1993.* Washington, D.C.: Office of the Coordinator for Counterterrorism, April 1994.

Wander, W. Thomas, Eric H. Arnett, and Paul Bracken, eds. *The Diffusion of Advanced Weaponry: Technologies, Regional Implications, and Responses.* Washington, D.C.: American Association for the Advancement of Science, 1994.

Wark, Wesley K., ed. *Espionage: Past, Present, Future?* London: Frank Cass, 1993.

Wriston, Walter B. *The Twilight of Sovereignty: How the Information Revolution Is Transforming Our World.* New York: Scribners, 1992.

INTELLIGENCE SINCE
COLD WAR'S END

Gregory F. Treverton

So far, the debate over American intelligence has been so limited as to imply that the fall of the Berlin Wall left intelligence pretty much unchanged. In fact, much has changed, but questions about whether there has been enough change remain. This paper describes the evolution of American intelligence since the cold war's end and outlines the issues that the changes raise for the future of intelligence.

The backdrop to these changes is uncertainty and turbulence. American foreign policy was upended by the disintegration of the Soviet bloc, and the shattering of concepts was as great for intelligence as for any other community. Intelligence is a service industry, meant to improve foreign policy and its execution. Now, not only are specific policies up for grabs, but so are priorities. Congress frequently criticizes intelligence for shopping for new business in such areas as peacekeeping, economics, or migration, but it also exhorts intelligence not to remain fixated on old threats.

All the while, the intelligence budget has been shrinking. The slide has so far been gentle, gentler than for defense. The budget has been held close to constant in recent years; due to inflation, then, the actual budgets have declined several percent per year. Given structures and fixed costs, those numbers translate into disproportionate cuts in personnel, ranging from 17 to 25 percent over five years throughout the intelligence community. Those cuts are no bad thing; intelligence, like all of America's national security establishment, grew too big too fast in the 1980s. But cutting has the usual unhappy implications: those that leave are not always the deadest embers, some are the liveliest sparks; hiring and advancement are constricted, so juniors chafe at being led by inferior seniors.

Under these circumstances, morale has been low, especially at the Central Intelligence Agency (CIA). Aldrich Ames has dominated the media discussion of intelligence. President Clinton's first director of central intelligence (DCI), R. James Woolsey, had a rocky two years; he was a victim of the Ames investigation and of his own distant relations to the president and increasingly bitter ones with Capitol Hill. Since the popular press nearly always conflates "intelligence" with "CIA," all of intelligence has been tarred with the same brush to some extent.

THE MILITARIZATION OF NATIONAL SYSTEMS

Expenditures on satellites and other sensors to intercept signals intelligence (SIGINT) and take pictures or other image intelligence (IMINT) already account for the bulk of the money devoted to collecting information, which in turn consumes about two-thirds of the total intelligence budget. To the extent that money is at issue in the future of intelligence, the money is here.

During the cold war, the United States built expensive national collection systems dedicated to fulfilling the overarching national purpose: understanding the Soviet Union. The agency titles bespeak that national focus: the National Reconnaissance Office (NRO), whose name remained an official secret until several years ago, for building, launching, and operating satellites; the National Security Agency (NSA) for code making and breaking, and for turning intercepted signals into useful intelligence, or SIGINT; and the Central Imagery Office (CIO), created more recently in an effort to mimic NSA for imagery, or IMINT.

By published accounts, the total intelligence budget is about $28 billion per year.[1] Of that, NRO spends about $7 billion, NSA about $4 billion, and the Pentagon budget for so-called Tactical Intelligence and Related Activities (TIARA) is on the order of $12 billion.[2] In comparison, the total CIA budget is about $3 billion. The total that all agencies spend for human intelligence (HUMINT)—mostly spying but also including everything else, including "open source" information collection—is also about $3 billion, about a tenth of intelligence's total budget.

Since the end of the cold war, old systems acquired for past concerns have been adapted to new missions. During the cold war, SIGINT satellites gobbled up Soviet communications wholesale, and IMINT painstakingly compared photos to try to understand the Soviet military. At the time, these processes were usually too slow to be of much use to tactical commanders. First-generation reconnaissance satellites, for instance, ejected film canisters with parachutes, which were then snagged in the air by U.S. military airplanes. It was a matter of some hours, at least, before film could be recovered and developed.[3] As then-Air Force chief of staff Lawrence Welch said: Back in 1986 "we never saw a [satellite] photo on the day it was produced."[4]

With digitized images, however, and improved communication, "pictures" can now be flashed from satellites to ground stations, to Washington, and out to field commanders in a matter of minutes. With some luck and advance preparation, communications of would-be enemy aircraft can be intercepted and returned to U.S. cockpits in time to provide detailed warning.

The IMINT and SIGINT satellites, originally intended to observe the Soviet empire, are not ideal for field purposes, but they are flexible enough to be of great use. Now, for instance, SIGINT must hone in on particular conversations between enemy units. What matters to combatants reliant on such information—call them info-warriors—is the location, and, with luck, the intended movements of a particular enemy unit.

The major action during Woolsey's unhappy tenure as DCI was reshaping intelligence's satellite architecture.[5] One aim of the restructuring was to cut costs by reducing the duplication resulting from the desire of every service—the Air Force and Navy, as well as the CIA—not to be left out of space. Thus, the total number of satellites was to be cut, and the number of ground stations cut still further.

The specifics of the reconfiguration, however, were ultimately driven by the requirement of precise geolocation for the info-warriors. The particular issue was the need for SIGINT satellites in highly elliptical orbit (HEO) as opposed to geosynchronous orbit. The latter, fixed over particular points on the Earth's surface, have the advantage of being able to dwell on specific points. HEO satellites also have long dwell times over those portions of the Earth they can see while in the long loop of their ellipses. They are helpful for locating particular points because they are in motion over the Earth's surface, in known tracks, making triangulation much more precise.

Desert Storm is a convenient demarcation point for the change in the mission of intelligence from keeping tabs on the Soviet Union to supporting warriors.[6] It was the first "information war," which systematically—if not always too coherently—used national systems for tactical purposes. For instance, the cold war's euphemistically named Defense Support Program (DSP) satellites are parked in geosynchronous orbits 24,000 miles above the Earth, staring with infrared eyes at particular sectors of the globe. They were designed for one purpose—to provide immediate warning of Soviet nuclear missile launches.

During Desert Storm, however, advances in software enabled the DSP satellites to see Iraqi Scud launches. Two satellites provided triangulation on the location of launches within 120 seconds of the launch.[7] Other cold war systems played an important role as well. The Air Force's system allowed satellite information to be relayed into aircraft cockpits in under ten minutes, versus the ninety minutes it had taken previously.[8]

Desert Storm also illustrated the technical obstacles to providing support to info-warriors. While the speed of retrieving images or signals from space has quickened, the air war often outpaced retrieval times. Moreover, warriors trust pictures much more than descriptions of pictures. While there is no surprise in that, transmitting pictures from national satellites to local commanders is no small feat. It requires a great deal of capacity and competes with a host of other communication needs. In particular, there was not enough communications satellite band width to serve all the users who wanted data.[9]

The developments from Desert Storm underscore how intelligence is increasingly responding to the needs of the military. While the benefits of informed warriors is clearly obvious, the militarization of intelligence raises a host of issues, from immediate to longer term.

Who Owns the Systems?

Before, support for warriors was a spill-over benefit. The cold war's end has reversed that priority, but structures may lag behind. Supporting warriors is now the main purpose of these national systems. There are important residual national purposes, like keeping tabs on North Korea's nuclear program, but these are now the spill-over. Thus, perhaps it is time to give the Pentagon direct control over the systems.

The trouble is that, on the battlefield warriors neither understand not trust what the national systems can do for them. General Norman Schwarzkopf, Desert Storm's commander, was eloquent, if perhaps overstated, on that score. Uncertain what they will get and unsure how to ask for it, tactical commanders tend to trust what is at hand. Schwarzkopf had more faith—misplaced, it turned out—in the damage assessments derived from pictures taken by aircraft than from space satellites.

The mismatch runs all the way through the Pentagon and intelligence organizations. Those, for instance, who design spy satellites and those who design precision-guided weapons work in different compartments, separated by walls of ignorance and classification. Thus, it is only a happy coincidence if weapons' capacity to hit targets matches intelligence's ability to find the targets.

There is some irony in the current state of affairs, given that the expansive national collection agencies already reside in the Pentagon. As technology improved, the Pentagon's infrastructure began to dwarf the CIA's entrepreneurial wizardry reflected in the U-2 spy plane. In the 1970s the White House proposed to give control of the collection agencies to the DCI. Then-Secretary of Defense Donald Rumsfeld defiantly replied, in effect if not in fact: "If they're in my budget, I'll run them."[10] Successive efforts since then have given the DCI more responsibility over the national collection agencies without giving him much more real authority.

If the big national systems are to support warriors, perhaps they should be managed by, and for, the Pentagon. At a minimum, technology is blurring the distinction between "national" and "tactical," and so it makes little sense to separate the national budget, which is overseen if not really controlled by the DCI, from the TIARA budget, which remains the province of the secretary of defense.[11] The logical response to the need to support info-warriors would be to reverse the efforts since Rumsfeld's tenure to give the DCI more control over the national collection agencies. National purposes, such as tracking would-be proliferators, would be served as spill-overs, reversing the cold war's priorities.

Indeed, in the current structure exactly *who* is responsible is not altogether clear. Taking a DCI perspective, I always assumed that DCIs had trouble getting a handle on the big collectors because secretaries of defense would not concede any power. However, recent interviews with Pentagon budgeteers have suggested defense officials held the obverse view: they were frozen out because the DCI was in control. Managers of the "stovepipes," as the collection structures are dubbed by officialdom, may have carved out considerable autonomy for themselves.

How Much Do the Systems Cost?

To be fair, the collection systems currently in place are impressive technical achievements. The question is: At what cost? More than one DCI or NSA director has complained about how much satellites cost. To detractors, the large system pricetags are the result of "gold plating." More neutrally, investment in these systems might be said to reflect the pursuit of technology with only secondary regard for cost. The NRO's recent troubles over a $350 million headquarters or a billion-dollar contingency fund might be testimony to either interpretation, though neither episode is very important in and of itself.[12]

Even in the best of cases, however, what might have been affordable during the cold war is not affordable now. The militarization of space is, in principle, open-ended: it will always be possible to provide better geolocation, more help to American warriors. To be fair, the same might have been said of knowing about the Soviet Union during the cold war: more was always better. At that time, however, the Soviet Union was the overriding threat, and learning about it provided lots of spill-over capability for other purposes.

There is room for argument over the current organization of collection by the major stovepipes—SIGINT and IMINT, in particular. A more rational alternative might be to unite the various collectors, allowing for continuous assessments of which system was best suited for a particular target. If such radical measures are ruled out, there is wide agreement that turning the CIO into a real stovepipe would be a desirable second-best path.[13]

At present, the CIO, created in 1992, does not monopolize IMINT to the same extent that NSA does with SIGINT. CIA's National Photographic Interpretation Center (NPIC) has the intelligence community's largest cadre of imagery analysts. Other agencies also play important roles in imagery. Consolidation would create an end-to-end organization for imagery, thus permitting choices among satellite and aircraft reconnaissance capabilities, as well as making clear to users exactly where and how to get their needs into the system.

What New Systems Should Be Developed?

The existing satellite constellation has been impressively flexible but is hardly ideal for today's needs. Support for info-warriors would best be provided through loitering over targets, passing images of the battlefield in real time. Satellites, however, many miles up and traveling thousands of miles an hour, can spend only minutes watching any given spot of interest to the warriors, and, since they are far away, their cameras can provide either area or resolution: they can look bluntly at larger areas or keenly at smaller ones, but not both. Over time, unmanned drones, small satellites, or something comparable but yet undreamed will better serve this need.[14]

SIGINT, too, will have to get closer to the signals it seeks. In war, urgent need will tempt opponents to use simpler communications, easier to intercept and decode, but American info-warriors will need ever-quicker answers. "It was *there* five minutes ago" may have been good enough for those warriors in Desert Storm, when they confronted an Iraqi tank column; it will not nearly be good enough for their counterparts in 2015 facing threats from fifth-generation Scud missiles.

In 1994 the CIA deployed drones—called unmanned aerial vehicles (UAVs)—into Albania in an experiment aimed at providing real-time intelligence on warring troop factions in former Yugoslavia.[15] The program objective was keeping a drone aloft for twenty-four hours at a height of about 25,000 feet. The Pentagon, too, has several kinds of UAVs on its drawing board for different altitude tiers—reflecting information needs not met in Desert Storm. As UAVs get larger, with more sensors aboard, they get more expensive. As they get more expensive, there is the temptation to protect them by making them stealthy, which would increase the cost even more. Still, UAVs cost a fraction of the $1 billion-plus that satellites cost.

The more serious question mark concerns access. Few nations could do anything about satellites flying over their territory. Over time this reluctant acquiescence softened into tacit acceptance; now hardly anyone complains about satellites as an infringement of national sovereignty. Encroachments into other nations' air space is a different matter, if only because they can do something about it. In shooting wars, such diplomatic niceties count for little, and the concern about UAVs is less that they might be shot at and more that they might be hit. But drones could be most useful in ambiguous situations that might or might not turn into wars. And it is precisely then that diplomatic sensitivities would be the sharpest: imagine the argument inside Washington if, in the late summer and early fall of 1990, intelligence had proposed sending up drones to keep tabs on Saddam Hussein's military exercises.

Small satellites, or "cheap-sats," are another possibility. In the early days of satellites, launching them was a significant fraction of their cost. But the cost of putting payloads into orbit has been declining. Thus, the United States might choose to do what the Soviet Union did out of necessity: build and stockpile satellites to be launched when circumstances dictate. These new satellites could be purpose-built, with single sensors or small packages of sensors, then launched into orbits tailor-made for seeing or listening to specific crises. The usual temptation to add just a little more capability to even these small satellites will drive costs up. But, in principle, cheap-sats could provide some of the advantages of both drones and satellites without entailing the enormous sunk costs of today's satellite models.

Over the longer term, both IMINT and SIGINT are in question. For IMINT the problem will be competition due to technological advances. Within a decade, imagery with one-meter resolution will be widely available on the open market. Two American firms already plan such systems, and three-meter resolution systems have already been licensed by the U.S. Commerce Department.[16] With access to this technology, potential targets would be able to see how others see them from the sky and act accordingly. The United States could continue to have advantages in its ability to integrate imagery into tactical battleplans and rapidly retarget, but those advantages will be of a different sort.

SIGINT faces three even sharper challenges. First, digitizing makes it possible to send incredible amounts of information over single channels, and so vastly compounds the challenge of sorting out particular communications of interest. Second, the use of fiber optics means that fewer messages get sent into open air, where satellites or ground stations can intercept them—if SIGINT is to be useful in the future, it will have to get physically close to the communications channels it seeks to intercept. Third, encryption means that soon, if not already, anyone will be able to buy essentially unbreakable coding systems at a local Radio Shack. Less sophisticated nations will make mistakes, and the pressures of war will lure opponents into shortcuts that will allow their messages to be read. But encryption will increasingly force the United States to practice "traffic analysis"—noticing when and where messages are being sent, without being able to read their contents.

How Much National Spill-over for How Much Money?

For the near future, the shift will be determined by sunk costs: the systems already exist. The systems themselves are flexible enough to serve national purposes. Over the longer term, however, the militarization of space will raise the issue of *which purposes* are to be served. Already, there is competition for satellite images during crises, when satellites are diverted from customary routines. Now satellites take many more images than can be processed. But if systems were fewer and more specialized, that competition would be even sharper.

PUZZLES VERSUS MYSTERIES:
THE "OPEN-SOURCE" REVOLUTION

Vast capacity to solve national puzzles, primarily about the Soviet Union, with a high secrets content: this is the intelligence legacy of the cold war. At that time, the most pressing questions were puzzles, matters that could, in principle, have been answered definitively had the necessary information been available. How big was the Soviet Union's economy? How many missiles did it have? Had it launched a "bolt-from-the-blue" attack? Such puzzles were intelligence's stock in trade during the cold war.

Mysteries differ from puzzles; they are questions that cannot be answered with certainty, regardless of how much quality information is amassed.[17] Russia's inflation rate next year is a mystery. Dissecting Boris Yeltsin's brain would not solve it, for he does not know the answer. No one does. It cannot be established with any real certainty.

Today's chaotic world still presents plenty of puzzles, such as whether China has sold M-11 missiles to Pakistan, or whether France has bribed Indonesia to give a contract to a French company. Yet most of the critical questions facing American foreign policy are mysteries: Will North Korea fulfill its nuclear agreement with the United States? Will Iraq again misbehave? Will China continue to grow rapidly, or will it fragment? Will reform and democracy take hold in eastern Europe—or South Africa?

Collecting secrets was, and continues to be, crucial for solving foreign policy puzzles. The potential foes of the United States do not advertise their military capacities; nor do proliferators of nuclear weapons or other weapons of mass destruction announce their deals; nor do nations disclose their bribes or other strategies in trade negotiations.

For addressing mysteries, however, information collected secretly may be helpful but seldom is as critical as it was for cold war puzzles. In the past, information was scarce; now it is overwhelming. During the cold war, the direction of Kremlin politics had to be gleaned from pieces of previously solved puzzles; now, Russia's politicians blab as much as any other. Then, it was not hard to see how secrets contributed to framing mysteries: even if the secret was small, its value was often magnified by the ignorance of the other pieces.

During the cold war, much of the globe was a "denied area." Now, only a few states are truly closed. Accessible parts of the world do not have to be photographed from thousands of feet in the sky. They can simply be looked at directly—"eyeball-intelligence," not IMINT. Of course, the lookers need to be trained to see a factory's output, technology, and morale where the rest of us would perceive only noise.

Now, surfing the Internet provides access to an exploding amount of information. By one estimate, the amount of stored information is doubling every two years.[18] The Net is a stew of fact, judgment, and fiction; in effect, anyone with a computer can now produce or "publish" information. The risk that hackers—curious kids or those with more evil motives—will enter restricted databases is well known if not yet well addressed. But in some respects the harder problem arises simply from volume, not malice: as "publishing" gets easier, standards of verification go down, and more of the stew is fiction, even if inadvertently so.

The challenge for intelligence—sorting fact from fiction, or signals from noise—is new only in magnitude. But the change in magnitude is awesome. There is so much more information out there, and a larger share of it, probably, is misleading.

Policymakers will be more, not less, reliant on information brokers. The images that are sometimes evoked of policymakers surfing the Net themselves, in direct touch with their own information sources, are dead wrong. Rather, as access to information multiplies, policymakers' need for processing—not to mention analyzing—that information will go up. If collection is easier, *selection* will be harder.

As more information becomes available, there will be more brokers and more competition among them. Intelligence analysts will be brokers, as will CNN anchors (or their producers), journalists, and academics. Amidst such competition, policymakers will want "pull," not "push" information: rather than being fed a firehose of factoids, they will want the ability to pull up puzzle answers or frames of reference when they need them.

Openness is blurring the distinction between collection and analysis. The best looker is not a spy-master, much less an impersonal satellite, but someone trained in the substance of the subject—an analyst. By the same token, reference librarians used to be able to point scholars toward reliable sources. On the Net, sources are many, but reliability is dubious. Beware those who surf the Net but are not experts: Who knows what they might make of the Net's hodgepodge of fact, fancy, and mistake?

It is no criticism to observe that this world is a far cry from the one to which intelligence has been accustomed: small amounts of information regarded, sometimes mistakenly, as reliable—satellite photos and spy reports. Now, it confronts a world of vast amounts of unreliable information. Then, collectors could be separated from analysts, since what to look for was not a problem; almost anything about the Soviet Union sufficed. Now, collection and analysis are merging. Then, communications had to be restricted lest secrets leak out. Now, communications need to be opened in a thousand directions.

The difficulty the intelligence community is having in systematically integrating "open source" collection into its structures reflects the culture of the past. "Open source" does not fit well alongside intelligence's specialized stovepipes. On the National Intelligence Council (NIC), we used to quip that if academics sometimes did better than intelligence analysts, it was because the former weren't denied access to open sources. Change comes hard to this system.

The intelligence community created the Community Open Source Office (COSO) as a focal point and gave it a fixed percentage of the intelligence budget. Its plan for analysts is "one screen and two boxes": in effect, a work-station would have two computer hard drives, one for classified information and the other for open source. Using Windows or equivalent software, analysts could shift from one drive to the other, but information would be able to move in one direction only: from open source into classified, not vice versa.

Meanwhile, various parts of the intelligence community have experimented with assembling databases. The DCI's Non-Proliferation Center (NPC) has been the most aggressive and, perhaps surprisingly, it has found them to be of real value. Proliferation would appear to be a secrets-rich area, but careful combing of databases and the foreign press provides hints, tip-offs, and partial confirmations. Since nefarious programs may depend on aggregations of apparently innocent imports, open sources can reveal who is buying what.

Yet there is a long way to go. In some ways, computers have reinforced the focus on secret sources. Analysts' computers provide only secret sources, and for many of those analysts, if information is not on the computer, it does not exist. For instance, analysts at the CIA's Office of Trans-National Security and Technology Issues (TSTI—formerly the office of Resources, Trade and Technology) could do competent assessments of particular industrial sectors in given foreign countries. Yet their analyses usually were done in ignorance of Wall Street or other private-sector sources that sometimes provided better results.

We tried a number of experiments at the NIC to extend or test openness.[19] We brainstormed almost every major estimate with outside experts in meetings that were seldom classified. On an important new subject, humanitarian crises, we began an estimate with a conference at which major nongovernmental organizations, like CARE, presented brief papers—an unusual and happy collaboration for both intelligence and its new-found partners outside government. In another experiment, we commissioned think tanks to write what were, in effect, "parallel estimates" to those being done in the usual way within intelligence. Our purpose was not to grade who did better—for good or ill, the work of investigating mysteries usually cannot be graded for years—but to see what we might learn about the process of framing these mysteries.

Another major innovation, Intelink, the intelligence community's classified version of the Internet, is for now a better way of communicating secret information within intelligence; it has not yet opened the community to the outside world.[20] But it could in the future. After all, it was the Pentagon that first created the Internet. Intelink is based on the same freely available software as the Internet. Different components of the community have their own home pages and decide which of their documents to put onto the system. At first the system was limited to just top secret material, thus eliminating the problem of compartmented intelligence. But next steps will include codes to identify authorized users, thus giving originating agencies a second check on who views their documents.

So far, the system is experimental and mostly a convenient means of sharing finished intelligence. Depending on how well prepared the system's documents are, users can click on key words to find additional biographical information or to move to related information. Logically, though, the system will permit communications among analysts and, eventually, question-asking and -answering between consumers and analysts. Again, though, it will not be senior policymakers who browse either the Net or the Link.

Intelligence or Information?

Determining the role of intelligence agencies first requires defining *intelligence*. Is it, as one of my colleagues used to put it, "the secret bits," or is it information? Choosing the broader definitions raises questions about how this information would be handled.

On reflection, there is little denying the need for more selection, for more information intermediaries. Yet if the data being processed contains few secrets, why should intelligence do the processing? None of the current reasons offered is entirely compelling.

The first reason is that no one else does it. When I was at the NIC, that was often the answer to questions about why we were starting a National Intelligence Estimate (NIE) about peacekeeping, or humanitarian issues, or the AIDS pandemic, or other issues of plain interest to policymakers but not of such plain interest to the intelligence community. For many, that answer was good enough. It isn't sufficient, though, for the government more broadly.

In principle, if the senior levels of the government need more information processing and more analysis, then why not create a kind of Congressional Research Service for the government as a whole? That service could be the government's designate surfer of the Internet and other open sources. Intelligence could then add "the secret bits" as appropriate for the relevant consumers.

The second rationale for having intelligence process the information is that intelligence does it anyway. Assessing the value of secrets requires knowing what is already available publicly. The CIA's clandestine service, the Directorate of Operations (DO), sustains a career structure of reports officers whose mission is to provide context and ranking to the reports of particular spies. (At the NIC, I kept my list of "howlers," recitations of the obvious obtained through circuitous means. "The French dislike GATT" might be an example. The spymaster that recorded that insight thought it was correct and important. It was—it just wasn't news.) Again, however, in principle the validators of secrets could be connected to the Internet surfers.

A third answer is that however little policymakers trust intelligence to do the processing, they trust everyone else even less. It is true that, overall, intelligence strives hard—too hard, in my view, a point for later—to be a truth-teller. It has its biases, but those are, on the whole, professional ones, matters of temperament and operating style, not views on substance.

The processors could, though, be dispersed to various policymakers. If Treasury needs information mediators, why not have them at Treasury, rather than in the intelligence community? Indeed, it is not obvious now why Treasury should have a person or two working on the German economy while the CIA has twice that capability. It might be convenient for the processors to have a role with respect to secret intelligence as well; those who surf the Internet need to be experts, as do those who judge the value of the secret bits.

There is a more telling, though seldom stated, reason for having the intelligence agencies do information processing or analysis even when the secrets content is low: other agencies would not do it, or at any rate much of it. Treasury or Commerce could have analysts if they chose, but they just haven't spent their money that way. The fate of the State Department's Bureau of Intelligence and Research (INR) is instructive. It does some very good work but remains a bureaucratic stepchild. Foreign service officers shun assignments there.

So, bureaucratically, analytic or information-processing capability might not easily be transferred from the intelligence agencies to their policy counterparts, although such a shift might be logical. The function might simply disappear, which would be a comment of sorts on the perceived value of analysis. But that perception might not be a shared one.

FOCUS: FROM THE SOVIET UNION TO . . . WHAT?

As the emphasis on supporting military operations bespeaks, there has been considerable reorientation in focus away from the former Soviet Union. According to its own statistics, the intelligence community spent about three-fifths of its resources on the Soviet target in 1980 but less than a fifth on the former Soviet Union in 1993.[21] Yet, military operations aside, the new focus is much less clear than the old. Indeed, because intelligence is a service industry, its quandary about mission is perhaps more intense than for any other part of the government's national security machinery. It is meant to serve, but what—and whom—does it serve? A host of new consumers has been not yet fully empowered, while old ones have not quite been disempowered.

Two examples, economics and peacekeeping, underscore the point.

Economics

Even before the Clinton administration's "It's the economy stupid!" self-admonition, it was clear that economics was becoming a higher national priority.[22] Intelligence's cold war economic task—keeping track of enemy economies, the Soviet Union's in particular—continued, although perhaps diminished in importance.

Three other tasks, none of them without precedent but all of them dealing primarily with friendly countries, were becoming more important. To visualize the spread of economic tasks, imagine a matrix (see Figure 1) differentiating between information or analysis that was *tactical* or *strategic*, *offensive* or *defensive*, intended to help the *government* or *private* Americans (even if private Americans never knew of the help).[23]

The result is eight cells, not all of which are of interest to policy-makers. Cold war analysis of the Soviet economy might be labeled strategic-defensive-government. If the CIA were to spy on foreign companies for the benefit of American companies, that would be tactical-offensive-private. An example of strategic-defensive-private might be helping American companies deal with potential threats from foreign intelligence services.

FIGURE 1	
Tactical-Offensive-Government	Strategic-Offensive-Government
Tactical-Offensive-Private	Strategic-Offensive-Private
Tactical-Defense-Government	Strategic-Defense-Government
Tactical-Defensive-Private	Strategic-Defensive-Private

Of the new or newly salient tasks, the first, leveling the playing field for American companies, would be tactical-defensive-private, though the companies helped may never know of this assistance. The area is intelligence rich, for just as nations seldom advertise their nefarious weapons programs, neither do they advertise their bribes or side payments in pursuit of international contracts. In effect, the United States seeks to enforce its own Foreign Corrupt Practices Act internationally.

Sometimes the American company that benefits remains unaware of the government action on its behalf. The CIA claims that in 1994 it uncovered fifty-one such cases involving contracts worth $28 billion.[24] In a 1993 case, the CIA found that France had bribed Brazil to land a $1.4 billion radar contract. The CIA then told the State Department, which complained to Brazil. In the end, Raytheon got the contract. In 1994, U.S. firms snatched a clutch of arms and aircraft sales to Saudi Arabia from France.[25]

Leveling the playing field is not only intelligence rich. It is also analysis rich. It is a major task for the CIA's TSTI. As with many intelligence puzzles, the work resembles peeling an onion: stopping a layer too soon can be a major mistake. In one recent case, for instance, a European company in pursuit of a Czech acquisition was allegedly competing unfairly against an American company. It turned out, though, that the American company itself was not very clean; it sought the Czech company, an arms maker, as a way to circumvent U.S. restrictions on arms transfers to the Middle East.

The second and third tasks both support U.S. policymakers working on economic topics. They are subtly distinguished by the kind of help being provided, strategic or tactical. Examples of strategic-defensive-government are current work on Japanese semiconductors and European civil aviation. Notice that the categories become arbitrary depending on how and when the information is used, and who is regarded as the ultimate beneficiary: chip research might be thought tactical and offensive if it issued into a specific U.S. demarche to Tokyo, and aviation work could be labeled private to the extent it provided arguments against buying Airbuses and for buying Boeings.

Similarly, tactical support might be labeled offensive or defensive, depending on its purpose. For instance, tipping-off U.S. negotiators in advance to their foreign interlocutors' position might be called tactical-offensive-government. Tactical help is secrets rich; it means providing trade negotiators hints about their opposite numbers or

their negotiating positions, just as intelligence would do if the negotiation were about arms control. Whatever the ultimate merits of
these tactical tidbits, they almost always win high praise from the
policymakers concerned.

The more strategic analysis is often the "politics of economics,"
not the "economics of economics." It seeks to display how economic
issues affect, or are affected by, political interplay in the country concerned: How will the state of Russia's economy affect Boris Yeltsin's
power? How will the latest Brazilian election influence prospects for
a serious economic stabilization program? By contrast, the CIA, whose
work on the Soviet economy was path-breaking economics, has been
abandoning the economics of economics. It is, for instance, giving
up its modeling of industrialized country economies.

Taken together, these newly prominent economic tasks illustrate
the mix of old and new consumers. At present, intelligence is asked a
dazzling range of questions about economics. At one end, some of the
most economically sophisticated consumers, at the Department of
the Treasury for instance, are uninterested in analysis (and quickly
turned off by political work with faulty economics). They want secret
tidbits, a leg up on their foreign interlocutors.

At the other end is the Commerce Department, which seeks to
elbow its way into policymaking. It needs staff help of any sort. In
developing its framework, the big emerging markets (BEMs) initiative,
Commerce leaned on the CIA, then-RTT in particular, for basic staff
work. This analysis would be strategic-offensive-government (or it
might be labeled strategic-offensive-private, since the private sector
was the intended beneficiary). It hardly mattered to Commerce that
little of this work depended on secret intelligence.

In between these two extremes, the newly created National
Economic Council (NEC) was a natural consumer for intelligence. Its
leadership has tended to use intelligence, which created a special publication for the NEC, the *Daily Economic Brief*, as a kind of designated
reader. As Bowman Cutter, then-NEC deputy director, put it: "I could
get most of what I want from the English *Nikkei* or the *Financial Times*,
but I don't have time to read those. If intelligence can glean the high
points for me, terrific. If it can add nuggets from secret sources, so much
the better."

In general, intelligence's concentration on tactics and on politics
probably makes sense. After all, the government can buy models of the
Japanese economy if it needs them. While it is convenient to have an

in-house model to manipulate in secret, it is not essential. And the CIA is not likely to surpass Wall Street at understanding the future of the Japanese biotechnology industry.

Yet the issue is how good the politics can be if the economic under-pinnings are not solid. Even if some senior consumers are economically literate and not very demanding now, more officials and policymakers will be in the future. The recent Mexican devaluation serves as a reminder that Wall Street analysts can be as myopic as any govern-ment analyst; when the stakes are so high, it does argue for at least retaining the independent capability to ask hard questions, and that, in turn, means having the people who can play in the same league as the Wall Streeters.

Peacekeeping

Peacekeeping is another example of the mix of old and new agen-das, old and new consumers.[26] Indeed, it raises the question of who intelligence's consumers should be.

When the cold war's end opened new possibilities for peacekeep-ing, the United Nations had almost no institutional capacity to handle these new responsibilities. Indeed, it was said, alas truthfully, that after hours in New York there was no one to take phone calls from far-flung peacekeepers.

The Clinton administration's Presidential Decision Directive 25, issued in May 1994, called for a UN information and research unit, linked to field operations, "to obtain and provide current information, manage a 24-hour watch center, and monitor open sources material and non-sensitive information submitted by governments."[27] For its part, the United States would "share information, as appropriate, while ensuring full protection of sources and methods." These words expand-ed the role of American intelligence beyond its traditional concern for security, and served as recognition that getting information in the hands—or U.S. interpretations in the heads—of foreigners could also serve America's purposes.

The United States designed a computer system using commercial-ly available technology, dubbed the Joint Deployable Intelligence Support System. Any member could hook into the system. Little by little, *intelligence*, which had been a dirty word at the UN—*information* was the politically correct term—became more accepted. The new assistant UN secretary-general for peacekeeping, Kofi Anan, was, perhaps ironically, much less sensitive about intelligence, and about material with American provenance, than was his predecessor, the Briton Maurice Goulding.

In practice, the Defense Intelligence Agency (DIA) became the focal point for this sharing once it was authorized—in Somalia, Bosnia, or Cambodia. Specially prepared reports—usually changed only to disguise the source of the information—would be transferred to the U.S. Mission to the United Nations, to be handed then to the UN Operations Center or other peacekeeping officials.

When American military forces themselves were involved, as in Somalia or Bosnia, there was in effect a second channel for intelligence through the U.S. chain of command. Reports could be transmitted to the field with a "tear line"—literally, a point at which the portion of a cable identifying sources of information could be ripped off. Tactical U.S. commanders could then pass the reports on to their non-American UN colleagues. The UN quietly facilitated these arrangements by appointing U.S. friends as the senior UN representatives on the scene: in Cambodia, the UN representative was an Australian, and in Somalia, it was an American, former admiral and National Security Council (NSC) official Jonathan Howe.

The Role of Secrets

The increasing importance of economic information raises a specific issue for the CIA's DO, which is now shambling and without mission. Of all the nation's cold war servants, its world has been upended the most. Young spy-masters echo in private the more public qualms about their trade. They say they were prepared and willing to entreat foreigners to betray their countries when America's survival was arguably at stake. Doing so to achieve economic advantage in trade negotiations is another matter, however.

While Washington can buy economic models if it needs them, no market can provide the specific negotiating positions of trading partners—and U.S. negotiators always relish knowing what those across the table will say. But spying for economic advantage runs against the American grain. Moreover, spying—more so than, for instance, intercepting communications—is inherently a target-of-opportunity enterprise. A spy may not be able to learn others' negotiating positions until it is too late, so counting on espionage to produce the missing puzzle piece is risky.

If spying on friends for economic purposes is an issue, so too is whether to eavesdrop or otherwise intercept their communications. The more frequently that intercepts are used tactically, the greater the chances that someone will suspect what is afoot. And so the practical question becomes whether the potential benefit is worth the risk of embarrassment if the source is ever disclosed. Similar issues must be considered in the field of peacekeeping—whether to spy or eavesdrop on international institutions in which the United States participates.

Looking versus Spying

The focus on economics exemplifies the possibilities that exist in a much more open world. During the cold war, it was necessary to spy; now, in most of the world, even those areas that used to be tightly closed, it is possible to simply *look*. Put differently, the United States maintains a diplomatic service to tend foreign office connections and a clandestine service to spy. But much interesting information falls outside those two channels. We can now visit Russian factories that we could previously have seen only in American satellite photos. To be sure, observers need to be trained to apprehend technology and efficiency where one might perceive only smoke and noise.

For instance, there is little need to spy on the German Bundesbank or other foreign economic institutions. In principle, diplomats or other trained lookers could report on these institutions in the usual way. The problem is that the American foreign service is stretched so thin that it is barely able to tend its foreign office channels, a problem intensified by the increased number of channels stemming from the creation of independent states from the former Soviet Union. At the same time, the number of lookers has decreased. For want of personnel as much as any reason, the CIA has, in effect, taken over State Department functions—either directly through assigning Washington-based analysts to foreign embassies or indirectly by CIA stations assuming tasks formerly performed by State Department officers.

Which New Tasks?

The focus on economics illustrates the kind of new tasks that intelligence might take on. Consider again the matrix and, especially, the overlap among the cells. The Mexican debt case of 1994–95 suggests the possibilities.[28] On the one hand, there seem to be powerful arguments against getting the government, especially intelligence, involved in international financial issues. It is hard to imagine how government could compete with Wall Street, and, moreover, trying to do so would require collecting information on American actors, which has been considered an intelligence "no-no."

Yet, on the other hand, literally no one knows or understands the cumulative impact of millions of financial transfers, as the Mexico case clearly demonstrates. The U.S. government has no way of keeping tabs on the movements of its currency, not to mention less tangible money. In principle, putting together the enormous puzzle of financial flows could be a job for NSA. It would be a logical extension of defensive-government work; whether it was regarded as tactical or strategic would depend on the nature of the crisis. It would be expensive and potentially intrusive, but the impact of sudden and unexpected currency crises on the United States could be as great as the impacts of past international security crises for which intelligence has been prepared.

Intelligence for Whom?

Again, the arbitrariness of the cells hints at possibilities. For instance, the arguments against government spying on behalf of private American firms are well known and require no rehashing here. The arguments are compelling, but they are also beside the point. The real issue is not whether to spy but what to do with the tidbits (or intercepts) of proprietary value that result from collecting information for other reasons. Now, it seems, such data are left on the cutting-room floor. But if intelligence were more focused on economics, there would be more such tidbits. (And despite the protestations, fair enough, by Robert Reich and others that what qualifies as an "American" company is now ambiguous, we usually know one when we see one. Like pornography, making definitions is hard but identifying actual objects is easier.)

Peacekeeping raises more immediate questions of whom intelligence is for. Not surprisingly, those questions parallel broader ones about America's role in the world. During the cold war, the space to be protected, America's security zone, was expansive—not just allies and friends but sometimes something uneasily called the "free world" as well. The protection, though, was mostly paternal, America doing the protecting with few constraints on its freedom of action. Intelligence was tightly restricted and shared sparingly with only a few (English-speaking) allies. The instinctive response to any request for sharing was, first, Why? The next question was, How little can we concede?

Now, the geography of interest to America's security may be shrinking. But, as with international finance, the spread of issues may be increasing. America's need for help may also be increasing. And so intelligence confronts the corresponding questions about for whom it works. Peacekeeping poses these issues most sharply: it is in this area that intelligence runs to foreigners and institutions, like the UN, for whom keeping secrets has not been mainline business.

Similar questions run through national institutions, as well. The most interesting of those is intelligence's relation to international crime. By custom and law, national intelligence and law enforcement have been separate compartments.

Because intelligence is loathe to reveal its sources and methods, intelligence officers are careful to stay out of the chain of evidence, so that they cannot be asked to testify in courts of law. As a practical matter, that means either that the intelligence role is limited to tipping law enforcement agencies or that intelligence officers are teamed with law enforcement counterparts.

Standards of evidence also differ between intelligence and law enforcement, a fact driven home in 1993 when the government sought to get to the bottom of alleged Iraqi plots to kill former president George Bush. The CIA and Justice Department formed a team—an unusual cooperation. What quickly became clear, though, was that what considered sufficient evidence for policy was not nearly good enough for law. Intelligence is used to inhabiting a world of uncertainty. But uncertainty is not good enough to take into a court of law where "beyond a reasonable doubt" is the prevailing norm.

This same difference was apparent in CIA analysis relevant to the UN war crimes proceedings in Bosnia. A careful 1995 analysis of ethnic cleansing was puzzle solving at its best, combining refugee accounts with satellite photos.[29] CIA analysts concluded that 90 percent of the cleansing had been done by Serbs against Muslims. Was it good enough as a guide for policy? It surely was.

But this was intelligence, discerning patterns rather than pointing to individuals. On the questions of most interest to the UN tribunal, it could say only that there was no conclusive evidence that Serbian leaders were involved in planning the ethnic cleansing. Yet "the systematic nature of the Serbian actions strongly suggests" that they "exercised a carefully veiled role in the purposeful destruction and dispersal of non-Serb populations." Thus, law enforcement officials were treated to the kind of fudged language that often has their policy counterparts pulling their hair!

TACTICS VERSUS STRATEGY: THE "GATES-IAN" REVOLUTION

Trends in intelligence analysis that began during the cold war have accelerated since its end. Intelligence officers have sought to get closer to their new consumers. In the process, intelligence has become more and more tactical.

The trends have been most apparent, for obvious reasons, at the CIA's Directorate of Intelligence (DI). Indeed, getting close to consumers might be called the "Gates-ian" revolution, after Robert Gates, who encouraged the trend during his tenure as both deputy director for intelligence (DDI) and as director of central intelligence.

In contrast to European traditions, since World War II Americans have drawn a bright white line between "intelligence" and "policy." This separation was less a reflection of wartime lessons than of the beliefs of cold war-intelligence's founding fathers, especially Sherman Kent, and of the CIA's improved standing in Washington. It was assumed that the operating agencies of government would want intelligence judgments cut to suit the cloth of ongoing policies. It was a natural concern, for instance, that the Air Force, charged with building American missiles, would relish higher estimates of the threat posed by Soviet weapons. Intelligence separated from policy would serve as a check on such proclivities.

Thus, conventional wisdom assumed that intelligence should not get too close to policy lest it be "politicized"—that is, have its detached objectivity tainted by the stakes of policy and policymakers. In the current structure, intelligence pays little price for irrelevance. It does, by contrast, pay a price for "politicization," for being seen to cross—or be pushed—across the line from objectivity to argument, for "joining the

policy team." Concern about such bias was vivid in Gates's own confirmation hearings to be DCI in 1991.[30]

There is plainly a lot to be said for this philosophy, especially for
analysts like those at State's Bureau of Intelligence and Research, whose
organizational position entangles them with policy. But for the DI,
detachment has meant disconnection, especially as the organization
has grown and become increasingly bureaucratic. Analysts can lose
sight of the fact that their papers are not written for their own sake, but
rather to help someone with concrete choices to make. Something of a
similar problem may afflict the Defense Intelligence Agency. Its analysts, though, know exactly for whom they work, a knowledge reinforced by military staffing procedures that produce a stream of taskings.

Gates and his colleagues began to alter the DI culture. During several stints on the National Security Council, and finally as President
Bush's deputy national security advisor, Gates had ample opportunity to
see which intelligence was helpful and which wasn't. An intelligence
careerist, he had come to know how different the intelligence and policy cultures are.

Indeed, the cultures are so different it is surprising that intelligence officials and policymakers connect at all. Intelligence analysts
still work in a world of paper, while policy relies mostly on discussion.
Analysts analyze what can go wrong, while policy types think wishful-
ly of what might go right. Analysts, focused on events abroad, take a
long-term view and tend to presume that the world is largely impervi-
ous to U.S. action. Indeed, they may understand the inner machina-
tions of Bonn or Tokyo better than they know the workings of
Washington.

Policy officials, by contrast, see foreign policy issues through the
prism of domestic consequences. Their time horizon is short, and they
are prone to overstate the potential impact of decisions made in
Washington. The average tenure of assistant secretaries is little more
than a year.

The physical separation of the CIA from policy agencies compounds the communication problem. Going downtown for lunch with
a policy colleague can be a half-day's endeavor. Moreover, the feeling in
the intelligence community is that, working for everyone, the CIA
risks working for no one. In answering broad questions, it answers no
one's specific question.

Gates and his successors have sought to change that culture in a
number of ways. DI analysts now frequently serve rotations in policy

agencies—the State Department, the NSC, the Pentagon, the U.S. trade representative, and elsewhere—where they serve as all-purpose staffers who just happen to have intelligence expertise. They acquire a feel for the pace and rhythm of policymaking that can be acquired no other way. By contrast to the rotations, permanent intelligence liaison operations that exist in many smaller agencies—Treasury and Commerce, for instance—seem more a part of the problem than a part of the solution. They are not experts but paper passers. They are naturally inclined to "scoops"—providing the latest secret tidbit, hopefully sooner than anyone else. Jealous of others' prerogatives, they often hinder, rather than facilitate, contact between their seniors and relevant experts in intelligence agencies.

The DI is still a "publish or perish" culture in which up-and-coming analysts are judged mostly on their written analytic outputs. So it should be, though the result is that much too much is "published"—that is, put between covers and distributed to large chunks of officialdom with the appropriate clearances. As with academics, it is not easy for analysts to realize that most of what they write, they are really writing for themselves, to build their own expertise.

Yet the DI culture has begun to reward and promote entrepreneurial analysts who are actively seeking contacts with policymakers. Not that policy types are besieged by intelligence—quite the contrary. But there has been a visible change in the old intelligence community attitude that said: "We're in the business of telling the truth. If policy doesn't listen, that's their fault." No longer does providing intelligence mean simply tossing papers over the transom. Five years ago, venturesome DI analysts spoke of "marketing" their products. Now, they realize that marketing isn't the right metaphor—their products need to be designed from the beginning with a clear eye to the detailed needs of those they would assist.

The DI's role with respect to the National Economic Council exemplifies this change. A DI officer was essentially assigned to the NEC deputy director. She would meet with the deputy director briefly several times a week, to get a sense of the NEC agenda. Out of these conversations grew the *Daily Economic Brief*, organized around the deputy director's concerns. On occasion, the DI official would have teams of analysts to meet with NEC staffers. For his part, the deputy director's insight was that, on the policy side, you get what you pay for, and in the government you pay with time.

The NIC's national intelligence officers (NIOs) have traditionally been a critical connection between intelligence and policy. Senior specialists from inside or outside intelligence, NIOs are in constant contact with what intelligence has to offer, and their stature usually gives them access to senior counterparts on the policy side. Good NIOs wind up spending half of their time out of the building, downtown, with policy officials, and unlike most intelligence analysts, they contribute more through what they *say*—in meetings or less formal conversations—than in what they *write*.

One of the innovations early in John Deutch's tenure as DCI was the introduction of a daily morning meeting, chaired by his deputy, of the CIA deputy directors for intelligence and operations, the chairman of the NIC, and other senior officers. The meeting's purpose was to share notes not just about what's happened in the world but also about what's going on in Washington. It resulted in some planning for the day's current intelligence publications and some ideas for longer-term work.

Both the NIC and the DI have tried to make their writings more useful, and the initiatives of both went in the same direction.[31] Getting the questions right is absolutely critical. Too many intelligence papers are of the "whither Uganda?" variety, even though policymakers are almost never interested in that question. Policymakers have more specific, more operational questions. The rub is that they aren't always very clear about the real question, or if they are, they aren't willing to share it with intelligence. On one occasion, the NIC learned from the NSC deputies' committee the menu of alternatives for decisions about trade with Japan. Alternatives aren't the same as key questions but are a considerable help in framing them. For that National Intelligence Estimate, we were able to point the analysis directly at the policy alternatives on the table—a circumstance more unusual than it should be.

Ideally, intelligence would interrogate policymakers about questions and presumptions and then try to validate or discredit those presumptions. But such conversations seldom happen; as a result, assumptions remain crucial. Often, lines of analysis, or of policy, are based on half-buried assumptions. For instance, thinking about the prospects for Castro's Cuba relies on assumptions about the Cuban military. Those assumptions are critical variables or linchpins for subsequent analysis. If getting the questions right is the first step toward making intelligence more useful for policymakers, being clear about assumptions and critical variables is the second.

The third analytic key is indicators. If the role and cohesiveness of the Cuban military is identified as a linchpin, then what are the indicators we should watch? In fancier words, How will we know that the world is moving from one envelope of possible Cuban futures to another? Identifying key variables but not indicators about them is more mystifying than helpful.

The fourth key is creativity in building scenarios. Used badly, scenarios merely confuse. There is a temptation to build broad scenarios that, in effect, cover all possibilities (not to mention analysts' anatomical parts). For instance, after knowing the election outcome in one foreign country, I read the preelection intelligence analysis, and I still couldn't decipher whether the analysis was right or wrong!

Scenarios should be used as checks on key variables. Once analysts identify their best bet about a particular future, constructing several improbable but high-impact excursions can not only stretch thinking. It can also identify the factors that would have to change to produce those radical excursions. Examining those changes may sharpen analysts' thoughts about how likely the excursions are; it will almost certainly be a test of whether previous analysis has correctly identified the key variables.

This discussion, though, has dealt primarily with strategic mysteries, not tactical puzzles. And it has been precisely tactical support, both to warriors and negotiators, that has become more and more prominent. Intelligence has been moving in a tactical direction, despite the emergence of so many mysteries after the cold war's end. In large part, the refocusing of national systems to suit warrior's tactical purposes is responsible for this shift. Perhaps the "Gates-ian" revolution is partly responsible too, for policy officials are most appreciative when intelligence tells them something they didn't know before. Solving a tactical puzzle is elegant and visibly helpful; putting some shape to a strategic mystery is much less so.

Tactical versus strategic, and puzzle versus mystery are related but separate dimensions. Some puzzles are strategic—Has China sold M-ll missiles to Pakistan? What is Iraq's order of battle?—and many mysteries are tactical—How will Milosevic respond to tomorrow's bombing of Serbian Bosnia? Secret versus open is a third, related dimension, in that the solutions to most puzzles require secret pieces. So the striking trend in intelligence now is best stated as tactical support, mostly puzzle solving (including some strategic puzzles, especially military) with a high secrets content.

MAGIC, a major CIA innovation after the fall of the Berlin Wall, was explicitly aimed at improving tactical support. It envisioned a network of interactive videos on a variety of intelligence topics on the desks of senior policymakers (or, more realistically, the desks of their special assistants). Those policy officials could then browse current intelligence as they chose, passing quickly over items of little interest and requesting more information on others. Over time, what they received would reflect their profile of interest. MAGIC would let those officials make immediate requests for more or different information, to be turned around within the day.

MAGIC was shelved due to lack of funds, but it represents the direction for the future. It would be a clear break with information *push*, the force feeding of officials with a torrent of factoids. It would permit policymakers to *pull* information. With its emphasis on question asking and answering, though, the needed analytic personnel would be extremely expensive; the number of officials who could receive full service would need to be limited. Its opportunity cost in more reflective, longer-term thinking would be high.

Organizations, too, have reflected this priority of the tactical. Other than the creation of a CIO, most of the organizational change that has occurred since the fall of the Berlin Wall has been tinkering within organizations, including both the CIA and DIA, to allow for better tactical support.

CIA: DI-DO Colocation

In 1994, the CIA finally decided to do what it had avoided for nearly a half century: make the DI and DO if not partners, then cohabitators—"colocation" in the CIA phrase. The logic was to put DI analysts close enough to the collection of secrets to influence what is sought to enable a CIA focused on tactical puzzles with a high secrets content. The DO, it was agreed, did not need its own cadre of reports officers to guide and grade field reporting when it had real customers in-house as guiders and graders—DI analysts.

In my view, colocation comes forty years late, when puzzle solving is less pressing, if no less popular, than during the cold war. But it does let the DI guide the DO, thus making for a shorter list of "howlers." To work well, though, the DI tactical brokers would need comparable access to the other collectors, SIGINT in particular (and they would need not to wind up as the tail of the much larger DO).

The choice turns on how the CIA's mission is defined. Colocation makes sense if the CIA is moving in a tactical direction. It does not if its mission is framing strategic mysteries. In that case, brokers would need access to secrets, but their crucial partnerships would be those with colleagues outside intelligence and outside government, in the academy and think-tank world.

DIA: Permanent Revolution

Since the Wall's fall, DIA has been through, if not permanent revolution, near-permanent reorganization. It first broke away from its organizational structure based on world regions and became an almost completely functional organization. The change was driven entirely by the desire to support military operations better. In a world of unpredictable conflicts arising in little-known places like Somalia, DIA couldn't afford cadres of dedicated regional specialists. It was bound to guess wrong.

Instead, it needed more fungible analysts composing a surge capacity. Thus, it reorganized by major battle functions—ground, sea, and air. When conflicts loomed, DIA would then be able to apply lots of analytic talent to the place or problem in question.

The logic was appealing, but the practice was awkward. DIA's regional analysts became orphans. More fundamentally, the new DIA sparked concerns over just how good military analysis could be if separated from regional expertise. During the cold war, Soviet military potential could be assessed without much regard for internal politics or economics. Now, however, that is no longer true for Russia, and it is still less true for other potential U.S. foes like Iraq, Iran, or North Korea. The functional organization was cumbersome and seemed to cut against the post-Colin Powell insistence on real jointedness among the ground, sea, and air services. Finally, even if DIA's organization had been ideal, the rest of the government remained organized by region, and so DIA was the odd agency out, including the Pentagon's own dominant regional commands. In 1995, it reversed the functional organization.

How Tactical?

This is, in many respects, the overarching question for intelligence's future. It can't and won't be decisively decided, but the broad choice of direction has enormous implications. Moving toward tactical, intelligence's implicit current choice, gives pride of place to secrets. It indicates putting the processors or analysts close to the ferreters of secrets.

Moving in the other direction, toward strategic, would define intelligence as information, not secrets. It would give priority to the torrent of information known as open source. It would not mean putting the processors close to the ferreters of secrets but, rather, linking them to colleagues elsewhere inside government and outside, at universities and think tanks.

Being responsive to consumers will almost surely reinforce the move toward the tactical. The broad choice can be seen as the degree to which consumer preferences should be followed and how much to lean against them. My own preference is unfashionably nonmarket. All the pressures in American political life shorten time horizons, and the more senior the official, the shorter the horizon. If most of intelligence moved toward tactics, it should still have some capacity to lean against that wind, to try to stretch time horizons and see issues in their time stream.

If the government is to do any serious foreign policy planning, intelligence can't be the planner but rather must initiate the process, for it has both the luxury of time and the focus on the right starting point, with a presence in foreign places America seeks to influence. Given time pressures, policy agencies, even those with planning titles and mandates either won't think seriously beyond current events or will do so only after adjusting for impacts on domestic politics.

I favor a mixed strategy. Most of intelligence should move in a tactical direction, but a central institutional capacity should be sustained, closely linked to the NSC and the NEC, should it continue. That central capacity might be called the National Intelligence Council, but it might just as well be labeled the National Estimates Council—or even the Central Intelligence Agency! Its focus would be strategic mysteries, and its mandate would be the intelligence side of the policy planning task.

The kind of people involved should plainly turn on the tasks at hand. Whether intelligence is tactical or strategic, the argument for a central check on departmental bias is weaker now. Analysts and policymakers need to work with one another. Relevance is the more urgent need.

In a world where both structures and U.S. interests are up for grabs, policymakers would be better served by intelligence brokers close at hand, down the hall, not out at Langley. In this confused world, Senator

Daniel Patrick Moynihan may be right for the wrong reasons.[32] Perhaps the CIA should be not abolished, but dispersed, its analytic pieces assigned to the Department of State, Treasury, Commerce, and elsewhere around official Washington.

Assessing the Changes

The bottom line of intelligence's change since the cold war is undramatic: no sweeping change in major systems or infrastructure. New missions have been found for old systems, particularly in collection.

The categories of changes since the cold war's end suggest similar categories of issues for the future. Those categories then become bench marks for evaluating proposals, more or less in this order. The militarization of intelligence raises questions: *What intelligence's primary mission will be? Who will be its primary consumers?* The open source revolution underscores the *role and relative importance of secrets.* Is the subject *intelligence,* defined primarily as secrets, or *information,* defined much more broadly? That same revolution, in the context of new or newly empowered consumers, raises the question of balance between *tactical* and *strategic.* The "Gates-ian" revolution makes us rethink *the relation between intelligence processing and analysis and policy.*

A follower of recent debate over intelligence might not know it, but organization should reflect, not precede, answers to these questions.

I Notes

1. This and every other number or detail about intelligence capabilities in this paper are derived from published sources. See, for instance, *Washington Post*, June 13, 1994, p. A8, or *New York Times*, November 5, 1994, p. 54. In 1994, a congressional committee inadvertently confirmed the numbers, publishing by mistake a committee print without the usual deletions. The CIA requested $3.1 billion, the Pentagon agencies (National Reconnaissance Organization, the National Security Agency, Central Imagery Office, and the Defense Intelligence Agency) $13.2 billion, and TIARA $10.4. See *New York Times*, November 5, 1994, p. 54.

2. The TIARA budget numbers are somewhat arbitrary, hence changeable, since many tactical activities could be labeled either "operations" or "intelligence" and so are labeled according to fashion in budgetary support.

3. For a review of the history of these procedures, see Jeffrey T. Richelson, "The Future of Space Reconnaissance," *Scientific American*, 264, no. 1 (January 1991): 38–44.

4. Quoted in *Washington Post*, March 17, 1995, p. A1.

5. See John D. Morrocco, "CIA Slashes Satellite Network," *Aviation Week and Space Technology* (hereafter "AWST"), January 16, 1995, p. 64.

6. James A. Winnefeld, Preston Niblack and Dana J. Johnson, *A League of Airmen: U.S. Air Power in the Gulf War* (Santa Monica, Calif.: Rand, 1994), esp. pp. 181–221.

7. *AWST*, April 8, 1991, p. 44.

8. *AWST*, August 23, 1993, p. 71.

9. *AWST*, April 22, 1991, p. 91.

10. Quoted in *Washington Post*, March 17, 1995, p. A1.

11. See John Hollister Hedley, *Checklist for the Future of Intelligence*, Occasional Paper, Georgetown University Institute for the Study of Diplomacy, Washington, D.C., 1995, p. 12.

12. On the headquarters affair, see *Washington Post*, October 6, 1994, p. A29.

13. See, for instance, Hedley, *Checklist for the Future of Intelligence*, p. 4.

14. For a nice, now slightly dated, summary of possible unmanned aerial vehicles roles in intelligence, see Richard A. Best, Jr., "Intelligence Technology in the Post-Cold War Era: The Role of Unmanned Aerial Vehicles (UAVs)," Congressional Research Service, Washington, D.C., July 26, 1993.

15. David A. Fulghum and John D. Morrocco, "CIA to Deploy UAVs in Albania," *AWST*, January 31, 1994, p. 21.

16. Russia already has sold images with two- to three-meter resolution, and there have been press reports of Russian readiness to market 0.75-meter resolution. James R. Asker, "High Resolution Imagery Seen as Threat, Opportunity," *AWST*, May 23, 1994, p. 51. See also *AWST*, July 11, 1994.

17. Joseph S. Nye, Jr., and I both found this distinction useful when we were colleagues at the National Intelligence Council. See his "Peering Into the Future," *Foreign Affairs*, 77, no. 4 (July/August 1994): 82–93.

18. The estimate is of the total capacity of all the world's computer hard drives. See John L. Simonds, "Magnetoelectronics Today and Tomorrow," *Physics Today*, April 1995, pp. 26–32.

19. These innovations, most of them not really new, are described in more detail in my "Estimating Beyond the Cold War," *Defense Intelligence Journal*, 3, no. 2 (Fall 1994): 5–20.

20. See *Washington Post*, December 28, 1994, p. A4.

21. In Hedley, *Checklist for the Future of Intelligence*, p. 27. Such numbers need to be treated with particular caution but not because they intentionally mislead. Relating outputs to inputs is just devilishly difficult. For instance, in the early 1990s about half of National Security Agency reports contained at least one paragraph of information judged "economic." Did that mean that half of NSA's infrastructure should be credited to economics? Probably not.

22. Philip Zelikow's excellent background paper in this volume, "American Intelligence and the World Economy," provides considerable detail. This section only highlights the more recent implications.

23. This matrix had been developed by Randall Fort within the CIA. I adopted and adapted it while I was on the National Intelligence Council.

24. Amy Borrus, "The New CIA: I Spy—for Business," *Business Week*, September 17, 1994, p. 23.

25. Reported in *New Republic*, March 27, 1995, p. 10.

26. Richard A. Best, Jr., "Peacekeeping: Intelligence Requirements," Congressional Research Service, Washington, D.C., May 6, 1994.

27. United States National Security Council, "The Clinton Administration's Policy on Reforming Multilateral Peace Operations," Washington, D.C., May 1994, pp. 7, 9.

28. Philip Zelikow's caselet for the Fund is the best treatment done so far.

29. This analysis is described in *New York Times*, March 12, 1995, sec. 4, p. 2.

30. For a thoughtful description of those hearings and the issues they raised, see James Worthen, "The Gates Hearings: Politicization and Soviet Analysis at CIA," *Studies in Intelligence*, Spring 1994, pp. 7–20.

31. See my and Joseph Nye's articles, cited above. For the Directorate of Intelligence, see then deputy director for intelligence Douglas MacEachin.

32. See his "Our Stupid but Permanent CIA," *Washington Post*, July 24, 1994, p. C3.

AMERICAN INTELLIGENCE AND THE WORLD ECONOMY

Philip Zelikow

I INTRODUCTION

The greatest concentration of analytical experts on international economic issues in the federal government resides not in any of the executive departments but in the Central Intelligence Agency. It is even possible that the ranks of CIA analysts contain about as much economic expertise on international problems as can be found in all the executive departments of the government put together. Within the Agency therefore the economic mission looms large: about one-third of its analytical talent concerns itself with economic issues of one kind or another.

This is not a new development. The CIA has been recruiting large numbers of economists for more than forty years. But there has never been a single, book-length study of the economic intelligence function in the U.S. government. The end of the cold war has, however, brought new interest and attention to this long-overlooked mission of the intelligence community.

The current organization of intelligence gathering and analysis for the government of the United States flows from the National Security Act of 1947. In that year, as in 1967 and 1987, the main job of American intelligence was to help policymakers meet the threat posed by the Soviet Union and its allies. This challenge shaped the intelligence community's structure, the capabilities it developed, and its sense of mission.

As the Soviet Union began to break apart in the autumn of 1991, retired Admiral Stansfield Turner, director of central intelligence during the Carter administration, explained how the transformation of world politics should have an equally dramatic effect on the intelligence community he once headed. "Are there," he asked, "topics of sufficient import to the nation's well-being to replace the Soviets as the focus of U.S. intelligence?" Indeed there were. For Turner believed "the most obvious specific impact of the new world order is that, except for Soviet nuclear weaponry, the preeminent threat to U.S. national security now lies in the economic sphere."[1]

To Turner, the need for "better economic intelligence" was a given. "The United States does not want to be surprised by such worldwide developments as technological breakthroughs, new mercantilist strategies, sudden shortages of raw materials or unfair or illegal economic practices that disadvantage the country."

This new intelligence mission meant new targets for American spies. Turner was worried about declining U.S. competitiveness in the world marketplace. Intelligence could help by spying for American business. "Economic intelligence can range from the broad trends that foreign businesses are pursuing, all the way to what individual foreign competitors are bidding against U.S. corporations on specific contracts overseas." To be sure, Turner noted, some might say it was wrong for the American government to intervene covertly in the operation of world markets, but Americans should think of the problem as one of national security. After all, the United States "would have no compunction about stealing military secrets to help it manufacture better weapons. If economic strength should now be recognized as a vital component of national security, parallel with military power, why should America be concerned about stealing and employing economic secrets?"[2]

This call to economic arms was soon echoed by the top congressman responsible for overseeing the intelligence community. Senator David Boren of Oklahoma, then chairman of the Senate's Select Committee on Intelligence, advocated renewed efforts to counter foreign spying against American industries and urged that the United States turn the tables by ferreting out the negotiating strategies of foreign countries and their collusion with their own firms. "In short, American intelligence assets should be used to level the playing field and give American companies an equal chance to compete."[3]

Boren and his staff, however, had been privately asking themselves just what the new economic mission would look like and had recognized there were some serious questions about legal requirements, protection of classified information, and ethical behavior in providing government benefits to certain companies. This unease shadowed Boren's public comments. "Defining the appropriate limits of economic intelligence will not be an easy task. . . . [C]aution must be used in the area of collecting economic intelligence." His conclusion was really a plea for the executive branch to take the lead. "It is important for policymakers to delineate the boundaries of economic intelligence activities. The intelligence community to date has received very little guidance in this sensitive area."[4]

In November 1991 President Bush signed a far-reaching classified directive, National Security Review (NSR) 29, ordering some twenty agencies and departments to assess their intelligence priorities to the year 2005. The responses were compiled into a list of new needs. Forty percent of these new intelligence requirements were economic in nature. A transition was under way. In 1980, 60 percent of intelligence community resources were directed at the Soviet Union; by fiscal year 1993 nearly two-thirds were tagged for issues unrelated to the former Soviet Union.[5]

This government study unearthed a crucial point. Industrial espionage to enhance American competitiveness might garner 95 percent of the publicity surrounding the new agenda for intelligence, but it was less than 5 percent of the problem. Director of Central Intelligence Robert Gates announced that policymakers wanted information, not only about general economic dangers, "but also the microeconomic concerns of potential allies or adversaries in any given policy initiative." Though a high priority would be given to countering foreign espionage against American companies, he thought the intelligence community had other economics tasks and "does not, should not, and will not engage in industrial espionage."[6]

Congress wondered if this guidance went far enough. "As far as I'm concerned, we don't have a workable policy to address this [economic] information in a meaningful manner," fumed Senator Frank Murkowski of Alaska, then the intelligence committee's ranking Republican.[7] Senator Boren announced, "I find as I talk to our people in our Intelligence Community, flung out around the world, they have very little idea about what they are supposed to do in terms of economic intelligence. They don't know what the guidelines are and they don't know what the policies are."[8]

As his administration prepared to take office in January 1993, President-elect Clinton promised to "make the economic security of our own nation a primary goal of our foreign policy." Trade, Clinton later added, would be "a priority element of American security."[9] The new administration reportedly reconsidered the issue of whether America should become more deeply engaged in industrial espionage. The new director of central intelligence, R. James Woolsey, told the Senate panel considering his confirmation that such espionage was "in some ways, the hottest current topic in intelligence policy."[10]

Yet, like Gates, Woolsey found that many subjects were covered by the label "economic intelligence." He observed that policymakers had recognized that "what other nations do with their interest rates, trade policies, or currencies can have an immediate and profound impact on our markets, our trade, our currency—in short, on our own economic security." So they wanted intelligence to help them. Woolsey, too, drew the line at industrial espionage. "The CIA is not going to be in the business that a number of our friends' and allies' intelligence services are in: spying on foreign corporations for the benefit of domestic businesses." Still, Woolsey hastened to promise that he would adopt other measures to help President Clinton ensure a level playing field for American business "with special enthusiasm and relish."[11]

Thus, by 1995 economic intelligence was vying with weapons proliferation and regional conflicts as the subject that would dominate American intelligence in the post-Soviet era. This seemed natural to those, like Turner, who saw economic clashes replacing ideological conflict as the new arena for global confrontation. From this perspective, winning the battle for "competitiveness" in world marketplaces is a prime new agenda for American security policy. More aggressive industrial espionage is only one of many implications for intelligence policy that would follow from such a worldview.[12] Some more traditional economists believe, though, that "the growing obsession in most advanced nations with international competitiveness should be seen, not as a well-founded concern, but as a view held in the face of overwhelming contrary evidence."[13]

However one may perceive the debate over "competitiveness," it is hard to argue against having useful intelligence on how economics can influence critical judgments about international policies. The demand for such intelligence had been evident for a long time. Testifying to Congress in 1992, former defense secretary and director of central intelligence James Schlesinger reminded his audience, "The notion that we should be doing a lot more in economic intelligence has been around for at least a quarter of a century, and probably longer than that. I remember former Governor Connally, when he was head of the PFIAB [the President's Foreign Intelligence Advisory Board], pressing President Nixon that we should be doing far more in this area."[14]

The end of the cold war did not make the economic dangers from abroad more acute. Trade deficits began declining in the late 1980s, though they have recently begun to rise sharply again. The persistence of the current account deficit is blamed more on the American recovery, stronger than that of its main trading partners, than on Japanese or European protectionism. Nor can foreign adversaries be blamed for the slumping value of the dollar in 1995. American companies are coping reasonably well, forging new and elaborate international corporate alliances.[15]

So what explains the resurgence of interest in economic intelligence? The best answer is that economic affairs have become more prominent not because the issues themselves have become more urgent but simply because the menace of a rival superpower no longer dominates the foreground.[16]

This sudden swing of the spotlight to economic intelligence is nevertheless fortunate. The subject was always important and remains so. But not one book has been written about the scope or quality of the U.S. government's efforts to obtain and use economic intelligence. The changed focus is an opportunity, first, to recognize the extraordinary breadth of the information challenge. Senator Boren hinted at the diversity of tasks ahead: "We're going to have to know about intentions about oil production levels and exchange rates and trade policy. We're going to have to protect our own commercial enterprises against the theft of commercial secrets. We're going to have to begin to think about the role that we want our own intelligence services to play in terms of protecting America's economic and commercial interests around the world."[17]

From sanctions against Bosnia to assistance for Russia, from G-7 macroeconomic coordination to the operation of foreign banks in the United States or most-favored-nation status for Beijing, economic intelligence of every kind informs policies fashioned throughout the American government. This study will try to comprehend what is essential for policymakers to know about the global economy and reflect on where specialized government agencies, rather than the private sector, have some comparative advantage in trying to satisfy these needs.

The problems of collection and analysis of relevant data are formidable and poorly understood. Though many scholars have considered how intelligence agencies can prevent new Pearl Harbors, few have reflected on the intelligence challenge of preventing politically and financially ruinous runs on the Mexican peso, or thwarting anticompetitive foreign business practices, or assessing the economic pressures that could spur revolution in Iran or armed aggression from Iraq.

The heightened visibility of economic intelligence offers a chance to ponder whether the laws, organization, or practices of the intelligence community fit well with policy needs of the 1990s. The CIA has not been traditionally a major actor in the formulation of international economic policy. Responsibilities for economic intelligence are spread unusually widely, with the departments of Treasury, Commerce, State, Agriculture, and Energy all having important roles to play.

Economic intelligence is indeed "emerging as one of the most vexing issues facing U.S. intelligence agencies in the wake of the Cold War."[18] But the issue is not yet well understood. Furthermore, it is not the intelligence agencies but the makers of American foreign policy who will have to account for the quality of the economic information and analysis that shapes their understanding of the world.

Chapter 1

ORGANIZATIONS AND MISSIONS

For the purpose of this paper, intelligence is treated as information collected by the government, overtly or covertly, to inform its international policy judgments. Economic intelligence is information about how those outside of the United States develop, produce, or manage their material goods, services, and resources. The term, as it is used here, encompasses the interpretation and presentation of raw knowledge or data as finished reports or analyses offered to inform policymaking consumers.

THE ORGANIZATION OF ECONOMIC INTELLIGENCE GATHERING

The United States government has always collected economic intelligence. In late 1776 the first U.S. intelligence agency, the Committee of Secret Correspondence of the Continental Congress, sent one William Carmichael to Europe, in the guise of a merchant, to report on a variety of economic topics of interest to the new government. Worried, for example, about foreign tobacco competition, the Congress instructed Carmichael to monitor European markets dealing in tobacco grown in the Ukrainian provinces of the Russian empire. In a November 1776 secret dispatch from Amsterdam, Carmichael reported reassuringly, "You have been threatened that the Ukraine would supply Europe with tobacco. It must be long before that time can arrive. I have seen some of its tobacco here, and the best of it is worse than the worst of our ground leaf."[1]

Once executive departments of the U.S. government were created, they began to satisfy their own needs for intelligence. No intelligence agency existed outside of these departments until the Second World War. As needed, departments collected and analyzed information on supply and demand of critical materials, the economies of particular countries, trade issues, or scientific and technological concerns. During World War I an economic intelligence section within the army's military intelligence operation was headed by John Foster Dulles. Preparing for the Versailles peace conference, President Wilson turned to a collection of private experts, the "Inquiry," which collected economic intelligence from its headquarters at the American Geographical Society in New York.

In World War II the traditional departments were supplemented by the Board of Economic Warfare, which studied the Japanese economy, for example, or analyzed the role of critical commodities,[2] and by the Office of Strategic Services (OSS). OSS collected information about tungsten and diamond smuggling or production of ball bearings, complemented by analytical models employing operations research to plot ways to attack German industry. A young petroleum analyst, Walter Levy, used the freight charges published by German railroads to deduce the location of oil refineries. The USSR division of OSS, directed by Abram Bergson and Wassily Leontief, offered prescient appraisals of the Soviet Union's postwar economic recovery.[3]

In 1945 OSS was dissolved. Whenever a successor organization was contemplated the traditional departments resisted surrendering any of their responsibilities for collection and analysis of information. Every department head insisted on the right to provide the intelligence affecting departmental issues. Not to be outdone, even the postmaster general declared that "it must be clear that any government intelligence service outside the Post Office Department must operate through the Post Office Department and recognize the absolute jurisdiction of the Department."[4] One important exception was evaluation of scientific intelligence and specific intelligence on foreign atomic energy work, a job turned over in 1946 and 1947 to the CIA's forerunner, the Central Intelligence Group.

The Central Intelligence Group concerned itself early with coordinating provision of adequate economic intelligence to top officials. In June 1946 a progress report to cabinet officials then constituting the "National Intelligence Authority" reported on success in gathering intelligence on "foreign industrial establishments" and ongoing work on foreign petroleum developments, compiling comprehensive geographical information and utilizing the services of attachés to gather data on strategic minerals. The next month the director of central intelligence, Lt. General Hoyt Vandenberg, offered the following example of the need for central intelligence coordination:

> . . . as regards a given steel plant, State is studying what products are made there and the rate of production. War Department, however, is interested in the construction and physical details of the plant, the railroads serving it, and other data required for target information. State Department, if it broadened the base of its studies, might well be able to furnish at least part of that type of economic intelligence. It is the job of C.I.G. [Central Intelligence Group], therefore, to find out the needs of all the departments and to meet them, either by recommending that one department expand its activities or by performing the necessary research in C.I.G.[5]

When the Central Intelligence Agency was established by the National Security Act of 1947, its role was limited. The State Department had primary responsibility for "political, cultural, sociological" intelligence; the uniformed services were responsible for military intelligence; and "economic, scientific, and technological intelligence" was assigned to "each agency in accordance with its respective needs."[6] The CIA's only duty was to provide "national intelligence" on transcendent issues, and to do this by coordinating the information collected by the various departments of government.

But there was growing recognition that while some economic intelligence did not fit in with the dominant interest of any particular department, it undoubtedly had value for the U.S. government. Following the 1949 recommendations of a review group chaired by Allen Dulles, the CIA created a new Office of Research Reports to collect and examine more economic information.[7]

This office was important because it was the only truly analytical office in the new CIA, separate from the personnel coordinating national estimates or providing daily or weekly intelligence summaries. In other words, most of the large analytical establishment of the CIA today can trace its lineage to the work on economic intelligence being done in the early days of the cold war. In a 1951 National Security Council (NSC) directive the U.S. government held the CIA responsible for determining the overall requirements for "foreign economic intelligence." The CIA was to insure that "the full economic knowledge and technical talent available in the Government" was applied to reports and discussions involving national security. It was also ordered to evaluate the "pertinence, extent, and quality of the foreign economic data available bearing on national security issues, and develop ways in which quality could be improved and gaps could be filled." Finally, as a service of "common concern" to various departments, the CIA was itself to conduct "such foreign economic research and produce such foreign economic intelligence" as was required to supplement work being done by other agencies.[8]

By 1952 the director of central intelligence, then General Walter Bedell Smith, was able to inform the National Security Council that the new Office of Research and Reports (ORR) was in full operation. He commented that "although accurate appraisal of an enemy's economic potential is a most important factor in estimating his military capabilities, this crucially important task had previously been scattered among twenty-four separate agencies of the Government." An interdepartmental Economic Intelligence Committee was also put in place, chaired by the assistant director of ORR.[9]

The allocation of responsibility for economic intelligence over the next twenty years was, in large part, a story of the shifting roles of the CIA and Department of State. The CIA and State had worked very closely together during the Truman administration. These were years when the economic mission was important and prestigious within State, supervised by powerful and capable officials like Will Clayton and Paul Nitze and harnessing the talents of economists like Edward S. Mason, Walt Rostow, Charles P. Kindleberger, and John Kenneth Galbraith. Over the years, however, as CIA's capabilities grew, the State Department retreated from its position as the primary U.S. government center for both economic data collection and economic analysis.

The Department of State felt it could collect and analyze foreign economic data, trends, and other intelligence without the CIA's help. The department conceded, however, that its diplomats could not readily evaluate the economies of countries in the Soviet bloc. The economies of these Communist countries therefore became the special responsibility of the CIA.[10] The bargain was put in writing. The State Department would produce "economic intelligence on countries outside the Sino-Soviet Bloc," and the CIA "shall produce economic intelligence on the Sino-Soviet Bloc and scientific and technical intelligence as a service of common concern."[10]

The job of coordinating economic intelligence for the U.S. government, assigned to the CIA in 1951, was a substantial challenge. The Economic Intelligence Committee worked to establish priorities and publish interdepartmental economic estimates. Since the various agencies' personnel still worked for their own bosses, however, this new committee's work often did little more than add to the flow of paper.[12]

It was the CIA's economic work on the Soviet bloc, though, that propelled its ascent to the status of a major source of intelligence analysis to the U.S. government. ORR's new head, a brilliant, young economics professor from MIT, Max Millikan, "had an electric effect" on the office and helped recruit a number of bright economics graduate students before he returned to Massachusetts. (He remained an influential consultant to ORR.) In 1955 there were nearly five hundred analysts in ORR, more than in the other offices of the CIA's analytical side, the Directorate of Intelligence, put together, and almost all these ORR analysts were working on Soviet bloc economies.[13] They had a formidable task, since there was little information available on any aspect of the Soviet economy. (Moscow did not begin publishing even basic economic statistics until 1957.) The office was generally credited with composing the first good pictures of Soviet economic capabilities—its transport system, current production, plant capability, and so on.[14]

This economic analysis became the CIA's route to challenging the military services' monopoly over the provision of strategic intelligence. In the mid-1950s the Agency was embroiled in a major controversy with the Air Force over Soviet bomber production. It argued that because of limited production capacity, the USSR could not possibly have built a force of the size claimed by the Air Force. The CIA was generally perceived to have won this fight. Its analysis was valued by the Kennedy administration, and it added to its luster by establishing dominance in the interpretation of the new photo imagery taken from aircraft and satellites. During the 1960s the CIA became the government's leading provider of strategic intelligence.[15]

The CIA also began expanding the scope of its analysis to cover "free world" economies, partly in response to specific requests and partly under the rubric of examining Soviet bloc economic activity in the developing world. In 1961 the State Department's Bureau of Intelligence and Research, faced with severe budget constraints, cut out the majority of its economic research in order to maintain its capabilities for political analysis. The CIA picked up most of State's responsibilities for providing regular economic contributions to national intelligence documents and also picked up substantial new demands from policymakers, especially for information on developing countries.[16] CIA director John McCone struck a new bargain with Secretary of State Dean Rusk in 1965, formally authorizing the CIA to pursue worldwide economic intelligence.[17] Still, relatively few policy officials thought they needed much intelligence about the economies of the developed world.

By 1967–68 a growing sense of European and Japanese competition sparked new interest in those economies, while the devaluation of sterling at the end of 1967 also created a demand to know more about international monetary problems. The CIA replaced ORR with a new office, the Office of Economic Research, which began receiving its first formal requests for intelligence from the Treasury Department in 1968. The President's Foreign Intelligence Advisory Board (PFIAB) reported to the White House on economic intelligence in December 1971. The State Department, it concluded, had not carried out its assigned responsibilities for collection and analysis on free world economic activity; only the CIA's Office of Economic Research could do the job. The PFIAB urged that the CIA get more resources in order to produce intelligence for the government's entire international economic agenda. As another sign of growing attention being given to economic intelligence, the Treasury Department became a formal member of the intelligence community in 1972.[18]

As in the period immediately after the end of the cold war, economics was suddenly the fashionable priority for international policymakers in the early 1970s. A 1974 issue of *Foreign Affairs* announced the "Year of Economics."[19] Close attention to various economic developments was ranked as one of the top five "substantive objectives" in guidance issued to the intelligence community for fiscal year 1976.[20]

These new demands meant that the CIA's economics capabilities were being spread more thinly. Diversion of analysts to studying Vietnam or other parts of the world caused a significant reduction in the effort devoted to tracking the Soviet economy during the 1960s and early 1970s. Demand for analysis from the CIA grew as other departments such as Treasury and Commerce increasingly challenged State's views on foreign economic policy. These agencies, along with the White House-organized Council for International Economic Policy (CIEP), sought information gathered or interpreted from outside of the State Department. The CIA built up its abilities to follow world commodity markets, especially gold, oil, and agricultural products (working closely with the Agriculture Department on problems like Soviet grain import requirements). It became the most important producer of intelligence for policymakers responding to the oil shocks of the 1970s. Meanwhile it remained a crucial source of information about Communist economies, especially China, which released no economic statistics at all between the late 1950s and the late 1970s.

Yet the CIA's overall importance in the provision of economic intelligence diminished during the 1980s. There was still little competition from the State Department; the analytical capabilities in its Intelligence and Research Bureau (as many as a hundred analysts in the 1950s) were never rebuilt and remain at a small fraction of their former strength. But other policy agencies had substantially bolstered their in-house expertise during the 1970s. The Treasury Department and the Federal Reserve Board both took steps to improve their monitoring of international financial issues. During the 1980s the Commerce Department built up a staff of hundreds of industry and country analysts.

The CIA's most important new competition, though, has been the new wealth and sophistication of international economic analysis available to policymakers from the private sector. Dramatic increases in international capital flows and trade have naturally been accompanied by a greater market interest in global economic information. Complementing this, the international financial institutions such as the International Monetary Fund and the World Bank have become strong, knowledgeable providers of the kind of information about the developing world that was once almost the exclusive province of the CIA. The result is a far greater volume of private and institutional information and analysis available to government officials, enhanced by more sophisticated information processing. On-line services now give private analysts access to a tremendous array of reports and data; their work in turn raises the general level of discussion in newspapers and trade publications.

Collection and Analysis: How Is It Produced?

While alternative sources of information and analysis, often produced outside of the U.S. government, have proliferated, the CIA's reservoir of experts has remained more or less constant for many years. The number of Agency analysts working on economic topics was at an all-time high in the 1950s, when creating a database for the Soviet economy was a labor-intensive task. Work on economic affairs now extends beyond the Directorate of Intelligence's economic office, renamed once again as the Office of Resources, Trade, and Technology (RTT), to analysts concerned with particular regions, with day-to-day intelligence briefings, or with special topics like export control and nonproliferation. But the total number of analysts working on economics throughout the Directorate of Intelligence has been fairly steady since the 1970s at about 250–270 professionals.[21] Overt government collection of economic information overseas, whether by State Department economic officers or by the Commerce Department's foreign commercial officers or by the Treasury's financial attachés, has also remained at roughly the same level for decades. The end of the cold war may have stimulated new interest in economic intelligence, but it has not had a dramatic effect on the resources available to perform this mission in any of the relevant agencies. The situation at the State Department has actually deteriorated.

The quality of the CIA's effort has been undermined by turbulence in the assignment of these analysts, as groups of people are moved from one hot topic to another. Talented economic analysts are also hired away to lucrative private work, and 20 percent turnover a year among the trained economists is not uncommon.

The main sources of economic intelligence are, in approximate order of importance, open sources, "overt" reporting, and clandestine reports. Open sources may range from official statistical publications, newspapers, radio broadcasts, and trade publications to IMF country studies. "Unclassified sources generally constitute the foundation of any economic analysis, even on the USSR and other communist countries, and provide an essential context to interpret classified material and how it fits into the overall picture."[22] The volume of records is massive, and the intelligent synthesis of such a vast quantity of material—in both English and foreign languages—is no mean feat. But the bulk of documents and transcripts that are made available is practically valueless without high-quality information processing.

The CIA is reluctant to acknowledge how much it relies on open sources. There is a fear that Congress will not appropriate money for experts who "just read the newspapers." But all agencies performing economic intelligence must admit the obvious: the world economy functions on the basis of publicly available information. In general, the CIA does more to aggregate and interpret open-source literature than any other government agency. The Agency has developed new computerized tools for sorting through open-source data that are virtually unrivaled in the U.S. government or even in the private sector.

Though it may seem that many agencies, including the Library of Congress, could do this job equally well, these others are not staffed or equipped to digest such a diverse quantity of data, match it against classified information, and provide a synthesis tailored to the needs of executive branch officials. To say that this task is little more than "reading the newspapers" is like saying that the navy's multibillion-dollar acoustic signal processing technology just "records sounds." The CIA's ability to process open-source literature can become an overexploited resource, since it is effectively free to users in the executive departments and no gatekeeper now sorts out which requests genuinely require extra attention from the CIA.

The second major source of economic intelligence is the reports from America's embassies and consulates penned by State Department economic officers, Treasury attaches (in some embassies), and officers of the Foreign Commercial Service. Since Foreign Commercial Service officers usually attend to aiding American businesses rather than providing systematic analysis of the local economy, the State and Treasury Department reports predominate. Unfortunately, the quality of overseas reporting varies greatly from post to post and officer to officer.

Few economic officers in the State Department are trained economists. The entry examination process for the Foreign Service "is almost obsessively neutral with regard to specialized qualifications."[23] Though mid-career economic training has improved, the State Department does not always prove to be an interested and critical audience that adequately develops and rewards outstanding systematic work and analytical talent. Instead economic officers are often burdened by "low-priority, even trivial, requests," related to State's own "lack of coordination and parochialism" in the economic field, promoting "a reactive, issue-specific focus."[24] The total number of economic officers in the Foreign Service actually declined between 1985 to 1992 by 7.5 percent, from 931 to 861 (about 600 of them overseas).[25] Limits on the deployment, training, and tasking of overt collection and analysis by State's economic officers are one of the most important constraints on the potential of American economic intelligence work.

Other overseas collectors also present a mixed picture. Treasury attachés are fewer in number (about 400 American staff overseas worldwide) and have a narrower focus, though the general standard of their reporting is regarded somewhat more highly. Commerce and Agriculture each employ about 250 Americans overseas, but Commerce does little mainstream economic reporting or analysis and Agriculture concentrates on only one sector.[26]

Clandestine information is data obtained without either the knowledge or consent of foreign governments. It can come from satellite pictures, intercepted communications, or the secrets stolen by a foreign national working for the United States. Such information rarely contributes vitally to the daily stream of economic intelligence flowing through government offices, but it often adds a special strategic insight or a tactical tip that instantly can catch the attention of top officials.

The economic information arriving in Washington from these various sources is processed, analyzed, and disseminated principally by the CIA, Treasury, and State. The other agencies tend to consume far more economic intelligence than they produce. As mentioned earlier, the CIA's base of economic analysts has remained roughly constant for decades while demands have grown, and it becomes harder to recruit and retain the best and most experienced analysts. Treasury was once considered to have an outstanding staff of economists in its Office of International Affairs, but the quality of their labors is widely believed to have suffered from benign neglect during the 1980s. The State Department has never recovered the economic expertise or mandate it sacrificed more than thirty years ago. Its Bureau of Economic Affairs has been hard hit by more budget cuts in the last few years, with declines in staffing, even while total domestic employment at State is remaining stable or growing. On the brighter side, the staff of the International Trade Commission and the Federal Reserve Board's Division of International Finance have, within their much narrower areas of responsibility, established excellent reputations for their interpretation and presentation of economic information. Overall, however, despite the louder rhetoric about the new challenge of securing international markets, there is no evidence of any significant change in the methods or resources devoted to the collection of economic intelligence in recent years. Nor are there signs of any major new investments in recruiting, developing, and retaining the staff needed to present such intelligence effectively to policymakers.

The CIA's role in providing economic intelligence to the U.S. policy community is now substantial. Hundreds of people work in the RTT office, which is divided into divisions working on international transactions (including sanctions enforcement and illicit finance), international economics and environmental problems (including trade and finance and competition), defense markets and logistics, geographic resources (including demographics and commodities), civil technology (including aerospace, advanced manufacturing, and emerging technologies), and energy resources.

These analysts join others, including those assigned to particular regions or countries, in preparing a variety of reports for policymakers. The Clinton administration's creation of the National Economic Council (NEC) has established an active new primary consumer of intelligence in the White House, stimulating publication of a *Daily Economic Brief* distributed to top officials around the government. CIA analysts personally brief senior NEC, Treasury, Commerce, and USTR (Office of the U.S. Trade Representative) officials almost every day.

WHEN TO RELY ON GOVERNMENT: FOUR PRINCIPLES

The growing availability of economic information from the private sector, international organizations, and the international financial institutions raises the question, should the U.S. government be in this business at all? If an outside entity can do the same work nearly as well as government agencies, or even better, why not let harried, budget-strapped agencies settle comfortably into the saddle of a free rider, using the products already produced for the marketplace at someone else's expense?

This paper presumes the agencies should do just that: they should take full advantage of the more extensive, more sophisticated flow of outside information and avoid duplicating tasks already performed adequately by others. The word "adequately" is especially important. The government may believe that it can do a better job collecting or analyzing certain information. The burden, though, is on government to show why taxpayers should be obliged to pay for this added increment in performance (if in fact the increment really exists outside the minds of those agencies asking for money).

However, the government does have some unique responsibilities in the collection and preparation of economic intelligence. As the various categories of economic intelligence are surveyed in subsequent chapters, four principles are proposed as a guide for sorting out the duties the U.S. government should perform on behalf of its citizens.

First, the United States should decide whether the collection or interpretation of the information is a public service that the private sector will not provide. There are certain kinds of information for which there is little market demand but significant public need. The CIA's economic intelligence function grew in response to the underserved need for more reliable estimates about Soviet-bloc economies and then the economies of the world's less developed and newly independent nations, decades before the international financial institutions began to accumulate impressive data about such problems. North Korea is an example of an economy that America needs to understand better but that offers little interest to either the private sector or the multilateral lending institutions. There are many other gaps in private-sector coverage of economic issues that justify public concern: the export efforts of the Ukrainian arms industry might be one; the finances of the Cali cocaine cartel might be another. U.S. government production of such intelligence is an expenditure in the public interest.

Second, the U.S. government has unique intelligence collection capabilities that can be applied to some economic questions. The government has both means of collection for which no substitute is available and special legal privileges. Washington has invested enormous sums of money in systems deployed, from outer space to the bottom of the sea, to record imagery, communications, other electronic emissions, and many other detectable physical phenomena.

Private citizens cannot afford to do most of these things, and they would go to jail for doing some of them.

The U.S. government sponsors clandestine intelligence collection by its officers overseas, or, put more bluntly, "it employs secret agents to perform acts that break foreign laws."[27] Further, U.S. intelligence agencies have a variety of "liaison" relationships with their counterparts in other countries. "Indeed, we have created whole national services, internal and external, from one end of the world to the other, trained them, vetted them, funded them, in order to be able to conduct liaison in their countries, and to get them to do work that we, though expending vast sums in training and subsidy of operations, thought we were too small or too poor to handle ourselves."[28]

Government officials unanimously praise the value of economic intelligence gathered by such means, even if the flashes of insight are unpredictable or episodic. These unique methods of extraction, as well as the craft that accompanies their use, also characterize counterintelligence (including working against some of the services with which the United States also has liaison relationships).

Third, there may be issues or questions for which the U.S. government does not wish to rely solely upon available outside sources of information. Outside information can be biased. The marketplace produces information in response to commercial interests. These interests may not coincide with what the government has defined as the public interest. The mining industry may not be an objective source on the question of whether the United States needs to enlarge its strategic stockpile of manganese. Motorola might not be the most objective judge of its competitors' pricing practices. Outside information can even be deliberately distorted. The Soviet Union never accurately reported its true defense spending. The United Nations might be obliged to rely on Iraq's reported GNP statistics because it would be impolitic to challenge a member state's veracity; the United States cannot afford to be so tolerant.

Outside information may also be too opaque to be useful. An institution might have a model for calculating China's use of fossil fuels, one so complex (or proprietary) that the crucial assumptions are invisible to all except the model's operators. Or construction company X might report that it lost a public building contract due to an unfair import restriction when actually that was just the excuse the overseas executive gave to his home office to conceal his mishandling of the bidding process. The government has no way of ascertaining the true provenance of such information.

Finally, the U.S. government may want to mold information to suit its own special requirements. A policymaker might read several different forecasts for Japan's economic future. Which forecast is best? A quick check of the literature reveals a good article in an economic journal, but it was written two years earlier. It does not reflect on the newly announced changes in Japanese fiscal policy. There may be no time to wait for another, more current academic paper or brokerage firm analysis to turn up. An answer must be provided, and it must take the latest developments into account as well as the fate of any new taxing or spending proposals in the Japanese Diet (a political dimension wholly ignored in the journal article). Another policymaker wants to know how the EC's latest carbon tax proposal would affect the American coal mining industry. The literature yields good treatments of the aggregate effect of alternative carbon tax regimes, but none of the alternatives matches up exactly with the EC proposal, and the work does not break out the impact into specific sectors like coal. In each of these hypothetical cases, the government needs to add something itself to the available information. Even where information is abundant and to the point—say, predictions for world oil supplies—government analysts might need to process a variety of judgments or methodologies into a terse, plausible synthesis.

Policy Issues

Has the U.S. government now organized effectively its collection and analysis of economic intelligence? The current system has evolved without central direction for economic intelligence. The authority of the director of central intelligence (DCI) in this area is not comparable to the post's authority in political and military intelligence. Policy responsibility in the economic field is more diffuse and compartmentalized. The most up-to-date information and the best experts are closely associated with agencies like the Treasury, the Federal Reserve Board, Commerce, or Agriculture. Neither the State Department nor the CIA seems prepared or able to assert a "lead" agency role.

Does the U.S. government have the general capacity to collect and analyze needed economic intelligence? Though particular analytical issues will be discussed in later chapters, there is a striking disjunction between the higher volume of rhetoric about the importance of economic intelligence and the constant or even diminishing resources allocated to the task at the CIA, State Department, and Treasury. Overseas reporting and analytical work in Washington depend on professional expertise. Yet the quality of the work produced by government experts is considered by many observers to be noticeably weaker today, in relation to the private sector, than was the case ten or fifteen years ago. Nowhere does the gap between rhetoric and reality seem wider than at the Department of State.

Chapter 2

THE ECONOMIES OF COUNTRIES

The United States government has always been interested in the economic condition of other states. Such intelligence can serve at least four purposes:

▲   General economic information about a country can provide material for other projections and analyses. German interest rate cuts might mean greater demand for goods throughout Western Europe, which is a major reference point for American macroeconomic forecasts. Or the rate of inflation in Japan might help predict Tokyo's position on cutting taxes.

▲   Estimates of potential military power have always taken into consideration projections about economic strength and production. The previous chapter offered the example of the CIA's successful use of economics to deflate estimates about Soviet bomber and missile production during the 1950s.

▲   Political deductions are often made on the basis of economic intelligence. If the United States wants to judge the prospects for South Africa's newly elected government, it must factor in some presumptions about how scarcities will constrain government choices and affect popular acceptance of democracy.

▲   Judging economic leverage depends especially heavily on good
intelligence. Whether designing economic assistance for Russia or
sanctions against Iraq, the government will wish to craft a policy
that achieves maximum results with the resources available.

Each of these four uses of economic intelligence for country analysis
will be discussed in turn.

GENERAL COUNTRY INFORMATION

Government often uses general economic information as an input to
devise projections or policy analyses. Environmental experts, for
example, use estimates about Chinese economic performance to feed
into models that predict China's use of fossil fuels or other energy
sources, a critical and poorly understood variable in developing policies to protect global climate. Others must incorporate judgments
about future economic growth or inflation in countries like Japan and
Germany into policies aiming to promote America's prosperity.

In 1969 the CIA's Office of Economic Research established a
systems development staff to provide high-quality, automated data
processing and methodological support. This function steadily
expanded into a Development and Analysis Center, so that by the
late 1970s OER "had one of the most sophisticated econometric
efforts in the world."[1] The office built its own model of the world
economy, linking major countries through trade flows, in order to
simulate the impact of changes in American economic policies or of
shocks to the world economy. This "Link" model, along with individual country models, was used to answer many "what if" questions
from government officials. What if the price of oil doubled? What
would be the economic impact on Japan of a 1 percent increase in
U.S. government spending? The energy sector of the "Link" model
was especially elaborate, dealing with questions of scarcity, price,
and patterns of consumption. Highly qualified experts were recruited to run these models, and the CIA held annual conferences with
leading economists and econometricians to develop further its
macroeconomic and energy analysis.[2]

CIA models have been developed for all the major OECD countries, the USSR, and several developing countries. The CIA also
draws upon commercially available data banks and models from the

IMF, the UN, and private forecasting firms such as DRI, Chase Econometrics, and Wharton, or it contracts for their use. Many intelligence officers prefer to rely on their own models whenever possible, however, because they thoroughly understand how these work and how much weight to place on a given conclusion. They can tailor their own models more precisely to the specific questions policymakers want answered. Some inquiries cannot be revealed to outsiders, in part because the knowledge that certain questions are being asked could affect world markets. Suppose, for example, it became known that a senior government official wanted to understand the macroeconomic impact of a 10 percent drop in the value of the yen?

Should the government then collect vast quantities of general macroeconomic data about the countries of the world, supplemented by its own econometric models to interpret the data and provide the needed insights? This is a difficult question to answer until more is known about the intended uses of the information. In principle, a strong case can be made that government duplication of private efforts is wasteful. A counterargument can be lodged, though, that the government must have its own in-house analysis, at least for certain kinds of questions.

Nevertheless, there is good reason to caution against extensive national macroeconomic data collection and econometric modeling by the U.S. government. The presumption against large-scale collection and modeling of general macroeconomic data stems, first and foremost, from the absence, at least as documented in the unclassified literature, of any notable occasion on which such intelligence was uniquely valuable to the leaders of the government. There is no doubt that scores of instances could be adduced when such intelligence was requested by policymakers. There are also probably many cases in which policymakers have attested that such intelligence is interesting, especially if they themselves did not have to pay for it.

America does not need to compile comprehensive macroeconomic information about other countries, with very few exceptions. And, fortunately, a considerable amount of macroeconomic data is already collected and maintained by international organizations and entities in the private sector. The United Nations (including its European and Asian economic commissions), the OECD, the European Union, the World Bank, and the International Monetary Fund all do a respectable job of collecting such data. At least some

U.S. government officials also consider IMF and World Bank analysts to be discreet as well as capable.

Most information relied upon by businesses and citizens in the developed countries of the OECD is published, debated, and available to interested foreigners. Private firms, research institutions like the National Bureau of Economic Research, and interested academics follow such data very closely and are constantly offering their own interpretations of it. The United Nations publishes a comprehensive guide, A System of National Accounts (SNA), to aid members in compiling national income accounts, including financial transactions by sector. The International Monetary Fund offers parallel guides for collection of balance of payments and government finance data, as well as standards for monetary statistics, in its monthly publication International Financial Statistics.[3]

Rather than rehash these efforts, the U.S. government could probably pick one among the databases that all agencies would use as a foundation, and then devote the effort of country specialists to critiquing and adapting it. The result could be a constantly updated, internal U.S. government "version" of the agreed database.[4] Washington's own country analysts would not develop econometric models of their own for most economies. Instead, resources should be devoted to assembling and evaluating outside interpretations and refinements, focused upon particular questions likely to trouble policymakers.

Reliance on outsiders has a downside. The quality of work obtained externally might leave significant room for improvement. Almost all the available data rely on national self-reporting, but not all nations report reliably, comprehensively, or truthfully. Reports are often about activities at least a year or two in the past, and even the most advanced countries file laggard and inconsistent statistical reports.[5] The data also have some methodological weaknesses. One is the way in which exchange rate differentials are handled in computing GDP or other statistical aggregates. If differently weighted exchange rates are applied to different kinds of transactions, then the dollar estimates of national income or purchasing power can vary dramatically depending on the controversial assumptions used in the weighing.[6]

However, the U.S. government is not likely to do much better itself in collecting the necessary information. Take the example of the amount of long-term debt held by other countries. The World Bank has a Debtor Reporting System with detailed guidelines for loan-by-loan reporting by member states. The Bank then checks this information against information major banks share through the private Bank for International Settlements and information about government-guaranteed debt and credits maintained by the OECD. It also checks with the regional development banks and interested governments.

Both the World Bank and the OECD maintain qualified staffs to work on these statistics. They can check the data with country analysts in the Bank and desk officers in the IMF. They go to the countries to examine the situation firsthand. The Bank and the IMF send missions to member countries, gathering information and providing technical assistance for national data collection.[7] The U.S. government would need to expend considerable resources to gain, at best, marginal improvements in data that may only be needed on a few occasions, for a few countries.

A major problem for the United States is those countries that provide limited or no useful national reports. Stay with the example of long-term debt: The World Bank receives no regular reports from countries like North Korea, Cuba, Iraq, Libya, South Africa, or even Greece. It gathers little of value from countries such as Egypt, Syria, or Haiti. Important states like Russia, China, and Iran only release partial data. Some of these deficiencies can be remedied with information from creditors and through estimates. But the Bank's own estimates are likely to be reasonably well informed. The international financial institutions have probably deployed more economics-related information gathering expertise in the field in Russia or Ukraine than have all the Western governments put together.[8]

The United States does not need fine detail for many of its judgments. The Bank estimates, for instance, that Cuba and Iraq are severely indebted, that is, their annual debt service obligations are more than 80 percent of their GNP or more than 220 percent of export earnings.[9] Absent some compelling contrary indicator, Washington can safely assume that these estimates are true, and concentrate its efforts on learning particular details about key payment obligations or efforts to obtain debt relief.

Naturally the United States would like to know more about the economies of some especially important countries that conceal significant productive activity, like China or North Korea. Yet rather than constructing its own macroeconomic database for the country, as was done for the Soviet Union, the intelligence community would be better off concentrating its scarce resources on information relevant to particular policy questions.

An even more radical thesis can be put forward. The U.S. intelligence agencies may actually perform the most useful economic analysis by bringing their political judgment to bear on someone else's economic data. Examine three hypothetical illustrations.

In the first case the U.S. government wants to estimate the likely consequences of French devaluation of the CFA franc used in Francophone Africa. The CIA and Treasury Department might, after checking with the international financial institutions, produce a rough estimate of the probable effects, a "reduced form" estimate. No fancy econometric modeling would be used. The problem has minor importance to the United States, and modest resources would be expended upon it. The agencies might arrange to have officers in overseas posts conduct controlled pricing checks to validate some of their hypotheses. The CIA and State Department could then add critical value to the raw forecast by integrating some political analysis of the effect of certain price increases on the stability of one government or another. That forms a direct link between the economic analysis and the interest of most American policymakers.

In the second case the government is preparing for a "jobs summit" of G-7 countries to discuss common efforts to combat unemployment. Briefing materials that analyze the nature and causes of persistently high unemployment in Western Europe are needed for the president and cabinet officials. The question is more important than the CFA-franc issue, but fewer resources are actually needed because so much literature is available off the shelf. The challenge is to sort from among the competing explanations for Europe's unemployment problem and reach an informed policy judgment. The analysts must be able to weigh the merits of the various theories or attempt some synthesis. They must make their arguments comprehensible to noneconomists but sophisticated enough to satisfy those familiar with the debate. Their product will be a kind of tutorial, but at the same time they will be performing a useful service if they can relate an abstract concept like "hysteresis" to the political dilemmas faced by the European politicians who will be leading their delegations to the summit.

In the third case Washington wants to know whether a Japanese pledge to the G-7 to increase spending and cut taxes is actually being kept. Both the Japanese government's budget proposal and a supplemental budget proposal must be analyzed carefully. The IMF has the official data on Japanese plans, part of its job of G-7 multilateral "surveillance." But for various reasons the IMF has difficulty probing beneath the surface of the official documents. So expertise is needed on Japanese fiscal policy, a subject that can mislead and confuse even Japanese officials. The expertise called for includes some knowledge of the general economic background but concentrates more on public finance, the structure of the Japanese budget, and the political process surrounding it. There are probably only a few such experts in the U.S. government, people who have studied the details of the budget process for years and who might be found in the CIA, in the Treasury, in the State Department, or perhaps at the U.S. embassy in Tokyo.

In all three of these cases general economic information is incorporated into the final intelligence product, yet the information itself did not have to come from inside the government. The intelligence agencies, fixated on their inside sources, often fail to digest what outsiders already know. One senior U.S. policymaker, commenting on the financial unrest after the 1994 assassination of Mexican presidential candidate Luís Donaldo Colosio, remembered that the "CIA had one-third of what we got by calling a few financial institutions." The ability to call "a few financial institutions" is only one aspect of a broader effort to assimilate what concerned private Americans might know about a given problem and then apply the government's unique assets for collecting and integrating intelligence from varied sources and its powers of analysis. Often, the primary value of intelligence agencies' work will come from its appraisal of the secondary economic and political repercussions of an economic event rather than from economic forecasting itself.

POTENTIAL MILITARY POWER

Economic strength has long been viewed as underpinning military power. Historically, the need to infer military capabilities has been the great motive behind collection of economic intelligence. The "most searching" intelligence reports coming to the British government about Germany before the First World War came from a commercial attaché, Sir Francis Oppenheimer. Concentrating on German

industry, finance, and commerce, Oppenheimer "could relate economic data to politics and external relations. His papers . . . were
'scoops.' People as varied as Lloyd George and Eyre Crowe regarded
Oppenheimer as a source of the highest quality."[10] Though the British
Navy ignored Oppenheimer's reports showing that Germany was relatively invulnerable to a blockade, Oppenheimer himself failed to
provide the intelligence revealing how dependent Britain was upon
Germany.[11]

Learning from this mistake, British intelligence gave considerable
attention to economic issues in the 1920s and 1930s, particularly in
regard to Germany, and put special focus on economic readiness for
war. Yet, despite good sources on German aircraft production, the
intelligence was not properly used, as the Air Ministry alternately
underestimated and overestimated German air strength with little
basis for either set of judgments.[12] More importantly, the British government, influenced by a false analogy to World War I, missed just
how dangerously short the Germans were of vital raw materials in
1938, before they had absorbed Czechoslovakia. While the military
leaders counseled caution in resisting Hitler, their intelligence had
not told them that the real resource situation "was catastrophic.
Throughout the 1930s the Germans had not possessed sufficient foreign exchange to build up stocks of raw material," especially petroleum
and rubber. In 1938 the economy had "reached a breaking point."
The British did not know.[13]

For their part, the Germans had developed a formidable body of
economic intelligence, relying on elaborate networks with private
businesses and economic think tanks. This operation was centered
in the War Economics Branch of the armed forces high command
(Oberkommando der Wehrmacht), a branch staffed by economists
and officers with business experience. But that agency "exhausted
itself in building up an archive rather than aiding political and military decisionmaking."[14]

After World War II, confronting its Soviet adversary, the
American government attempted to build up an "archive" and at the
same time provide strategic assistance to decisionmakers. Washington
made an unprecedented effort to integrate economic analysis into its
fundamental assessment of the Soviet military threat. "I believe it
may be safe to say," commented Nick Eberstadt, "that the U.S. government's effort to describe the Soviet economy may be the largest
single project in social science research ever undertaken."[15]

THE SOVIET ECONOMY CASE

When the CIA began trying to construct a database about the Soviet economy in the early 1950s, little was known and much was feared. "People thought the whole country had been turned into an arsenal," recalled one veteran analyst. The underlying reason for the CIA initiative was to better calibrate the scope of Soviet military preparedness and strength. As recounted earlier, the CIA's work on Soviet industrial capacity became its pathway into officially approved direct collection and analysis of military intelligence.

But the United States could not help being curious about the general size of the Soviet economy. Khrushchev's promise to "bury" the capitalists and his bragging about Soviet economic achievement (Moscow was claiming 12 percent economic growth per year) made the curiosity unbearable. The worry was of some imaginary "crossover" point at which the Soviet Union would actually pass the United States. Back in this age of New Dealers and ex-New Dealers, when America's own wartime command economy was still a fresh memory to government officials, there was genuine fear of the industrial potential that years of ruthless, totalitarian compulsion might succeed in harnessing. The 1957 Gaither report to President Eisenhower warned, "The gross national product of the USSR is now more than one-third that of the United States and is increasing half again as fast." Eisenhower was skeptical, but Washington's anxiety had to be satisfied with a number.

Since general statistical data about the Soviet system was unavailable or unreliable, and since the prices of goods were denominated administratively in a nonconvertible currency, rubles, there was no obvious way to calculate Soviet GNP. The method eventually adopted, pioneered by Abram Bergson (a professor at Columbia, then Harvard, who had worked on the Soviet economy for OSS during the war), was to calculate "adjusted factor cost": goods would be examined and priced by Western standards in order to evaluate their worth. The method was better than the alternatives at hand, but it required a vast, labor-intensive effort. The CIA fostered an academic working environment for highly trained economists, however, hiring and retaining many of them. Using a relationship with Congress's Joint Economic Committee as an outlet for publishing their research and methodologies and interacting with other academic economists, the CIA's Soviet project had a powerful, even dominant, influence on the developing study of East bloc and other command economies. Meanwhile the CIA began preparing its own GNP figures. Its estimates seemed to confirm substantial Soviet growth but cast doubt on worries about a "crossover." Through the 1960s and into the 1970s the CIA's work commanded respect and a substantial audience both inside and outside of the U.S. government. The CIA could examine Soviet consumer consumption, for example, by comparing 334 different American and Soviet items, from food products to durable goods to 59 household services and even health care. A fifth of the food items and nearly all of the durable goods were brought to the United States and, if necessary, disassembled and matched to relevant products by U.S. businesses. Throughout these decades the CIA estimated Soviet GNP to be growing at between 3 and 5 percent annually.

These estimates became more controversial in the early 1980s. Herbert Meyer, an economic journalist, was an aide to President Reagan's CIA director, William Casey. Meyer thought the CIA estimates of Soviet growth were too rosy. "It simply couldn't be true," he remembered later. "I know what an economy looks like when it's growing three percent a year, and that isn't what it looks like. . . . You cannot have food shortages getting worse, production shortages growing worse, bottlenecks—all those things we knew were going on—and still have an economy growing at the rate the agency said it was—which the United States was barely doing at that point." The analysts disagreed with Meyer, showing him a Wharton School computer simulation model (SOVMOD), which he found incomprehensible. Meyer wrote a memo to Casey on his views. Casey liked it; the memo leaked. The conservative critique became public in 1983, as it came to be linked to underlying judgments of military strength. The conservatives maintained that since the Soviet economy was really smaller than previously thought, Moscow must have been spending an even larger share of resources on defense, thus revealing its confrontational priorities. Further, a smaller Soviet economy would be less able to sustain a competition with Reagan's defense buildup.

The CIA's estimates of Soviet GNP had already begun to go down. By the end of the 1970s annual growth was estimated at about 1.9 percent, and guesses averaged 1.8 percent from 1981 to 1985. Teams of outside economists were brought in by CIA officials in 1983 and 1985 to pore through the files and analyses. The outsiders said the work was sound. GNP aside, though, CIA reports regularly portrayed a Soviet economy under serious stress. The USSR, one analyst noted at the end of the 1970s, was "sort of a poor Portugal." Soviet foreign policy burdens, a 1980 study declared, "will place substantial additional claims on an already strained economy." Another study called the USSR, in a phrase quoted by the *Washington Post*, the world's "most underdeveloped developed country."

The GNP issue continued to dog the Agency. The CIA thought the Soviet GNP was about half that of the United States. Stanford University's Henry Rowen and the RAND Corporation's Charles Wolf published conclusions from a dissenting group of experts, claiming the USSR's national income was "in fact less than a third" the size of America's. Anders Aslund contributed an article pointing to new Soviet contentions that the old statistics were a sham and that Soviet GNP and consumption were about a third lower than estimated by CIA. The main methodological criticisms were a failure to account adequately for wasted production, which translated into visibly widespread shortages, and the notoriously poor, practically useless, quality of many goods. Yet Aslund's conclusion, likening the USSR to a "reasonably well-developed Third World country," was little different from that reached by Agency analysts. A 1990 Airlie House conference bringing together these dissident Soviet and Western experts caused a stir, especially since the CIA was already talking about the need for more economic intelligence as the cold war wound down. William Safire scoffed that the CIA's past overestimation of Soviet GNP was a "fiasco" that was being "ignored and concealed even as the future CIA mission must be redirected toward realistic assessments of economic and scientific strength. . . . As the Bay of Pigs was to intelligence operations, the extended misreading of the Soviet economic debacle is to intelligence evaluation."

Beset by conservatives, the CIA found that the same supposed overestimates also enraged more liberal commentators, who accused the Agency of having exaggerated the Soviet threat during the cold war. "The fact is that for 40 years American presidents were near to traumatized by the prospect of the Soviets becoming economically and militarily stronger than us," stormed Senator Daniel Patrick Moynihan, "when in fact the opposite was happening."

George Kolt, who headed the CIA's analysis of the Soviet Union, made the organization's case to Congress in July 1990. "Soviet GNP may be somewhat lower than we have stated, but not to the extent portrayed by the more dramatic criticisms," he said. Once reasonable amounts for defense, investment, and government administration were accounted for, some allowance had to be made for consumption. An estimate of 25 percent of the size of the U.S. economy left a little room for consumption, but only enough to put the Soviet Union on a par with "Pakistan, Botswana, and Swaziland." Thirty-five percent got the Soviet Union into the same range as Panama, Jordan, and Turkey. "Here," Kolt testified, "we are getting to [perhaps the lower boundary of] what is not an entirely implausible number for per capita consumption."

The debate over GNP, however, bore an increasingly tenuous link to any material policy question. GNP estimation had always been imperfect, and the settling of the "crossover" debate had taken place long before. Since the figures were inherently somewhat unreliable, they had little independent value as a basis for other projections. A senior intelligence official acknowledged publicly that "we have always been much more confident in our estimates of the structure and trends of the Soviet economy than in our estimate of size." Nor did a GNP estimate say much about actual Soviet military capability that was not known from direct measurement and assessment of military industry and output.[16]

True, the GNP data might yield inferences about Soviet economic performance and strains on productive capacity. But the clashes over measuring output actually obscured a fairly broad consensus about the poor quality of Soviet goods and the sacrifice of consumption, the portrait of "sort of a poor Portugal." Contrary to critics such as Moynihan, the CIA had repeatedly warned about how these economic strains would affect political stability and military potential. As early as 1985, in evaluating Gorbachev's first reforms, it called attention to the inadequacy of his "marginal tinkering" and, in a notable National Intelligence Estimate, concluded: "Unless the system is reformed in fundamental ways, it will hamper the growth its leaders seek because it stifles the innovation on which technological and social progress depends. . . . We do not exclude the possibility that these tensions could eventually confront the regime with challenges that it cannot effectively contain without system change and the risks to control that would accompany such change."[17] The CIA continued to provide reasonably accurate, though general, judgments on the way economic stress was affecting Soviet military plans.[18]

Using Economic Intelligence to Infer Military Power

Two conclusions emerge from this history. First, country economic intelligence has been able to place upper and lower bounds on projections of military strength, but seldom yields reliable inferences about relative advantage or disadvantage. The CIA's economic work helped contain fears about Soviet military production in the 1950s and 1960s, but its economic intelligence was soon eclipsed by the direct collection and analysis of order of battle, military planning, and specific military technologies.

Second, the accumulation of general economic data can actually divert attention from policy-relevant conclusions. It is hard to avoid the impression that the CIA would have been better off altogether abandoning the quest to derive GNP estimates for the Soviet Union and sticking instead to data offering more reliable, and more applicable, comparisons and inferences. Just such a practice is evident in some of the Agency's 1993 unclassified country profiles for states like Kazakhstan and Uzbekistan.

CIA's handling of China estimates seems to have incorporated some of the lessons of the controversy over the size of the Soviet economy. In 1990 the Agency fused political and economic analysis to predict accurately that austerity policies would be replaced by a rapid expansion of credit that would cause a sharp rise in inflation. The CIA forecast further erratic macroeconomic policies from Beijing because of the difficulty in managing inflationary pressures without a more comprehensive program of market reform. On the other hand, Agency analysts have studiously avoided attention-getting estimates of China's GNP. Instead they cited the problems encountered in providing such estimates, including the unreliability of Chinese statistics and flaws in alternative methodologies.[19]

POLITICAL DEDUCTIONS

Just as economic intelligence allows inferences to be drawn about military potential, so can inductive reasoning be applied to a country's political intentions. As early as 1985 the CIA derived very important political conclusions from its assessment of economic strains in the Soviet Union. Before World War II the superb French intelligence service accumulated economic intelligence that, as in Britain, was misused to produce greatly inflated estimates of German air strength. But the French also developed a shrewd argument that "the Nazi regime was producing itself into a severe economic crisis from which the most radical political solutions might come" as the Germans exhausted their domestic resources.[20] More extended illustrations of how country economic intelligence can be converted into political analysis may be found in the cases of Iran and Iraq.

Economic Intelligence, the United States, and the Iranian Revolution

A great deal has been written about Iran's economic performance between the oil bonanza of 1974 and the outbreak of revolutionary violence in 1978. Though many specific points remain uncertain or controversial, the broad outlines of the story have emerged.

The tremendous rise in oil prices during 1973–74 produced vast windfall earnings for Iran. These earnings turned already rapid economic growth into a boom that quickly overheated, as the Shah tried to turn Iran into one of the world's leading industrial powers, another Japan, in a generation (while also procuring a large and modern military establishment). Domestic demand for goods and services skyrocketed; freighters bringing goods to Iran backed up in ports and had to wait months to offload their cargoes. (Iran paid nearly $1 billion in foreign exchange just in the freight charges incurred by these delays.) The government adopted an overly ambitious program of domestic investment, especially industrialization, that more than doubled public spending in a single year. Inflation rose to 25–35 percent, relatively low by the standards of other developing countries but a new high for Iran. With expenditures running out of control (especially those to buy and support new military hardware), fantastic amounts of government waste, and an inflating economy, the government adopted an austerity plan in 1975–76 that slowed the rate of growth and dashed cold water on many Iranians whose expectations of wealth and government largess had run far ahead of what the economy could sustain.[21]

Jahangir Amuzegar has pointed out that none of the standard economic arguments explain the Iranian revolution. The austerity measures were not exceptionally harsh. Inflation was not unbearably high, nor was unemployment or debt a problem. The income gap between rich and poor did not widen by a great margin. Nevertheless, the Shah's economic strategy

> inadvertently bolstered the opposition forces by acts of both omission and commission. . . . On the omission side, the

regime overlooked, underestimated, or dismissed the mundane realities that the country lacked adequate infrastructure for sustaining an increase in national gross investment from a total of only $5.3 billion in 1963–67, and $10.8 billion in 1968–72 to nearly $70 billion in 1973–77, and a projected $129 billion in 1978–82. . . . On the commission side, the hasty expenditures of oil revenues on projects that did not quickly add to capacity expansion in food, raw materials, manufactured items, or basic infrastructures made both industrial and agricultural sectors more reliant on imports in 1977 compared to 1973 or 1963 [with sociopolitical implications for Iranian nationalists]. An old-fashioned anti-inflation campaign in the mid-1970s added to the economy's growing problems. Hasty land reform and industrial reorganization measures lacked sufficient time to bear anticipated fruit. The result of these overconfident and risky policies [was] to weaken the regime's economic backbone, and to progressively alienate every politically active group in society from the crown. . . . [22]

Though most people were better off than they had been, and though the economy continued to grow at a solid pace, these turbulent years undermined public support for the Shah. Growth had brought tens of thousands to the cities, where especially high local inflation priced many of them out of decent housing. The sharp rise and then cutback in government investment deflated the expectations of many in the business community. Growing bottlenecks in public infrastructure and competition for scarce supply inputs (like construction materials and labor) aggravated corruption and favoritism, since so many sectors of the economy remained under government control. Traditional positions in society were being undermined by the Shah's attempt to remake Iran, yet the new elites joined some of those displaced by social change in expressing rising dissatisfaction.[23]

Economic developments were not a primary cause of the Iranian revolution, but they contributed significantly to it. With the Shah's dynastic legitimacy never completely firm, his great solution to containing dissent would be material prosperity. Though he in fact had delivered great new wealth to Iran, the exclusion of the new elites from real political power, the appearance of chaos, the special pain inflicted on rural migrants by the urban inflation, the combination of conspicuous consumption with evident public corruption, the obvious overextension of the national development plan, and the perception of boom/bust all undercut the Shah's hopes for building a wide base of public support. Instead it was the revolutionaries who were able to draw support from almost every segment of the population. In other words, faced with fundamental societal upheaval, the Shah adopted economic policies that heightened the potential for political instability.[24]

American intelligence on Iran observed almost all of the key facts about the Shah's economic situation, but little was inferred about the significance of these developments. In 1975 the CIA informed Washington officials that the Shah would not be able to achieve his ambitious development goals. Shortages of labor, housing, food, transport, and sensible planning were all noted. As for the outlook, growth would slow to no more than 15 percent yearly, but this was "still an enviable rate." Income levels were expected to stay ahead of inflation. The CIA's economic office did comment, in a study issued in April of that year, that "a significant economic, and potentially important political, problem centers on the rising expectations that for many can not be fulfilled." But its exploration did not venture beyond rhetorical questions. "Can the government move rapidly enough to respond to their needs . . . ?" After several more such idle inquiries the paper moved on to balance of payments issues.[25]

The embassy's financial/economic development officer did somewhat better, writing a long paper for his end-of-tour assessment that captures the peculiar, upbeat yet ambivalent tone characteristic of much reporting from Iran at the time. The magnitude of the economic transformation signaled that political change had to be coming. But the report concluded that

> while the economic outlook for the country is very favorable, increasing U.S. involvement in the economy contains the seeds of potential, though probably not serious, bilateral conflict. . . . The conflict between rapid economic growth and modernization vis-a-vis a still autocratic rule . . . is the greatest uncertainty marring an otherwise optimistic prognosis for Iran. If the country manages to maintain relative stability by somehow working out an evolutionary rather than revolutionary means of liberalizing its system of government, then the long range outlook for its continued prosperity is as encouraging as for any developing country in the world.[26]

In late 1976 the national intelligence officer for the Middle East chaired a committee of more than forty officials, from the White House to the National Security Agency, to consider the quality of reporting about events in Iran. Economics came up in the political discussions only in the desire for more grassroots reactions to the country's anti-inflation and anticorruption campaigns. When economic concerns more generally were on the agenda, the committee merely decided, "The obvious bottlenecks to economic development are being covered well. . . . More in-depth reporting on the industry-wide development of key industrial sectors (e.g., steel, petrochemicals, copper) would be appreciated" along with more information about the shortage of skilled manpower.[27] The State Department's transition briefing paper for President-elect Carter's team stated flatly that "all indications" point toward continuation of the Shah's preeminence and Iran's political stability "for at least the years immediately ahead."[28]

In 1977 a new American ambassador arrived in Tehran, William Sullivan. Before departing overseas Sullivan spoke with thirty American business executives with interests in Iran. They were "universally optimistic" about the Iranian economy.[29] Sullivan was more skeptical, and, as his memoirs recounted, he had a clear grasp of some of the social consequences of the Shah's economic policies, including rising public corruption and the resentments of rural migrants to the cities. Sullivan asked the State Department to send a researcher to study the impact of the Shah's industrialization program. He complained in his memoirs that State complied but added so many questions that the project became "infeasible, and the study, to the best of my knowledge, was never completed." Sullivan then turned to CIA analysts. "They sent an officer who spent several months in the embassy attempting to accumulate information for a study along the lines I had proposed, but I never saw the results of that effort either." Sullivan wrote that he just maintained his general skepticism, "proceeding on instinct and without the benefit of a good, solid statistical analysis."[30]

This sense of largely accurate but superficial U.S. economic intelligence about Iran in the 1970s is reinforced not only by comparison with the retrospective academic assessments mentioned earlier but also by what the British ambassador at the time says he was observing. Though Ambassador Anthony Parsons felt the Shah's position was stable, he wrote plainly and at length in his memoirs about the obvious

"economic malaise of 1975" and the "social upheaval, serious inflation, and rising expectations which could not be fully met." One year
later, he thought "agriculture was a disaster and the government's
assertion of a growth rate of 7 per cent a year was a lie." He summed
up the year 1976 by explaining that "Iran was still enveloped in a
miasma of uncertainty and malaise in the aftermath of the boom."
Government was doing better, but "inflation was still hitting all class-
es of society hard, exaggerated expectations had not been met, and
social conditions in the poorer areas of the great cities were bad. . . .
However, although active discontent was probably running at a *higher* level amongst most elements of society than in the years before
the boom, manifestations of discontent were likely to remain diffuse
and without central leadership."[31] Parsons's account, suffused by
impressions of economic malaise and government unease, appears
credible.

Note that Parsons's bottom line is not so different from that of
the Americans. Both thought the Shah's hold on power was still
secure. But the British ambassador's plain discussions of malaise and
recognition of the widespread alienation offer a far clearer picture of
the underlying situation. It is known that reports of rising turmoil in
the fall of 1978 came as a real shock to President Carter and other
senior officials, prompting him to complain to Secretary of State Cyrus
Vance and the director of central intelligence, Stansfield Turner,
about the quality of the political intelligence he was getting.[32] Surely
the shock would not have been so great if for years the economic
intelligence about Iran had vividly conveyed the sense of despair
among the population, and not just dry reports of a country outgrow-
ing its infrastructure.

Economic Intelligence and Iraq's Invasion of Kuwait

The U.S. government was to be shocked again by events in the
Persian Gulf, this time by Iraq's invasion and conquest of Kuwait in
August 1990. For more than a week the intelligence community had
provided warning that an invasion was likely, based largely on Iraq's
observed military movements. But President Bush was receiving contrary assessments from the regional Arab leaders who knew Saddam
Hussein best, and, with Iraqi forces already massing on the Kuwaiti
frontier, he had few options. To even have a chance of developing a

credible policy to deter or confront Hussein in July 1990, the U.S. government would have had to appreciate the full danger he posed to other Arabs weeks or months earlier. For that, the United States needed not only better political intelligence but better economic intelligence as well. After all, the long-standing dispute between Iraq and Kuwait was reignited by a quarrel about money.

In 1989 Iraq was a country judged by outsiders to be under severe economic strain. Burdened by enormous debts incurred during the war with Iran and struggling to rebuild foreign exchange reserves from revived oil exports, Iraq was expected to concentrate on rebuilding. A National Intelligence Estimate, "Iraq: Foreign Policy of a Major Regional Power," was issued in the fall of 1989. The estimate stated clearly that Iraq suffered from a chronic shortage of cash and would be inclined to put pressure on its major creditors, which were Saudi Arabia and Kuwait. The oil-rich Kuwaiti islands of Bubiyan and Warba were mentioned as potential targets of Iraqi expansion, though Baghdad was expected to seek a way to do this without using force. The possibility of Iraqi aggression against Kuwait was buried in the back pages of the estimate, not highlighted in its "key judgments."[33]

In the first months of 1990 the United States became more worried about Iraq, but concern focused on Baghdad's effort to acquire weapons of mass destruction and the threat of conflict between Iraq and Israel. Though American intelligence reported that Iraq owed at least $80 billion to foreign creditors, including $10 billion to Kuwait alone, the implications of this situation received less attention, particularly since Hussein carefully kept up to date in his payments to American banks. Full payment of just the interest on its other debts would have forced Iraq to curtail or terminate its military buildup and domestic subsidies. The intelligence community had expected a drawdown in Iraqi military strength from the high levels reached during the war with Iran, but this was not happening.

In February 1990 Saddam Hussein openly broke with his fellow Arab leaders over financial issues as they gathered for a summit of the Arab Cooperation Council in Baghdad. Iraq, he said, had championed the Arab cause during the war with Iran. Since Iraq had supplied the manpower, it was only fair for the other Arabs to provide the money. Iraq should no more have to repay these loans than should the other Arab states have to provide men to replace those Iraq lost during the war. "Let the Gulf regimes know," Hussein warned, "that if they do not give this money to me, I will know how to get it."

But U.S. attention was diverted in March and April by Saddam Hussein's more publicized threats against Israel and the seizure by American customs officials of goods being smuggled to Iraq to support his nuclear weapons program and construction of an extremely long-range "supergun." During the subsequent review of policy toward Iraq in April and May, Washington decided to suspend most government support for commerce with Iraq and tightened export control rules. But the CIA did not update its National Intelligence Estimate on Iraq's overall intentions, nor was there any fundamental reorientation of policy in the Persian Gulf, even to the extent of holding military discussions with the Gulf states threatened by Hussein.

Iraq clearly had an acute foreign exchange problem. The intelligence community knew that Baghdad had tried, and failed, to get new credits from Western banks. The country was already failing to meet repayment schedules on loans from the Arab states; now the Iraqis were also on the verge of defaulting on debts owed to Western creditors, which would have had quick and severe repercussions for his domestic plans. Saddam Hussein urgently faced two basic choices: either he curtailed imports of foreign goods and correspondingly reduced domestic investment, including military spending, that relied on such imports or he would have to find some other way to get a great deal of money. In Washington, this dilemma was not spelled out to policymakers during the spring 1990 policy review. Recognition of it would instantly have raised troubling questions, since there was no evidence that Hussein was prepared to rein in his demand for foreign goods and the only obvious source of big money was his rich neighbors to the south.

The falling price of oil made Iraq's economic dilemma even more acute. Iraq focused its anger on Kuwait, which was contributing to the price drop by producing beyond its OPEC quota. At a May 30 Arab League meeting Saddam Hussein vented his accusations and not only demanded a debt moratorium but began insisting on getting billions of additional dollars from Kuwait in compensation for the oil it was allegedly stealing from a field pooled under both countries. On July 15 Iraq began assembling troops on the Kuwaiti border. The United States was slow to react, especially since the Kuwaitis themselves, joined by other Arab leaders, urged Washington to let them work the problem out with "Arab diplomacy" and not inflame the situation by taking any provocative action. On August 2 Hussein invaded Kuwait.

As in the Iranian case, U.S. economic intelligence had accurately reported on the fundamentals. Iraq's foreign exchange problem was understood; Baghdad's difficulties with its creditors were also known. But the implications for Iraq's political and economic choices were not spelled out, even after it became clear that its response was inconsistent with the "rebuilding" scenario offered in 1989. These implications were not obvious. Iraq's currency problem had to be matched with estimates of Iraqi domestic plans in order to draw a persuasive picture of the dilemma Saddam Hussein faced, simulate his timetable for resolving it, and point out the indicators that would reveal what choices he had made. American economic intelligence did not perform this task. So although the intelligence community provided good tactical warning of Iraq's military moves once they were imminent, it failed to provide the effective strategic warning needed for timely consideration of possible deterrent responses.[34]

JUDGING ECONOMIC LEVERAGE

Countries often seek to use their economic influence to persuade or coerce another state. Sometimes these levers are positive, as in the offer of foreign assistance. Other times they are negative, as with sanctions or a blockade. The U.S. government relies especially heavily on economic intelligence in devising such policies.

Early Attempts to Calculate the Probable Effect of Sanctions

Without economic intelligence, countries can get into serious trouble. In 1914 Britain's plans for a European war turned on the conviction that a blockade of Germany would soon cause the German economy to collapse. Hence the General Staff's case for preparing a major land force commitment was all the more easily rejected. The Royal Navy's plans assumed that Germany was extremely vulnerable to economic pressure, even though the secretary of the committee drawing up the relevant war plans later admitted that "we could not judge whether it would be possible to squeeze [Germany] into submission, or how long it would take." One historian has commented, "This vital question, which was fundamental to any judgment about the effectiveness of the blockade, was never properly answered before 1914."[35]

An even greater gamble was made by the German government during the winter of 1916–17. After years of arguing over the advantages of unrestricted submarine warfare against Britain compared with the disadvantage of giving cause for American entry into the war on the side of the Allies, the German government decided firmly in favor of the submarine blockade. Economic analysis was at the heart of the debate. The German Navy circulated memorandums detailing evidence that Britain could be starved into submission within six months, based on a projected ability to sink 600,000 tons of British shipping a month. The German chancellor marshaled arguments to the contrary, stressing the decisive contribution America could make to the Allied war effort and focusing on America's ability to finance the strained Allied governments. The Kaiser's military believed, in contrast, that America could not supply more shipping or war materiel to the Allies, that the dollars were unimportant, and that American soldiers would be slow to arrive in Europe (a calculation also based largely on economic factors such as shipping capacity and munitions production). Such estimates strongly influenced the German decisions that brought America into the war.[36]

The U.S. intelligence community has long supplied estimates to inform the American government's use of coercive diplomacy. Economic sanctions of varying kinds were applied in the postwar period against the Soviet Union, China, North Korea, Cuba, Vietnam, Nicaragua, Libya, Iran, Rhodesia, and South Africa. Though not rising to the level of sanctions, economic coercion was a feature of American diplomacy during the Suez crisis of 1956. But American intelligence agencies appear to have contributed little to Eisenhower's use of such pressure, as he relied instead on Treasury officials and his own grasp of the situation. At the height of tension with the British, the American government may even have underestimated the extent of its perceived economic leverage.[37]

As the CIA became fully involved in economic and political analysis during the 1960s, it began providing more intelligence on the extent of American leverage. During the 1981–83 controversy over European assistance in construction of a Soviet gas pipeline, the intelligence community and the CIA provided influential prognostications of Washington's inability to prevent pipeline construction and the likely ineffectiveness of U.S. sanctions. These judgments effectively integrated the Agency's own engineering expertise, its political analysis, and its knowledge of the Soviet energy industry. When needed, the intelligence community could also bring government and private-sector analysts together to offer a complete picture to top officials.[38] Yet few debates put the intelligence community under as much pressure as the 1990–91 controversy over the effectiveness of economic sanctions against Iraq.

Judging Leverage: Sanctions against Iraq, 1990–91

When freezing and blocking of Kuwaiti and Iraqi assets was ordered on the morning of August 2, 1990, the government obliged private banks and the firms "most knowledgeable concerning the ownership" of property to identify assets subject to the order so that intelligence efforts could concentrate on the biggest threats of evasion. The crucial roles were played by Treasury, the Federal Reserve Board of New York, and various policy and law enforcement agencies, backed by the intelligence community. The American efforts were augmented by Treasury and State Department contacts with Kuwaiti officials, the United Nations, the OECD, the EC, and participants in the Bank for International Settlements.[39]

By the end of 1990 many prominent experts had adopted the position that economic sanctions would alone be sufficient to compel Iraq's withdrawal from Kuwait, probably with eighteen to twenty-four months. They therefore thought the United States did not need to risk an armed conflict against Iraq after the UN ultimatum expired in January 1991. These experts included retired Admiral William Crowe, retired General David Jones, John Kenneth Galbraith, Robert McNamara, Arthur Schlesinger, Graham Fuller (former national intelligence officer for the Middle East), and Judith Kipper (of the Brookings Institution).

The most prominent scholar of economic sanctions, Gary Hufbauer, Wallenberg Professor of International Financial Diplomacy at Georgetown University, testified before the Senate Foreign Relations Committee. He and others had used the full panoply of social science methods to extract every significant variable from past cases of economic sanctions.[40] Based on this formidable effort, backed by 116 prior examples, Hufbauer calculated, testifying before Congress, "History suggests that 1 or 2 years will pass before the sanctions prevail." This argument was based less on an analysis of Saddam

Hussein's political quandary than on Hufbauer's inferences from the empirical record. Sanctions would cost in excess of 40 percent of Iraq's GNP, he said. "The cost to the target country reached double digits on only three previous occasions of sanctions in this century, and in all three of those cases, sanctions contributed to a positive outcome."[41]

The CIA disagreed. On December 5, 1990, Director of Central Intelligence William Webster testified before the House Armed Services Committee. Webster's conclusions, on behalf of the intelligence community, were:

▲   Sanctions dealt a serious blow to the Iraqi economy.

▲   "Our judgment has been and continues to be that there is no assurance or guarantee that economic hardships will compel Saddam to change his policies or lead to internal unrest that would threaten his regime."

▲   Although sanctions were hurting Iraq's civilian economy, they were affecting the Iraqi military only at the margins.

▲   Probably only energy-related and some military industries would still be fully functioning by the following spring [1991].[42]

Oddly, the New York Times published a story the next day asserting that the CIA had now "appeared to part company with the administration on the question of whether and when the sanctions might erode Iraq's military forces." No other news stories shared this interpretation, which was incorrect.[43]

The New York Times story was, however, circulated among Congress, and it was soon widely believed that Webster's analysis undermined the administration's position, which stood by a January 15 deadline for Iraqi withdrawal before using force. On January 9, at the height of the congressional debate over war, Representative Les Aspin of Wisconsin—who backed the Bush administration's stance—asked Webster to update his testimony and answer some specific questions. Webster's reply, written by the same analysts who had prepared his December 5 testimony, referred to that earlier testimony and elaborated on his previous points:

▲   The ability of the Iraqi ground forces to defend Kuwait and southern Iraq was unlikely to be substantially eroded over the next six to twelve months even if effective sanctions could be maintained.

▲   Sanctions had shut off nearly all Iraq's trade and financial activity and weakened its economy, but disruption in most sectors was not serious.

▲   The DCI continued to believe that economic hardships were unlikely to compel Saddam Hussein to retreat from Kuwait.

Since many congresspeople mistakenly thought Webster had "parted company" from the administration in his earlier assessments, they were suspicious of the clarification he offered. Senator Hollings said, "I do not care what CIA Director Webster says now, politicizing his intelligence report as he does." A month later, Sidney Blumenthal wrote an article in the *New Republic* accusing the CIA of "cooking" testimony and shifting its position to suit the administration.

But in fact Webster had testified explicitly in his earlier appearance before the Armed Services Committee that, "at present, Saddam almost certainly assumes that he is coping effectively with the sanctions. He appears confident in the ability of his security services to contain potential discontent, and we do not believe he is troubled by the hardships Iraqis will be forced to endure."[44] There is no evidence that any CIA officials or analysts felt their conclusions were distorted by political pressure; indeed, the analysts worded their reports carefully to avoid any such inference.[45]

More significant for the purpose of this study is the substance of the CIA analysis. With sanctions having been imposed on Iraq for more than four years now, it is increasingly difficult to refute any of the specific predictions about their efficacy offered by the intelligence community in 1990. Iraq is presently willing to tolerate continued imposition of sanctions rather than accept Western demands that seem far less onerous than the original demand for the total and unconditional withdrawal from Kuwait. It is noteworthy that, despite the strong categorical conclusions of economically knowledgeable witnesses like Hufbauer and McNamara, none of them actually addressed in detail the very specific judgments itemized in the CIA's assessment.[46]

Economic sanctions remain a popular instrument of policy. The Clinton administration has utilized such sanctions against Iraq, Iran, Serbia, Libya, and Haiti (before the American occupation), to name just the more notable examples. All of them except Libya are countries that meet Hufbauer's "double-digit" criterion yet defy easy predictions of success or failure. The CIA and other U.S. agencies provide the more nuanced data and analysis demanded by such coercive diplomacy. The analysts are obliged to consider not just the way sanctions will affect a country's macroeconomic condition but also how they may influence the particular calculations going on in the minds of the targeted adversaries. The recent record for such analysis has been positive, at least by inducing appropriately modest expectations of what sanctions can accomplish. The intelligence community may thus have helped the U.S. government avoid the sort of overestimates that, as mentioned before, misled the British and German governments earlier in the century and could have misled the U.S. government, or the U.S. Congress, into an overreliance on sanctions in the 1990–91 confrontation with Iraq.

Chapter 3

CRITICAL RESOURCES

Governments have always sought intelligence about resources that seemed to possess the worrisome quality of being vital and at the same time precariously supplied. Eighteenth-century Britain kept a constant eye on the disposition of territories that supplied the timber for its warships. In the Second World War, strategic planning in every capital was strongly influenced by worries about critical resources—oil, iron ore, rubber, tungsten, and uranium topped the list.

When the war ended and the new American president, Harry Truman, arrived in Europe for the Potsdam Conference to determine the immediate fate of occupied Germany, he was briefed on popular unrest and international Communist agitation. But it was a resource issue that was "far more significant," according to historian Melvyn Leffler. Truman had received a report on an imminent shortage of coal in northwestern Europe, warning of "a coal famine of such severity as to destroy all semblance of law and order, and thus delay any chance of reasonable stability."[1] Hence Truman felt he had to help restore German coal production. The United States thereby committed itself to at least some measure of German economic revival. That meant resistance to the most ardent reparations claims of the Soviet Union and France, setting the scene for the emerging quarrels over the postwar administration of a divided Germany.

Economic intelligence about strategic resources should help policymakers identify which resources are genuinely critical in terms of

their importance to manufacturing. Such intelligence should also provide useful advice on how the United States or countries of interest to
Washington could be vulnerable to disruptions of supply serious
enough to cause scarcities (real or perceived) and price shocks that
might trigger instability or violent conflict, impair American defens-
es, or threaten a country's economic health.

A list of natural resources of major interest to the U.S. government could include petroleum, fresh water, grain, fish, platinum-group
metals, chromium, and possibly cobalt. Though experts might dis-
agree about which materials belong on such a list, few would argue
with the inclusion of petroleum. The U.S. government has paid close
attention to world oil supplies for more than half a century.
Washington has not been alone. Worries about the availability of oil
in the 1930s and 1940s helped drive Japan to war in the Pacific, influenced German grand strategy in both the North Africa campaign and
the war against the Soviet Union, and shaped Allied strategy, from the
strategic bombing offensive against Germany to the Anglo-American-
Soviet occupation of Iran. The postwar period saw sustained
American interest in getting good intelligence about the likely availability and price of oil.

OIL: IRAN AND SUEZ

The first postwar threat to oil supplies came in Iran. Growing disputes between the Iranian government and the Anglo-Iranian Oil
Company (AIOC) during 1950 prompted analysis of possible consequences of nationalization and interruption in the Iranian oil supply.
Predictions were dire but were based on outside information from a
less than disinterested source: "According to our oil companies,"
warned the State Department's oil adviser, "loss of Iranian oil *could not
be replaced.*"[2] These fears were subsequently shown to be unfounded.
Iran did nationalize AIOC, and Iranian exports of oil products were
halted by unrest during 1951. But it proved to be relatively easy to
replace Iranian crude with oil from Arab and American producers.
The Western position was so strong that it could actually turn the
tables and engage in a buyers' boycott of Iran. Unable to find foreign
buyers for its oil, Iran quickly ran out of foreign exchange and was
facing economic collapse by the time the Iranian leader was over-
thrown (with clandestine help from the CIA) in 1953.[3]

As an intelligence case, at least three points are worth noting about the Iranian crisis of 1950–53. First, the U.S. government was apparently influenced by warnings that were too pessimistic. Second, the government relied on American oil companies for crucial information. While the companies may have been gravely worried, American oil companies had a stake in playing up such fears, since Washington was as a result more likely to pressure the British to accept Iranian demands, demands that would inevitably undermine European competition and open up new opportunities for American companies in Iran while strengthening the market position of crude from Texas or American consortia in Saudi Arabia and Kuwait. Third, there was no problem of marginal shortfalls in oil or oil products for America's European allies, particularly Britain, because London had reliable, profit-seeking, oil-rich friends in America and the Near East.

The next major disruption in oil supply came in 1956 during the crisis stemming from Egypt's nationalization of the Suez Canal. As the crisis broke, the Defense Department's Office of Defense Mobilization sponsored a meeting of the Foreign Petroleum Supply Committee, composed of oil company officials gathering under the chairmanship of the Department of the Interior. The Defense Mobilization director reported to President Eisenhower and other cabinet officials that a closure of the Suez Canal could oblige the United States to increase its oil production, but the companies thought they were capable of doing so. Washington recognized that, as in the Iranian case, the problem was not an absolute shortage of supply, but American willingness and ability to make its own ample supplies available to the British and French. This intelligence was accurate and helpful, though Eisenhower already seemed to be remarkably well informed in discussing Western Hemisphere oil production.[4] Indeed, after the British and French invaded Egypt, the American government used its oil leverage in pressing London and Paris to accept UN cease-fire terms in November.[5]

The only apparent intelligence lapse during the Suez crisis by the government-organized committee of oil company officials was not in assessing a foreign government like Nasser's Egypt or Saudi Arabia. It was a failure to anticipate actions closer to home, by the government of Texas—more specifically, the Texas Railroad Commission (TRC). The TRC, then a very powerful agency that set ceilings on Texas oil production, refused to let production expand. It wanted to drive up prices and profits for small producers. Eisenhower ultimately had to threaten to use federal emergency powers against the TRC in order to get it to allow the needed surge in Texan production.[6] If the big oil company officials advising Washington failed to anticipate the TRC's behavior, one explanation could be that the TRC was motivated by concerns the big companies simply did not share.

The Six Day War

The next challenge for intelligence came in 1967, with the outbreak of another war in the Middle East. By 1967 the CIA had obtained official responsibility for gathering economic intelligence regarding the free world, including Middle Eastern oil. In May 1967, as the crisis intensified, the White House formed a "Working Group on Economic Vulnerabilities," which thought an Arab oil embargo could have "devastating economic impact."[7] On June 6, 1967, during the second day of the Six Day War, the major Arab oil producers called a halt to all oil exports. The next day the CIA provided an estimate that, during the first six months of embargo, the loss of Arab oil would "be inconvenient" to Western Europe "but not seriously damaging" to its economies. After six months, the effect would be much more severe. The report also called attention to the stress such a crisis would place on Britain's modest foreign exchange reserves.[8]

But only a few days after providing its estimate the CIA noticed that West European officials were not particularly alarmed by the oil danger.[9] As in 1951 and 1956, strong American action to increase oil production and rearrange worldwide delivery patterns offset the effect of the Arab embargo, which fell apart after less than a month. What, then, went wrong with the CIA estimate? The Agency's assumptions were explicit and not unduly pessimistic. It was assumed that all Arabs would cut off oil. In the event, Algeria did not join the embargo. Yet this fortunate circumstance was canceled out because Nigerian exports were suddenly cut off at the end of May by developments in the Biafran civil war.

The main component entirely absent from the CIA estimate was any analysis of possible Western responses to such an oil cutoff. That was still the business of others, such as the Department of Interior's reactivated Foreign Petroleum Supply Committee of oil company officials. Though the CIA was not in the business of collecting information on American activities, surely it was not beyond its institutional capacities to consider openly available data on how much or how quickly oil production could be increased in the Western Hemisphere and diverted across the Atlantic (even if the oil needs of the war in Vietnam were a major complication in this analysis). So while the estimate usefully could have been a spur to Washington to prepare to meet European needs, it offered no net assessment of how well Europe could cope if Washington exerted itself to help.

In the years after the Six Day War the CIA created a group of economists, geologists, and petroleum engineers to follow the international oil market.[10] Despite this new cadre, despite substantial interest and expertise in the State Department, and constant public discussion of an "energy crisis" notwithstanding, the Arab oil embargo of October 1973 plainly caught top U.S. decisionmakers by surprise. "While it may be overstatement to call it an economic Pearl Harbor," wrote former joint chiefs of staff chairman Maxwell Taylor, "at a minimum our unpreparedness certainly demonstrates a lack of institutionalized responsibility in the executive branch for anticipating nonmilitary dangers and developing plans and programs to forestall them." Having sorted through various explanations for the seeming inaction in Washington at the outset of the embargo, Raymond Vernon concluded that "there is a much simpler explanation of United States behavior, one that is more in keeping with the scraps of evidence. A full realization of the implications of the crisis did not appear at the highest levels of government until early 1974."[11]

THE ENERGY CRISIS OF 1973–74

Despite years of building concern about the trend toward greater U.S. vulnerability to an oil cutoff in the Middle East, Henry Kissinger commented in his memoirs that "amazingly, the full implications of it had not yet been absorbed when the [October 1973] war was started."[12] This unpreparedness seems, on the surface at least, to imply an intelligence failure of the first magnitude.

Decisive evidence on what Washington knew about its growing dependence on Middle Eastern suppliers is still elusive, or classified. But some fragments can be assembled. A major governmental effort to marshal information occurred in 1969–70 and was constituted as the U.S. Cabinet Task Force on Oil Import Controls, chaired by Secretary of Labor George Shultz. After a year of work, thousands of pages of testimony, and involvement by every relevant policy agency of the government, the report did point out one fundamental new fact, that the United States would no longer have spare capacity to supply "anything like the deficit in . . . free world requirements brought about by a prolonged curtailment of Eastern Hemisphere supplies."[13] However, practically all public forecasts properly anticipated the rapid growth in world energy demand, the continued shift toward reliance on oil for fuel needs, and the full extent of rising American oil imports.[14]

Two flaws in the Nixon administration's assessment of the energy situation seemed to emerge from the varying accounts. One was a common belief, at least among some officials at the State Department, that OPEC could not or would not maintain a united front to fix higher prices. Saudi warnings in the summer of 1973 were, according to one former official at State, dismissed "airily" by a senior official, "noting that a boycott was scarcely feasible; but even if there were one, we could not be hurt he said, as we imported only 2 percent of our needs from the Arabs [an inaccurate figure] and we could make this up by turning valves in Venezuela and Canada."[15] Officials from President Nixon on down were also misled by their reliance on historical analogies to the Iranian crisis of 1950-53, or to 1956 and 1967. In September 1973 Nixon reacted to Libyan nationalization of Occidental Oil by recalling publicly, "Oil without a market, as Mr. Mossadegh learned many, many years ago, does not do a country much good."[16] Kissinger recalled that when the October 1973 war began, "there was vague talk in our government about a possible oil embargo. Remembering the experience of 1967, few believed that it could have any lasting impact."[17]

The other mistaken judgment was an apparent notion, rooted in traditional economics, that there was no real energy crisis because price increases would inevitably find a market-clearing equilibrium between supply and demand. This seemed especially likely since there was plainly no absolute global shortage of oil production capacity, despite widely varying projections of exploitable oil reserves.[18] This view of a phantom shortage is sometimes associated mistakenly with MIT economist Morris Adelman, whose early 1973 *Foreign Policy* article bore a title ("Is the Oil Shortage Real?") that led people to identify him with this economic argument. In fact Adelman quite rightly pointed out that prices were not below a market-clearing level, as theory would dictate, but many times higher. This was because the price was moving toward a monopoly equilibrium. As Adelman explained, "*supply and demand are irrelevant to the current and expected price of crude oil. All that matters is whether the [OPEC] monopoly will flourish or fade.*"[19]

Rising OPEC oil prices did not stimulate new U.S. production because the Nixon administration had begun controlling domestic oil prices along with other prices in August 1971, because relaxed import regulations offered U.S. producers no protection against OPEC undercutting, and because rates of return on investment for the multinationals were higher outside of the United States—where both production costs and regulatory hurdles were much lower.[20]

These two errors were compounded, when the crisis broke, by the immediate reaction to the embargo: a focus on the danger of supply shortages owing to cutbacks in OPEC production. When the dust settled later it became clear that the fear of absolute scarcity was overdrawn. Targeting the United States for an embargo merely meant that oil companies swapped customers (so that, for instance, more Nigerian oil went to U.S. markets or Libyan oil was redirected from the United States to France). The embargo itself had little effect. What mattered were cutbacks in the total quantity of oil being produced, induced shortages that affected all consumers more or less equally. Indeed, some of those states most anxious to strike special arrangements with the Arabs actually experienced larger shortfalls than those endured by the United States.[21] Yet the fear of scarcity encouraged panicky bidding for oil, rapidly driving up prices. These prices did not subside after the panic disappeared because the market had not yet reached a monopoly equilibrium. The fear of supply shortfalls had thus divided the West and secured its acquiescence to the new monopoly prices.

U.S. government estimates contributed to the exaggerated fear of scarcity rather than concentrating on the monopoly pricing. As Kissinger put it,

> The structure of the oil market was so little understood that the embargo became the principal focus of concern. Lifting it turned almost into an obsession for the next five months. . . . In fact, the Arab embargo was a symbolic gesture of limited practical impact. . . . The true impact of the embargo was psychological. The fear that it might be extended—that Arab production might shut down further—triggered a wave of panic buying by Europe and Japan, which constricted supplies and drove prices up even more.[22]

Yet during the winter of 1973–74 the White House, Treasury Department, State Department, Pentagon, and the newly created Federal Energy Administration delivered somber estimates of a short-fall in the United States of more than 3 million barrels of oil a day. Actual shortfalls were much smaller. In April 1974 the deputy head of the Federal Energy Administration acknowledged that previous esti-mates had been excessive because they "did not take into considera-tion price elasticity or embargo leakages."[23] These phenomena were, of course, perfectly foreseeable and indeed had been forecasted by Morris Adelman nearly a year earlier.[24]

It is still hard to tell just how much of the responsibility for these inaccurate estimates should fall upon the intelligence community. In bureaucratic terms, at least, the energy crisis was a success story for the CIA. The crisis created an enormous demand for information, and the CIA took the lead in satisfying it. The former director of the CIA's economic office has written, "Although there was only a limit-ed amount of information from special intelligence sources, CIA was the only agency capable of putting all available information together into a coherent, up-to-date picture useful to policy officials."[25]

Responding to a request from NSC staff, the CIA began pub-lishing a regular, classified product that became a "best-seller," first called *International Oil Developments* and later called *International Energy Weekly*. The CIA developed its first econometric models in order to forecast world oil developments. "Before long CIA had become a dominant source of information and analysis in the US Government on international oil issues."[26]

NEW OIL ESTIMATES AND IRAN AGAIN

The CIA's new role as the government's key source of expertise on world oil markets was publicized when President Carter referred to CIA estimates of coming supply shortages in an April 1977 news conference. The Agency thereupon released two of its estimates, one calculating that reduced oil supplies and rising demand would cause another massive round of price increases and an inability of suppliers to meet global demand for oil. The other study forecast a drop in Soviet oil production (seen as contributing to the tight supply situ-ation overall). Both of these predictions prompted a good deal of controversy.

The first estimate declared that OPEC would be both unable and unwilling to meet rising world demand for oil. Without major conservation efforts, "projected world demand for oil will approach productive capacity by the early 1980's. In these circumstances prices will rise sharply to ration available supplies."[27] This conclusion was widely thought to have been vindicated when another major price shock did occur, practically on schedule, in 1979–80. Maurice Ernst, then director of the CIA's Office of Economic Research, testified that "we have been widely criticized for having been overly pessimistic in our assessment. We turned out not to be pessimistic enough; witness the 60 percent increase in oil prices since 1978."[28]

Yet Ernst himself later conceded that "OER was right but in part for the wrong reasons. It was of course the Iranian revolution that triggered the price rise although many other forces to set up the rise were in place."[29] Even this judgment may be too generous. It now appears clear that the price increases were, just as in 1973–74, aggravated by too much attention to supposed supply shortfalls. Once again the gap was relatively modest but had disproportionate impact on prices due to poor information among consumers about the real situation and consequent panic bidding for oil.[30] The CIA's dramatic warnings thus may genuinely have become a self-fulfilling prophecy.

The Agency had clearly pegged its analysis to fundamental constraints on supply. In 1979 Ernst explained that although oil stocks were being rebuilt, "the international oil market is in precarious balance. . . . Even if there are no accidents, the outlook for oil supply is dim. Although the emerging economic slowdown will moderate oil demand, we cannot count on increased supplies being available to meet rising demand during the next upswing of the business cycle."[31] That the prices did not reflect a true shortage of supply was soon shown by their short-lived nature, however. Rather than supply shortages worsening, real oil prices actually declined.

The CIA had predicted petroleum companies' inability to supply a demand of about 17.5 billion barrels a year (about 48 million barrels per day). Since 1968, however, world oil production has been relatively stable at about 20 billion barrels a year. Since the costs of production are still well below the price being charged by many producers, oil prices have drifted steadily downward as the OPEC cartel's ability to impose monopoly prices has weakened. It is even possible that the "monopoly price equilibrium" was increasingly disturbed after 1974 by the ways in which the cartel members had come to depend on their newfound wealth, forcing them to compete with one another to sustain their share of the cartel rents. The analytical basis for the CIA's 1977–79 predictions appears to have been fundamentally flawed.[32]

Nevertheless, the CIA was praised for having hit the target. The Agency's other well-publicized estimate, the one about Soviet oil production, seems to have suffered the opposite fate. In 1977 the CIA estimated that the Soviet yield of about 10 million barrels a day (MBD) might increase to as much as 12 MBD before slumping to 10 or even 8 MBD by 1985, forcing the Soviet Union to begin importing substantial quantities of oil.[33] This estimate was criticized as much too pessimistic, and the Defense Intelligence Agency's director testified in 1981 that "the outlook for Soviet energy, from the perspective of the USSR's leadership, is highly favorable."[34] Maurice Ernst admitted that "OER began to back off from its Soviet oil estimate as early as 1978," having "underestimated Moscow's willingness to pour added resources into oil development."[35] Yet by the end of the 1980s (before the Soviet breakup), oil production in the Soviet Union had indeed fallen to the 8–9 MBD range, making the country a significant net importer of petroleum. The original conclusions may have overstated the rate of decline, but the fundamental analysis appeared to be sound—and important.

Accumulating and disseminating accurate, timely information about world oil markets soon proved to be more valuable than dire forecasts of oil shortages. The Iran-Iraq war resulted in supply disruptions as great as those caused by the Iranian revolution, but there was far less disturbance on the market, in part because governments had learned lessons from experience and treated the disruption as a short-term phenomenon to be managed with sensible policies. Another disruption of oil markets following Iraq's 1990 invasion of Kuwait, combined with a significant drop in Soviet production, was also managed with only a brief spike in oil prices—and even that price jump may have been caused less by any absolute shortage than by Western delay in signaling readiness to draw on national stockpiles to make up shortages on the spot market.[36]

The U.S. government now receives voluminous intelligence about the world energy situation. In Washington the CIA retains a strong and well-regarded staff of energy experts, complemented by the massive data-gathering capacity of the Energy Information Administration of the Department of Energy.[37] An international organization, the International Energy Agency, was established as part of the OECD in 1974. It has purposefully set out to gather the market information that was so vitally needed in 1973–74 (and 1979–80). According to a former IEA employee, the agency's information systems on energy markets now "are without equal." As a requirement of membership, states in the IEA must allow the IEA secretariat to conduct annual audits of their energy policies, a form of peer review that enlarges the pool of available information.[38]

BEYOND OIL

The history of economic intelligence concerning oil supply and prices is humbling. The major assessments were often fundamentally wrong, and in some cases may even have aggravated a crisis. Classical economics was of little use in predicting the aggregate behavior of such a distorted market, but the relationship between supplies and prices remained important even if the relationship was counterintuitive (supplies growing even after prices dropped). Clearly the explanation was rooted in a more complex evaluation of the political economy of the cartel, and of individual oil producers. "In reality, oil can be understood most effectively through integrating insights from both economics and politics."[39] The CIA employed such a methodology, but it looks more like geology added to economics added to politics, like three overlays on a transparency. That is not the same thing as a true synthesis of the international political economy of the oil producing states. Assessing OPEC pricing may be a function of establishing where the monopoly equilibrium lies, a calculation that concerns itself less with world oil supply than it does with the fiscal policies, foreign investments, foreign exchange positions, and other—mostly political—encumbrances burdening the major supplier countries.

The substantial literature on nonfuel critical resources, from fresh water to cobalt, suggests that intelligence estimates on these resources must overcome some of the same analytical problems found in the case of oil. Estimates of world grain supplies are also complicated by many market distortions. Both the Department of Agriculture's Economic Research Service and the CIA, in its estimates of Soviet crop yields, established good reputations for providing fairly reliable assessments and analysis against tough methodological challenges. But the Defense Department's standard methodology for identifying critical materials (for stockpiling purposes) is little more sophisticated than what the CIA used in the oil estimate it prepared at the time of the Six Day War, observing that a material is important and then simply tabulating the extent of current import dependence.[40]

As with oil, a more accurate picture of critical resource dependence must encompass: (a) the political scenario for supply disruption, figuring into the calculus the potential severity and duration of a cutoff; (b) the extent of market impairment (including underutilized capacity); (c) logistics for transfer or substitution of new or alternative supplies; and (d) the elasticity of demand (especially taking account of externalities, from climate to conservation inducements).[41] A crucial dimension, illuminated by the experiences with oil, is national competition for resources that are perceived (rightly or wrongly) to be scarce.[42] Since, for example, "many water data are still classified as secret by national governments . . . changes in flow could therefore be perceived and misinterpreted by downstream nations as intentional manipulations rather than geophysical events, thereby provoking conflict."[43]

The CIA has supplemented its analytical capabilities with complex engineering and agronomic models. Agronomic models can simulate plant growth under various climate conditions, aiding predictions of Russian crop yields, for example. Engineering models of major oil fields can be used to estimate oil reserves and production potential, or the impact of damage to oil facilities.

But even the best analytical approaches can be stymied by basic problems in data collection. Scholars working on resource scarcity often complain about the quality of available data. Basic data about oil production are abundant; after all, there is substantial private-sector demand for such information. Even so, governments have found it necessary to collect and interpret such data on their own. Some resources are not as well-served from the standpoint of information as oil. Government action might be needed to secure reliable information about cobalt production and reserves in Zaire, for instance, or in Russia. The government might also wish to vet the methodologies employed in varying estimates of agricultural production or fish harvesting.

Finally, the way statistics, observations, and estimates are handled and synthesized to produce resource projections, from population growth to the intensity of energy usage, calls for great breadth in interpretation. A comprehensive study of the U.S. government's methods for estimating future consumption and prices of resources was undertaken by the Global 2000 study, requested by President Carter and sponsored by the Council on Environmental Quality and the Department of State. Comparing the models and efforts of different agencies, the study found their conclusions inconsistent, the essential problem being that the government's various projections "were designed to simulate sectoral aspects of long-term global trends largely to the exclusion of interactions between and among sectors. This design is no institutional accident but is in conformity with the bureaucratic division of responsibility within the executive agencies."[44]

Specifically, forecasts varied materially on vital measures like population growth and projected GNP. Some agencies would use Census Bureau population projections; others would turn to the UN or USAID and get quite different figures. Some agencies used World Bank GNP projections from the Bank's forecasting department; AID employed the Bank's more optimistic individual country analyses; the Agriculture Department relied on sources from the UN's Food and Agriculture Organization; the Energy Department plugged in OECD numbers; the Interior Department went with calculations developed by a professor at the University of Pennsylvania. "Major disparities" were found in commodity price projections. "Not merely the extent of real-price changes, but even the direction of such changes, is inconsistently projected with regard to fundamental price variables involving fertilizer, nonfuel minerals, food, and energy."[45] The Commerce and Agriculture Departments each had their own way of estimating the fish catch, producing substantially different conclusions. Resource utilization, such as water or minerals, was considered in models developed by the World Bank, the Energy Department, the Interior Department, and the CIA; none of the methodologies used comparable assumptions. Hardly any of the models incorporated much in the way of feedback from other projections, which led to "frozen" sets of assumptions.[46]

Many of the differences were not inadvertent. As the Global 2000 study noted, "an agency finds it helpful to use advanced analytic techniques (and associated projections) as weapons in the adversary process of initiating, justifying, and defending its programs." The consequences can be significant. "The complex patterns of bias caused by the inconsistent variable values used by different elements . . . make adjustment extremely difficult. In particular, a chicken-and-egg problem is encountered in attempting to make simple quantitative adjustments to any single set of projections developed by a single element. . . ."[47]

CONCLUSION

The main points of the foregoing discussion of economic intelligence available for government policy on critical resources can be summarized as follows:

▲   The government has a legitimate requirement for such intelligence on resources that can genuinely be defined as critical—a relatively short list.

▲   Adequate basic data is already available for some key resources, such as oil, and the government should not duplicate this effort (acknowledging the value of the clearinghouse service now provided by the Department of Energy and the International Energy Agency). Direct government collection of information on certain vital resources can, however, be justified in order to exploit special collection capabilities and avoid undue reliance on one or two dominant firms.

▲   Serious problems are presented in the useful assimilation of this data for presentation to policymakers. Methodologies are seldom integrated across agency boundaries. In the oil crises, data was presented in ways that were either plainly inaccurate or, at best, failed to dissuade policymakers from drawing misleading and damaging inferences.

▲   Traditional econometric projections of supply were not especially helpful in understanding the impact of supply disruptions. Policy judgments hinged on political and market considerations that may not have been emphasized sufficiently in the selection and presentation of available intelligence. Information may have been set forth too neutrally, without adequate guidance to how particular theories of market behavior would determine the relevance or irrelevance of proffered information to the policy challenges at hand.

Chapter 4

HIGH FINANCE

The U.S. government is very interested in the large-scale movement of money, or capital, outside of the United States. It is concerned about how much money is coming into the United States and why it comes in; it also cares about how and why money leaves the United States. On occasion, the government must even follow how money is moving between foreign countries—not just when the money being moved is dollars, as in the Eurodollar market, but when these foreign activities will somehow affect the value of America's currency or macroeconomic policies. Sometimes the movement of money is linked not simply to America's international economic policies but also to the financing of illicit activities that also preoccupy the United States.

Therefore the U.S. government collects intelligence, both overt and clandestine, about international capital flows. In 1989 Director of Central Intelligence William Webster explained to a Los Angeles audience:

> Traditional distinctions have blurred between domestic and international markets, between the different kinds of financial transactions, and even between who is a market participant and who is not. . . . foreign exchange transactions now exceed 300 billion dollars per day, and one week of funds

transferred on the international market is larger than the size of the third world debt. The number of international banks is now in the hundreds, up from just a handful in the 1970s; and new financial instruments, such as currency and interest rate swaps, are growing in the market faster than either the traders or the regulators can fully understand them. . . . Just a few years ago, a rumor spread through the market that there would be an emergency "Group of Five" meeting to stabilize the U.S. dollar. Within 30 minutes the deutsche mark and the yen dropped more than two percent against the dollar. Given the size of outstanding foreign exchange positions, the drop represented a shift in wealth of about 1 billion dollars on the market.[1]

Yet there is no major area of economic activity where basic information is so elusive.

CAPITAL FLOWS

The scale of international capital flows has grown almost exponentially during the past twenty years, to the point where such transfers of money or financial assets greatly exceed the value of goods or services passing across borders in international trade. Although total trade flows still affect a relatively small proportion of U.S. GDP, capital flows can have a larger, if more subtle, effect. Not only do capital flows influence the value of the dollar, but they can also affect the stability of U.S. financial and securities markets in ways that are increasingly difficult to track and comprehend yet undeniably significant.

At the very least it would be helpful to have some grasp of the quantity of dollars in circulation throughout the world and the various forces influencing the value at which these dollars are traded. The government's basic information about these phenomena is, however, ever less certain. For example, "the existing data system for reporting U.S. capital transactions was basically designed some 50 years ago; it collects primarily from large domestic financial intermediaries and other corporations, missing many new participants and new modes of transactions. There are both clear gaps and major obstacles to tracking the many kinds of increasingly complex transactions that now occur."[2]

Even measures of the simplest forms of money flow, the movement of American currency, are suspect. A substantial portion of U.S. currency, perhaps as much as one-third to two-thirds of all paper money, circulates outside of the United States in ways that are poorly understood, undermining the Federal Reserve Board's use of monetary aggregates (such as M1) as a guide to determining monetary policy.[3] "There is now no official recording of international shipments of U.S. currency."[4] The problem is not unique to dollar capital flows. Neither the United States nor Japan have reliable data on the amount of yen flowing every year from Japan to North Korea, though it is apparently vital to North Korea's foreign exchange position and is a matter of intense interest in both Washington and Tokyo.

Information about capital flows as part of the balance of payments is collected by the Commerce Department's Bureau of Economic Analysis and the Treasury Department's Treasury International Capital data system. But since both American and foreign companies have operations that cross the border and constantly transfer money within the firm among its global subsidiaries, the collection and interpretation of data about such flows has become problematic. Data collection, concentrated on banks, is fragmentary for important nonbank movers of capital, such as institutional investors and professional money managers.[5] Foreign market behavior can also sway U.S. markets in ways that are not captured at all by measurements of the balance of payments because of both the globalization of "American" assets and the growing trade in derivative financial instruments linked to the performance of foreign markets. "As a result of the surge in derivatives transactions, the capital flow data in the U.S. balance-of-payments accounts no longer serve as adequate indicators of international sources of exchange market and interest rate pressures."[6]

One consequence is that many American economic policy decisions must now be informed by some judgment about their relationship to world markets. If, for instance, Washington decides to boost savings with tax incentives, it must determine whether these incentives outweigh comparable investment opportunities overseas before it can count on a marked rise in domestic savings. In fact, though, the U.S. government still does not understand quite why much more capital comes into the United States than goes out, despite data indicating that rates of return for American overseas investments are significantly higher than the returns on investment at home. Among the possibilities are inadequate data on the true extent of American overseas investment or errors in estimating the real returns on capital, especially the investments of foreigners in the United States.[7] There is a worldwide pattern of investors underreporting the flow of money out of their home countries.[8]

A panel of the National Research Council of the National Academy of Sciences has already made a number of useful recommendations about ways to improve government collection of information about international capital flows. Among these are adoption of the more rigorous and streamlined reporting requirements devised by the Commerce Department, the Treasury, and the Federal Reserve Bank of New York. In 1994 the Treasury Department began its first systematic survey of U.S. holdings of foreign securities since the end of World War II. Other recommendations involve more sharing of data between the United States and foreign central banks.[9]

The report also recommends improved collection of government information on capital flows from the electronic networks that process a large portion of such transactions. Some of these networks are based in the United States, such as the Federal Reserve Board's wire transfer system (Fedwire) and the private system (CHIPS) maintained by the New York Clearing House Association. The European Community is also encouraging a standardized network for electronic transactions (EDIFACT) for use among its member states.

If the U.S. government wishes to obtain better access to the data handled by these and other networks, especially those located overseas, it will need to consider the terms for any formal international cooperation. One important issue will be the protection of individual privacy and confidential corporate information. The United States might also consider whether investing resources in international data collection could be both a sound investment for the public good and an incentive for other countries to join in a new cooperative regime.

Interpreting the Intelligence: The LDC Debt Case

The underlying uncertainty about the causes and nature of capital flow has a pervasive effect upon government policy. The pattern of the past decade or more has been to rely on certain fundamental verities, such as belief in the relationship between interest rates and currency value, and then guess at the consequences of government policy. Such uncertainty encouraged caution, and the more experienced the officials, the more cautious they tended to be. Their natural caution was reinforced by the widespread belief that a more adventuresome course, like the so-called locomotive concept for stimulating demand associated with the 1978 Bonn G-7 summit, which had turned out quite badly, illustrated the danger of miscalculation.[10] So the first Reagan administration's Treasury Department, led by Don Regan and Beryl Sprinkel, tended to avoid any government intervention in international financial markets or international coordination of macroeconomic policy. They were reinforced by Fed chairman Paul Volcker's strong skepticism about the Treasury ideas advanced for his consideration.

One problem, however, could not be ignored: the dangerous possibility that less-developed debtor nations (LDCs) might default on their obligations to Western banks. The intelligence community, especially the CIA, played an active part in trying to alert top officials in 1981 and 1982; despite rising interest rates and a debt default by Poland in March 1981, senior officials had not seen a serious, systemic problem. According to Norman Bailey, then serving on the NSC staff, "The story was, it was Poland. Nobody could expect the Poles to manage their affairs properly. The government wasn't concerned about it."[11]

At first the CIA just called attention to individual country problems. A September 1981 report warned that Brazil could go into default. But in the spring of 1982 the CIA's Office of Global Issues first called attention to rising debt burdens throughout Latin America. Other than Norman Bailey, no one appeared to be listening. In fact, the Treasury and the Fed understood the situation well; they just preferred not to broadcast their fears. By early 1982 Mexican officials were warning Volcker that their finances were in dire straits. An officer of the New York Fed met weekly with officials from the Mexican finance ministry. On four occasions between April and August 1982 Volcker secretly arranged currency swaps to keep up an appearance of Mexican solvency. The CIA, and indeed the NSC staff, knew little or nothing about this.

When the Mexican finance minister arrived in Washington in August 1982 to announce that his government could no longer pay its bills, the U.S. government realized it had to deal with a major crisis. Mexico owed $80 billion, and its debts represented 44 percent of the capital of the nine largest U.S. banks and large portions of the capital assets of many others. Volcker led an intense effort to mix a short-term cash infusion with structural reforms in Mexico, which in turn would be backed by IMF loans and a rescheduling of private debt. The precedent of this "Mexican rescue" encouraged Treasury officials to believe they could deal with other country debt problems on a case-by-case basis.

CIA analysts visited with American bankers and drew more ominous conclusions about an oncoming global debt crisis. As banks curtailed new lending to LDCs after the Mexican scare, the CIA's worries seemed vindicated. Brazil and Venezuela went into default; each was bailed out with a mix of structural reform, IMF lending, and debt rescheduling. CIA analysts kept warning of a systemic crisis, publishing pieces to that effect in the president's daily brief (given to the president and a few other top officials) and the National Intelligence Daily (widely circulated among subcabinet officials). "I had to use a lot of capital to get those pieces in," one CIA economist recalled later. "People didn't understand these issues, and they had trouble with the fact that we didn't have [secret] sources. I could say that we had information that they were borrowing, and now they weren't borrowing" (but this lacked the impact of a clandestine intelligence item). CIA began publishing a newsletter, the *International Financial Situation Report*, with debt updates. Agency analysts thought the IMF-imposed corrections would take a long time to work, at best, and would not ease LDC shortages of foreign exchange.

The CIA analysis made little headway. Paul Krugman, then a Council of Economic Advisers staff economist, remembered that "there was this weird coalition—basically the NSC, the CIA, the Council of Economic Advisers, and Commerce—that would . . . needle Treasury, saying, are you really sure this is going to work? What kind of assumptions are underlying it—shouldn't we have a study?" But "Treasury didn't want to share the issue with anyone else. It didn't have any analysis . . . it was all very slapdash. Treasury's strategy, as it emerged during this time, was basically to do as little as possible, as late as possible: and the less said the better." A Treasury official later acknowledged, "We're not the CIA, and we're not the Federal Reserve Board or anything like that. The amount of sophisticated economic analysis we can do is virtually nil."

Yet, as another Treasury official remembered, the CIA was involved in extended projections that did not help much with the day's problem. "We weren't working long-term. The CIA was doing ten-year balance of payments projections for debtors. We couldn't do anything like that." The Treasury tried to visualize the next year or two, "enough to deal with the crisis." Treasury officials were also not terribly impressed with the quality of the CIA's macroeconomic modeling of the debt crisis.

The Treasury Department felt it had to confront concrete policy dilemmas. It did not want to cause a panic that would shut off the extension of credit to the developing world. In any case, respectable economic theory held that LDCs should run current account deficits, financed by developed country surpluses, if the borrowing improved their capacity to sustain long-term economic growth. Nor did the Treasury want to endanger American banks. A case-by-case policy might at least buy time for U.S. banks to build up their reserves so that they were able to deal with an eventual write-down, or write-off, of some of their LDC debts and avoid a market stampede. Finally, the Treasury could not accept a solution that would write off debts or dispense money without forcing individual countries to accept the necessity of painful structural reform. So the Treasury stayed with its case-by-case approach through 1983, resisting calls for more comprehensive debt reduction.

The CIA, as one of its officials conceded, "never tried to come up with a solution." It just warned that the problem was not being solved. It also began integrating its analysis of IMF-imposed austerity with threats to political stability, even starting another newsletter, the *Political Instability Quarterly*, to track indicators of unrest. But to some its products still seemed aimed more at potential than present problems. Krugman remembers that

> they [the CIA] were just not responsive to what was happening in the internal process. There would be an argument in the interagency group [about the package for Brazil or Mexico]. . . . And the CIA would not join in that discussion. They'd say, we're working on it, we will come out with a study. And the study would come out, with four-color maps, several months after whatever was at issue was over and done with.

That, he thought, was unfortunate because the process was starved for good analysis. Krugman ended up participating in an interagency study that vindicated Treasury's basic approach, though it called for more bank lending.

Frustrated, the NSC staff organized a CIA briefing on the debt problem directly for President Reagan and relevant cabinet officials. The CIA laid out the scale of indebtedness and debtors' inabilities to pay. The NSC staff then gave their interpretation of the implications—this was a systemic solvency problem requiring a radical solution. But Reagan turned the problem over to Treasury, and there was no change in policy.

As the years passed the CIA kept telling officials the debt problem was not solved, but as the director of the Office of Global Issues said later, the briefing for Reagan "was the pinnacle. Everything after that was really just keeping people informed, monitoring." In fact the case-by-case approach appeared to buy the time Treasury wanted while forcing the pace of structural reform in the third world. The process of adjustment proceeded, despite various reversals, and banks built up their reserves and began selling off their Latin debt portfolios on a secondary market. The Bush administration was consequently able to move toward debt reduction in the 1989 Brady plan without encountering the dilemmas such a plan would have faced several years earlier.

Treasury officials, considering their strategy reaffirmed, felt little gratitude for the CIA's contribution. Indeed, one official thought "the CIA was one enormous pain in the ass." He went on:

> Time after time the CIA took what I felt to be irresponsible positions in terms of playing up the benefits of debt relief, and advocating debtor points of view. Predicting disaster, year after year. . . . I mean, they weren't saying, look, this country has a miserable foreign investment regime, it is never going to grow if it doesn't [correct it]. Instead, they [CIA] say look at how much debt it has, look at the 50 percent debt service ratio, our interests in this country are going to be compromised by debt. Well, we knew that. We knew that was unhealthy, the Secretary of the Treasury knew, everybody who worked on these things knew it was not good to have a 50 percent debt service ratio.

The third world debt crisis did not reveal an inability to gather needed intelligence. Substantial data about the extent of LDC indebtedness were available to the U.S. government. Lessons about how to close some gaps in data have been learned. In the early 1980s it might have taken nine months to find out how much Turkey owed to international banks. The Turks themselves did not know the total figure. Deficiencies in knowledge have been remedied by the growing use of the IMF's Debt Reporting System and the clearinghouse/credit bureau function of the private Institute for International Finance.

The CIA's interpretation of the available intelligence made little impression upon the Treasury or the Fed because those agencies felt reasonably well informed from their own information and their own contacts with private banks. Therefore the CIA was not perceived to be adding much to what they already had. Further, they did not believe that the CIA understood the policy dilemmas constraining any reaction to the information. The CIA's effort to broaden bureaucratic interest in the scale of the debt crisis could be viewed by the Treasury and the Fed as an attempt to challenge their primacy in international economic policy. If the Agency actually entertained the idea of using debt to become a policy "player," it had no chance without vigorous support from the president, or at least the secretary of state. This was not forthcoming.

THE MEXICO CASE, 1994–95

During the winter of 1995 the U.S. government was confronted with a severe financial panic in Mexico. Washington quickly crafted a heroic package of international economic assistance for the Mexican government. This included the provision of up to $20 billion from the Treasury's Exchange Stabilization Fund (ESF) and nearly $18 billion in loans from the International Monetary Fund. The expenditure, disbursed without congressional authorization, was 2000 percent larger than any such previous ESF commitment. The IMF loans were the largest in the institution's fifty-year history and amounted to more than 700 percent of Mexico's quota in the Fund. Plainly the United States had been confronted with a grave crisis that forced unprecedented and risky exertions of government power. The turbulent consequences are still being played out, as Mexicans suffer from an acute recession while there is no ease in sight for the worried American creditors.

Why was Washington caught by surprise? Certainly American government agencies had been watching Mexico. They had encouraged adoption of policies that had by 1993 reduced inflation but had also stopped economic growth. In 1994 real estate interest rates remained stiflingly high. These high rates attracted investment in peso holdings so that the value of the currency rose. Mexican exports declined and imports gained, yielding massive current account deficits. Interest rates remained high in order to attract foreign investment that would finance these deficits, investment that might otherwise be scared off by political uncertainties stemming from a peasant revolt in Chiapas and the assassination of presidential candidate Luis Donaldo Colosio. The dependence of Mexico's currency reserves on investors from abroad created noticeable volatility in foreign exchange markets requiring repeated large-scale interventions by the Bank of Mexico in the spring.

By this time two schools of thought had emerged about the Mexican financial situation. The optimists argued that the high interest rates were a natural product of the disinflationary measures Mexico needed and that the country should stay with the current policy, in the hope that government determination would reassure investors. Then interest rates could eventually come down and allow renewed domestic economic growth. The pessimists, including prominent MIT economist Rudiger Dornbusch, argued that the peso had risen too much, fueled by speculative investment, and had for some time been overvalued by at least 10 percent and as much as 20 or even 25 percent. The result was harm to the competitive position of domestic producers, a high current account deficit, and a dangerous dependence on a bubble of speculative foreign investment. Dornbusch warned that the peso needed to be devalued immediately by about 20 percent if a new wage-price pact could be achieved. If not, the peso should be allowed to float.[12]

The leading U.S. agency for Mexican financial issues, Treasury, seemed to acknowledge the arguments on both sides but to side with the optimists. Secretary Lloyd Bentsen was repeatedly advised in May 1994 by Under Secretary Lawrence Summers and Assistant Secretary Jeffrey Shafer that "in our view, Mexico's current exchange rate policy is sustainable." The declassified documents do not, however, reveal the data or assessments that underpinned this presumption other than occasional references to contacts on Wall Street.[13] The Mexican government had begun to promote the large-scale inflow of foreign capital by the issuance of *tesobonos*, instruments that promised high short-term returns to investors and shielded them from the danger of peso devaluation because they were denominated in dollars (though redeemable in pesos). There were few cautions expressed in the Treasury documents about Mexico's growing reliance on *tesobonos*, even though these dramatically increased Mexican government exposure in the event of a devaluation. Hence, at this time, Treasury officials demonstrated no belief that a significant peso devaluation was inevitable or necessary.

The Federal Reserve Bank of New York staff did not agree. Confidential Fed memos reported, "Staff analyses indicate that the Mexican peso is significantly 'overvalued' . . . somewhere on the order of 20%." Devaluation was inevitable. Though the peso might be maintained for the near term, "its position is clearly quite precarious."[14] The Fed assessment was not based on special data. Instead it was grounded on a general analysis of Mexico's historical performance and comparisons with countries that had encountered similar current account deficits. An earlier Fed analysis had called attention to a worrisome point in the data available from the IMF and its own staff studies, notably that Mexican imports were principally of consumer rather than capital goods. Fed staff, both in New York and in headquarters' Division of International Finance, was also noting the growing use of high-yield *tesobonos* to defend the peso. (Mexico sold nearly a billion dollars of such instruments during just the first week of July 1994.) The issue engaged the members of the Federal Reserve Board, including Chairman Alan Greenspan. A memo to Greenspan and Vice-Chairman Alan Blinder showed how the yields reflected rising market fears not only of peso devaluation but also of a default that would abrogate Mexico's *tesobono* obligations.[15]

Relevant CIA estimates have not been declassified. But in response to press criticism of the CIA's performance, the Republican chair and Democratic vice-chair of the Senate Select Committee on Intelligence wrote to the Senate Banking Committee. They had asked their staff to examine all pertinent CIA analyses. They concluded, "While the classified nature of U.S. intelligence analyses precludes us from providing the details of these analyses, we were frankly impressed with their quality." The senators added that the CIA's work "made clear that a large, delayed devaluation of the peso would have significant ramifications for Mexico's economy and political situation." It illuminated "the difficult dilemma that Mexican policymakers faced in deciding whether to take painful economic steps before an election, when such actions might affect the very outcome of that election, or to delay those steps and accept the risk that the economic situation might get out of hand as a result."[16] A study group that examined the Mexico crisis also found that, "as early as the spring of 1993, the CIA privately warned the U.S. Treasury Department of the dangers of a Mexican collapse."[17]

To the extent they have been declassified, Treasury analyses during the fall of 1994 did not focus on this dilemma, tending instead to dwell on short-term influences on the peso, with little assessment of the underlying macroeconomic presumptions.[18] Yet, by October, Fed staff were directly advising Greenspan to warn Mexican officials about the "risks and costs of trying to defend an unsustainable exchange rate."[19] A month later, after serious attacks on the peso had begun, Summers negotiated language of reassurance with his Mexican counterpart for Secretary Bentsen to announce in public, assuring everyone that: "I have been much impressed by Mexico's strong economic fundamentals" and "[I welcome] President-elect Zedillo's commitment to stability and the consolidation of economic reform."[20] There is little evidence of any effort to develop a coordinated message, or underlying set of intelligence assessments, between the Fed and Treasury. The State Department does not appear to have played any role at all.

In early December Treasury staff began exploring options for dealing with a Mexican devaluation that was coming to be seen as inevitable. Its summary report incorporated some staff analysis of the current account deficit and monetary policy and attached a paper on Mexico produced by J. P. Morgan.[21] On December 20 the Mexican government announced a 15 percent devaluation of the peso. Treasury's analysts were optimistic about what would happen next. "When all the smoke clears, probably by early next year, we expect the peso will settle about 8–12 percent below what it was trading at prior to the new policy." On the key question of market reaction, they thought, "Some short term turmoil is almost inevitable but a significant question mark has been removed and investors are more likely to react favorably than unfavorably to the new policy." Though it is unclear what evidence informed this assessment, the conclusion was clear: "Our best guess is that the devaluation will not affect Mexico's basic macroeconomic course or fundamentally alter the country's brighter economic prospects in 1995."[22]

Within a week the peso had lost a third of its value, and the Mexican government abandoned any effort to defend it. The currency would float. For the first time the United States began offering direct financial aid. Summers blandly explained to the new Treasury secretary, Robert Rubin, that, following the devaluation, "Secretary Bentsen made a supportive statement about Mexican fundamentals. Unfortunately, investors continued to sell pesos for dollars, drawing down Mexico's reserves."[23] Washington activated a $6 billion credit line first created in the spring of 1994 after the Colosio assassination. Summers's memo to Rubin did not appear to analyze broader market implications, but he announced on December 27 that the decline of the peso had gone "considerably beyond what can be justified by Mexican economic fundamentals" and emphasized his "confidence in the underlying soundness of Mexican economic policies." Treasury staff talked to IMF staff and found some agreement that "Mexican banks do not have a foreign currency exposure problem," though they did have a solvency problem from an excess of bad loans. For data the Treasury used a table that had appeared in the *Economist*, sourced to J. P. Morgan and Baring Securities.[24]

Mexico did, however, face early repayment of more than $29 billion in *tesobonos*, indexed to the now much more expensive dollar. The investors made their worries known to Washington, which feared the consequence of a sovereign default both for Mexico and for the investors. Further, the U.S. Government began noticing a much wider impact of the Mexican crisis on other Latin American debtor countries seeking external financing. For these reasons, and with little warning, the U.S. government now confronted demands for a far larger package of aid for Mexico. The Clinton administration first proposed congressional passage of government guarantees for massive private loans to Mexico. When Congress balked, the administration prepared the ESF/IMF package that would bypass Capitol Hill, signing a series of agreements with Mexico. To secure the loans, these agreements gave America the right to garnish all income from sales of Mexican oil, the country's most valuable export and a major source of national pride.

In a prepared address, President Clinton offered this initial explanation of the origin of the troubles: "It is clear that this crisis came about because Mexico relied too heavily upon short-term foreign loans to pay for the huge upsurge in its imports from the United States and from other countries. A large amount of these debts came due at a time when, because of the nature of the debts, it caused a serious cash flow problem for Mexico, much like a family that expects to pay for a new home with the proceeds from the sale from its old house only to have the sale fall through."[25] Shortly afterward, a different explanation was drafted for a speech by Summers, observing that "American officials and others expressed concerns repeatedly that Mexico's exchange rates were unsustainable." The final draft said only that Mexico had maintained an exchange rate that "ultimately proved not to be defensible."[26]

President Clinton's emphasis on *tesobono* exposure had been previously noted by the Federal Reserve Board's staff, but his proffered theory of the shock's being caused by a large amount of these debts coming due at a bad moment suggests unlucky timing rather than disastrous economic policies. There are also, naturally, questions about why Mexico was relying on *tesobonos*. Had the American government noticed this troubling behavior? Had Washington tried to do anything about this behavior before accepting the responsibility of bailing out both the speculators and the debtor? Nor is there any available evidence to confirm the draft Summers assertion that American officials (again possibly excepting the Fed) had ever told Mexican officials that their exchange rate was unsustainable. In fact, Treasury memos from mid-1994 repeatedly made just the opposite point.

The Mexico case indicates some gaps in the evaluation and integration of relevant economic intelligence. The most comprehensive macroeconomic analysis and tracking of *tesobono* trading appears to have been done by staff of the Fed in New York and Washington but its research does not appear to have been plugged into the policy questions considered or presumptions made in either Mexico City or Washington. The CIA appears to have understood the seriousness of the economic and political dilemmas confronting the Mexican government and accurately projected possible choices. It did not, however, alert officials—at the White House, for example—by linking prospective Mexican actions to likely reactions from the market. Since the crisis developed precisely out of the interaction between Mexican deeds and market responses, the seriousness of the danger was therefore not adequately portrayed. The job of integrating the various strands of information, which ought to have been taken up by an interested policy agency, the Treasury, was not performed. When Treasury attempted to assess the situation, it looked to recent market behavior, studies produced by market risk analysts, or the occasional call to someone at Bear Stearns or elsewhere on Wall Street.

First, the case starkly illustrates the danger of relying on Wall Street to provide vital economic intelligence. Most firms failed to anticipate the crisis, to the extent of explaining in detail to their clients why no devaluation would happen. When the crisis broke, the investment community reactions "frequently displayed more emotion than insight."[27] Investment banks trusted statements of Ivy League-educated Mexican officials; they had difficulty visualizing a catastrophe; and many firms had large sums tied up in the country or were marketing Mexican debt to their clients.

The deficiencies of this structure for providing assessments are obvious. There appears to have been little targeted collection of data. Analyses were compartmentalized and disjointed. There was no serious method employed for gauging likely market behavior. This latter omission is especially stark since firms advising clients on Mexican investments, or holding positions in such investments themselves, should not be asked sensitive questions or trusted to give objective answers.

Since direct dialogue with investors, advisers, and traders is so problematic, the government must be able to form its own independent opinion of what the market will do under various circumstances. In this effort Treasury and the Fed may have few comparative advantages, except in constructing the relevant scenarios. The task that they are probably best suited for is to evaluate the copious open-source information used by financial advisers and attempt to infer: (1) the "conventional wisdom" that will animate similarly well-informed traders; and (2) the likely contours of relevant computerized trading programs. A range of potential outcomes could then be attached to the postulated government actions, with critical variables highlighted for policymakers.

The CIA convened a postmortem conference that included some outside experts to reflect on the Mexican experience. One immediate result has been the development of new intelligence tools that can convey possible macroeconomic risks more vividly to decisionmakers.

The International Monetary Fund has also pondered the Mexican crisis to evaluate its own capacity to gather needed economic intelligence. The managing director of the Fund, Michel Camdessus, has called attention to this "first financial crisis of the 21st century . . . that abundantly illustrated the rapid contagion effects in integrated financial markets of major disturbances in particular countries [as well as] the more rapid marginalization of countries that fail to integrate themselves into the globalized economy" as "national economies have become more vulnerable to international capital flows." One conclusion Camdessus drew was the need to strengthen IMF "surveillance . . . in order to improve our capacity to work as an early warning system."[28]

Unfortunately, IMF early warning assumes that the IMF has much better information, or is more able to challenge statements by government officials. Neither may be true. The IMF would become a very different institution, with much more difficult relations with member governments, if it became responsible for the reliability of its data and relaxed the secrecy surrounding its reports. While the IMF does not have the profit motives that can compromise private sector analysis, the IMF may fear that sounding an alarm would cause the problem it seeks to avert. The IMF may also worry that its warnings might jeopardize the IMF's own structural adjustment programs.[29] The American government can seek IMF help and support IMF surveillance, but cannot rely on the IMF to satisfy its own needs for accurate and timely intelligence.[30]

INTELLIGENCE AND COORDINATION OF NATIONAL MACROECONOMIC POLICIES

During the second Reagan administration, the Treasury, led by James Baker and Richard Darman, embarked on an ambitious effort to coordinate national economic policies with the other major industrial powers (the G-7). The coordinated exchange rate interventions of 1985 to lower the value of the dollar (the Plaza accords) relied on several sets of judgments, such as the effect on the balance of trade, how far the dollar would fall in response to a given amount of intervention, or how the European Monetary System (and particular European central banks) would discharge its intervention responsibilities and simultaneously cope with the destabilizing effects of dollar devaluation on its member currencies. Almost none of these appear to have been significantly influenced, however, by intelligence about either capital flows or the tendencies or activities of foreign governments.[31]

The need for information grew as Baker insisted on matching exchange rate intervention with pledges from his counterparts to adjust their countries' macroeconomic policies. From the start there was a need for a process of "surveillance" to determine whether pledges were being carried out. The May 1986 Tokyo G-7 summit explicitly adopted a set of economic indicators to measure the compatibility of each country's economic plans and forecasts. Though these indicators never became a basis for automatic policy coordination (even the reference "ranges" agreed in the Louvre accord of 1987 really only applied to exchange rates), the Tokyo initiatives did formalize multilateral observation of other countries' policies and forecasts.

This monitoring, which has continued to the present, does not impose a major new requirement on American intelligence agencies. In the G-7 process the role of impartial information provider is played by the International Monetary Fund. The economic counselor of the Fund is invited to join G-7 deputies at their meetings. National representatives present their country's projections on the chosen indicators, such as GNP growth, consumer price inflation, current account balances, and real domestic demand. The IMF puts its own projections before the deputies and analyzes the "compatibility" of the various national plans. (This analysis has usually been circulated beforehand for comment.)

There appears to be little role for intelligence in this process. While it could divine specific tactical information, such as Bundesbank willingness to consider cutting the discount rate, the value of this information is unclear. Certainly the ambitious attempt to coordinate macroeconomic policy in 1986 and 1987 had its problems beyond the capacity of intelligence to predict. The dollar fell more sharply than was expected. Exchange rate intervention to stabilize the dollar after the Louvre accord was less effective than was hoped. It was hard to determine a notional "equilibrium" value for the currencies. Government outlays for intervention far exceeded the sum thought to be necessary, and still failed to prevent appreciation of the yen against the dollar.

Meanwhile tension grew between the United States and Germany, or more precisely between the Treasury Department and the Bundesbank, because the Germans refused even to acknowledge the desirability of stimulating their domestic economy and appeared to undermine American efforts to stabilize the dollar. The U.S.-German clash may have contributed to the sudden plunge of the stock market on Black Monday in October 1987.

If intelligence could not contribute valuably through its interpretation of available economic information, it still could bring its knowledge of foreign politics to bear upon that data. Although many Treasury and Fed officials understood some aspects of how other governments worked, their grasp was often narrow. The same official who could interpret the real impact of a proposed Japanese tax cut plan might not be the person who could explain the inner politics of the governing council of the Bundesbank. Intelligence agencies could bring such expertise together and combine with it some insight into the local political environment. Such a synthesis could, in principle, help anticipate the dynamics of a G-7 meeting.

From public accounts, economic intelligence appeared to have given some help to Washington, especially in understanding Japanese fiscal policy and bureaucratic politics. More information was also collected about foreign central bank operations. But though the information may have been very interesting, how to employ it in practical policy terms remained elusive.

THE POLITICAL COMPONENT OF FINANCIAL INTELLIGENCE: "BLACK WEDNESDAY"

The relationship between institutional and financial analysis is close and important. The fracturing of the European Monetary System on "Black Wednesday" in September 1992, leading to the exit of sterling from the exchange rate mechanism and the devaluation of other currencies, can be understood as a product of underlying economic tensions. But the British government was taken by surprise when word came on a Sunday of the Bundesbank's planned Monday announcement of an interest rate cut British officials knew would be inadequate to ease pressure on weaker currencies paired to a lira devaluation that they expected would be perceived as insufficient by the markets.

Also, though London had ruled out a general realignment of European currencies, it did not know that Germany was newly willing to contemplate a significant interest rate cut in exchange for such a realignment. These and other misunderstandings meant that opportunities to defuse the crisis or diminish its impact were lost, along with the large sums of money vainly invested by the British government in its short-lived effort to prop up the pound. Intelligence apparently did not warn the British government of the results of consultations between the Bundesbank and Chancellor Helmut Kohl shortly before the Bundesbank's announcement, or the content of the German-Italian conversations or German-French discussions that might have revealed what was coming. On the German side, whatever the Bundesbank's preference might have been, the Bonn government surely did not intend to trigger a monetary crisis—especially a fortnight before the French referendum on the important Maastricht Treaty (which concerned steps toward European political and economic integration). Yet the Germans did not know that French officials had failed to relay news of their interest rate proposal to other EC capitals—another intelligence failure.

Recent evidence suggests that intelligence, either in the various policy agencies or in the CIA, has an important role to play in traditional financial and macroeconomic issues. The problem of improving the tracking of capital flows is, principally, a problem of overt data gathering, especially by the Commerce and Treasury Departments and the Fed. Basic information about national economic indicators or indebtedness is relatively well understood by policymakers without help from the intelligence agencies. The challenge is to interpret and analyze this information, both from an economic and a political perspective. For example, could the intelligence agencies explain why the United States apparently had so little difficulty financing its current account deficits during the early 1990s even though Washington was cutting interest rates and the dollar continued to sink? The task is more than just a sophisticated restatement of a familiar problem. The synthesis of specialized economic and political knowledge for American officials should convey a sharper understanding of the way their foreign counterparts view a given situation, reflect the accumulated memories that foreigners bring to the table, and spotlight the bureaucratic fissures in overseas capitals or other opportunities for American influence.

Watching Financial Institutions

A newer role for intelligence agencies is to study some of the nonstate institutions that hold and channel global flows of money. Such intelligence may have political rather than economic value. The collapse of the Bank of Credit and Commerce International and the indictment of the branch manager of the Atlanta branch of Italy's Banca

Nazionale del Lavoro have both revealed much more about this mission of the intelligence community.

The CIA began collecting information about the Bank of Credit and Commerce International in the mid-1980s, after clandestine sources passed on information implicating the bank in the laundering of drug money. The Directorate of Operations developed a larger, covert collection program targeting this Middle East-based bank from 1986 until its collapse in 1990. The collection effort successfully focused on the management of the bank and the way it was laundering money. The CIA also began learning about possible manipulation of financial markets, involvement in illicit purchases of military technology, and alleged relationships between the bank and terrorist groups. The Agency reported in early 1985 that BCCI had succeeded in gaining control of an American bank holding company in late 1981, which later became First American Bankshares.[32]

The CIA produced "several hundred" reports on BCCI's activities. These sensitive documents from clandestine intelligence gathering were distributed to different individuals, depending on the report's sensitivity, but BCCI reports went to all the relevant policy agencies, including Treasury, Customs, Commerce, DEA, FBI, and the Federal Reserve Board. The CIA did not develop materials for criminal investigations, since, as its acting director put it, "what we were interested in doing was not trying to find wrong-doing per se and trying to follow the individuals to detail their involvement. Our focus was on the activities that BCCI was involved in with regard to drug traffickers or trafficking, money laundering, terrorism, or arms deals. We were focused on larger strategic problems and issues, not on the bank itself or the individuals involved."[33]

The Agency was criticized, however, for not referring the information to appropriate law enforcement bodies. The 1985 report on BCCI's ownership of First American Bankshares went, for example, to the Commerce Department and the Treasury, including the Comptroller of the Currency, but not to the Justice Department or the Federal Reserve Board. The CIA trusted the intelligence liaison office at the Treasury to figure out which agencies should hear about the report. In his confirmation hearings for director of central intelligence, Robert Gates promised to be sure the Justice Department was informed in the future about such investigative leads. A large number of reports on other law enforcement issues connected to BCCI did go to the FBI and DEA, though it appears this information did not help in the particular investigation and grand jury proceedings being conducted against BCCI officials by U.S. attorneys in Florida. This is no surprise; the CIA reports, though they might cue an investigation, are not tailored to legal procedures on gathering or presenting evidence.[34]

The Banca Nazionale del Lavoro (BNL), based in Rome, is one of the largest banks in Italy. It is owned by the Italian government. In 1981, the bank established a branch in Atlanta that began doing business with Iraq. From 1985 to 1988 BNL-Atlanta advanced money to American agricultural exporters shipping rice and other grain to Iraq, with the loans secured by Iraqi letters of credit guaranteed under the U.S. Department of Agriculture's Commodity Credit Corporation program. Iraq made all its scheduled payments on these letters of credit until the invasion of Kuwait. Unrelated to the CCC-endorsed trade, in 1988 and 1989 the Iraqis obtained cash loans from BNL-Atlanta of more than $2 billion, loans that were not adequately secured and were said to be unauthorized by the head office in Rome. Some of this money was reportedly used in secret purchases of arms and military technology. In July 1989 two Atlanta employees reported these unauthorized loans to federal authorities. On August 4, 1989, FBI agents raided BNL-Atlanta and seized its records.

The CIA knew little about BNL-Atlanta's relationship with Iraq. A subsequent investigation by the Senate Select Committee on Intelligence found a few reports mentioning both BNL and Iraq, but none suggested any awareness of the links between Iraq and BNL's Atlanta branch. The only intelligence assessment between 1983 and 1989 of Iraq's arms procurement network, a June 1989 Defense Intelligence Agency report, described the financial structure for these activities but did not mention Iraqi ties to BNL-Atlanta. CIA economic analysts apparently knew nothing of interest about BNL and Iraq before the FBI's raid.[35]

After the FBI raid, the CIA assumed that BNL-Atlanta was also part of Iraq's arms procurement network. Though the Agency had no contact with the Atlanta investigators, it received information suggesting or speculating that Rome knew of the "unauthorized" loans to Iraq. This information would have been important to the investigation, since the government prosecutors' theory was that headquarters had been a victim of its branch manager's fraud, not its author.

Almost all of the reports CIA received on BNL-Rome's rumored involvement were duly disseminated to the Justice Department, but none of the Justice attorneys involved in the case could recall having received them because of the "normal" way intelligence was distributed (through liaison at the top of the department with limited dissemination to line offices).[36] The CIA forwarded a report about BNL to the Agriculture Department in January 1990 with a letter asserting that BNL's Rome managers were involved in the scandal. This assertion, based primarily on an analyst's reading of a Financial Times article quoting an Italian treasury official, was not passed to Justice. The CIA did not know that Justice had developed an entirely different theory of the case.[37] The Justice handling of the case against BNL-Atlanta was subsequently plagued by constant questions about possible CIA reports and failures to know what reports they had already received. The CIA aggravated matters through its neglecting to tell Justice what it was telling the Congress or through its inability to find promptly everything that was in its own files. Information was not deliberately withheld, however, and the material ultimately unearthed did not appear to have added important new information about the issue of Rome's involvement in Atlanta's loans to Iraq.

By law the CIA has no enforcement powers, and by executive order it is expressly precluded from targeting "U.S. persons" for law enforcement purposes. The intelligence agencies tend to stay away from collection for the benefit of law enforcement even in the case of foreigners fearing the disclosure of their "sources and methods" in court. The intelligence community may know more about foreign banks than most other agencies, and it has unique abilities to monitor electronic communications and monetary transactions. Though the value of the intelligence is clear, it is less clear how or whether this intelligence is usually put to use effectively by criminal justice agencies in the United States. There are some indications that such information might not be sufficiently available to prosecutors or agents in the field and is rarely, if ever, used to help the government if a case goes to trial (due to classification and heresy problems).

The Senate Select Committee on Intelligence's staff report on the BNL-Atlanta problem noted that both the Justice Department and the CIA were confused about the relationship between law enforcement and intelligence needs. The practice of avoiding any purposeful collection of intelligence against foreigners suspected of U.S. crimes needed, according to the report, to be "thoroughly assessed."[38] It also observed that CIA analysts writing about BNL in

1990 and 1991 "were largely oblivious to the evidence being developed by the criminal investigation," although the Agency had a copy of the government's detailed indictment. The result was "intelligence analysis which was largely uninformed as well as subsequent consternation for the prosecution when the competing intelligence analysis was unexpectedly cited by defense counsel. . . . " For its part, Justice's procedures for disseminating intelligence and dealing with the intelligence community also did not bear up well under scrutiny.[39]

The information revealed by the Senate Select Committee on Intelligence about the CIA's information gathering on BCCI and BNL-Atlanta shows the strengths and weaknesses of financial intelligence collection. CIA was apparently effective in collecting valuable information about the activities of BCCI, whether or not the knowledge was actually used in subsequent prosecutions of BCCI officials. Yet both the BCCI and BNL cases show that the CIA and Justice Department were ill-prepared for systematic cooperation in gathering intelligence on foreign financial institutions. The CIA shies away from a law enforcement function, and Justice did not appear to have sought out the Agency's help in either of these two cases.

Chapter 5

FAIR AND UNFAIR COMPETITION

In the last years of the nineteenth century British politics was divided by debates over whether Britain's economy was experiencing
decline and whether the Empire ought to turn from free trade to protectionism. There was a sense that Britain's relative dominance in
manufacturing, so clear in 1870, was eroding against the burgeoning
industrial might of France, Germany, and the United States. The
debate at the highest levels of government was fairly starved of reliable
information. Practically the only statistics kept over a long period of
time were the Customs Department's records of imports and exports.
Therefore, "as discussion of the nation's condition progressed, the
trade returns emerged as *the* indicator of Britain's economic performance."[1] Yet these figures were not an especially good measure of
Britain's overseas commerce, much less of its relative economic prosperity. Still, then as now, policy was shaped around the available intelligence, for better or worse. The numerical indicators in the trade
returns "tended to cut deep grooves in the minds of Britain's leaders
and to become invested with a symbolic significance that far exceeded their actual usefulness."[2]

In the last years of the twentieth century, American politics is
divided by debates over whether the U.S. economy is in relative
decline and whether the country ought to turn from free trade.[3]
American officials, though, are assured that the state of the art in

compiling international economic information is well beyond anything imaginable a century ago. They would agree, regardless of ideology, that the government needs to have information about the
extent of international trade in goods and services, the intracompany
trade of multinational firms operating in the United States, the
employment statistics and investments of foreign firms in America
and American firms abroad, and the relationship between all this
information and domestic economic prosperity. It is not really clear,
however, that American officials have avoided the danger of being dis-
tracted by other misleading and poor-quality numerical indicators of
economic performance.

The National Research Council's Panel on Foreign Trade
Statistics studied the quality of international economic data in
1991–92. It concluded that data on U.S. international economic
activity were seldom comparable to analogous data on domestic production, so that much of the international data have limited analytic value. Information about services and financial transactions was
especially hard to match up.

Comparability aside, "there are major data gaps and quality problems with existing data on U.S. international transactions." Statistical
discrepancies in U.S. balance of payments accounts amounted to
$63.5 billion in 1990, or about 70 percent of the entire current
account deficit. Data collection systems were weak, and information
was lacking on the foreign goods and services used as intermediate
inputs in domestic production. Also, "there is almost no evidence of
modern process quality management in the statistical agencies that
produce the data on U.S. international transactions." One study of
U.S. trade with Canada showed that U.S. exports north of the border
were underreported by about 20 percent.[4]

The NRC panel went on to note that few users of trade data realized the inherent flaws. Fluctuations in the trade balance caused significant market reactions, yet consumers probably did not know that
"monthly changes in the U.S. merchandise trade balance over the
period from February 1987 through February 1991, corrected for trend
and for correlation over time, have a mean value which is *small*, $249
million, and a *large* standard error, $1.4 billion." In other words, rad-
ical monthly changes bore little relation to reliably measured, long-
term trends in the trade balance. The statistics compiled by the
Census Bureau and the U.S. Customs Service included no real, consistent time series of merchandise trade data.

The situation was worse for services, since, unlike for merchandise, there can be no continuous tabulation of things being moved physically in and out of the United States. Instead the collection system depends on periodic surveys of representative firms; the Commerce Department's Bureau of Economic Analysis then produces estimates based on these samples. Many kinds of transactions in this fast-changing area are probably missed altogether. As a result of this and other problems, "large errors and omissions have diminished the meaning of individual trade balance figures and compounded the difficulty of assessing the economic standing of the United States in the international economy."[5] Some of the NRC's recommendations for improving the database have been adopted by federal agencies, others have not; still others depend on allocating more money to the government's statistical efforts.

RECOGNIZING COMPETITIVE OPPORTUNITIES

Though the U.S. government has a formidable task in developing meaningful aggregate figures about international trade and competitiveness, the task would be made easier, at least in theory, if the government concentrated on particular industries or products. Following this logic, the government has pledged to identify competitive opportunities for American business. An interagency task force, the Trade Promotion Coordinating Committee (TPCC), was created in 1990 to help Washington coordinate its various efforts to help companies export their products. Most recently, President Clinton announced a National Export Strategy in September 1993 that promises even better coordination of federal and state government efforts to help American businesses find foreign customers.

The Commerce Department has established a database of information on major project and procurement contracts for which American firms can compete. Export promotion is the major task of Commerce's Foreign Commercial Service, which posts about two hundred Americans overseas and employs an additional twelve hundred foreign nationals in its efforts. Agricultural exporters are helped by the USDA's Foreign Agricultural Service. The Commerce Department publishes commercial guides to specific countries, maintains a trade information center, and posts export "leads" both electronically and in the *Commerce Business Daily*. All U.S. embassies in countries with "significant market potential" are required to develop Strategic

Commercial Plans. A team, directed by the ambassador, is to "identify goals, strategies, and performance measures."[6] Commerce has asked the intelligence community as well to join in its quest to identify the "big emerging markets"[7] of the future.

All of these efforts require information about commercial opportunities. In principle, all U.S. government commercial information is to be included in a National Trade Data Bank, regularly reviewed by the Commerce Department for its timeliness and continued relevance. The data bank already contains more than 100,000 documents along with basic information about exports, particular industries, market research reports, and an index of foreign distributors interested in American products. Few businesses actually use the service, however, either because they do not have the needed CD-ROM technology or because they find it difficult.[8]

Almost all of this substantial effort, led by the Department of Commerce, consists of the compilation of publicly available material so that businesses can more easily use it, presumably as a supplement to their own private sources of information. The Commerce Department has, in Washington, hundreds of country desk officers and hundreds more industry desk officers, ranging from "abrasive products" to "zinc." They are all ready to help advise companies about export opportunities.

There is no evidence that intelligence agencies systematically collect clandestine information about competitive opportunities for American businesses. Intelligence officers may learn of an upcoming chance to bid for a contract in a foreign country. If they do, under current procedures, the information will probably be passed on to the State and Commerce Departments for further action. Similarly, if intelligence officers learned that a foreign country has bribed a third country's official to win a contract, that too would be passed along to Commerce and State, and those agencies would consider how to react. In 1990 Indonesia was considering competing bids from AT&T and a Japanese consortium. Intelligence reporting indicated that Indonesia was about to give the contract to the Japanese, partly because Japanese officials were promising that such a decision would mean more foreign aid from Tokyo. Duly alerted, Bush administration officials urged Indonesia to reconsider, and ultimately the work was divided between the American and Japanese bidders.[9]

A more difficult case is presented when an important opportunity, such as the recent Saudi decision to buy a large number of new passenger aircraft, has been identified well in advance as vital for American industry. Instead of hoping for some windfall tip-off, would the intelligence community be recruited to develop information about the way in which bids will be considered or about the competitors? Assume that the foreign bidders are actively collecting intelligence of their own, so Americans feel no particular compunction about responding in kind. Assume further that there are no opportunity costs to making available intelligence resources for this purpose.

Two important issues need to be addressed before the question can be answered. First, Washington would have to decide whether American national interests in the case were clear-cut enough to warrant a deliberate collection effort. For instance, suppose that Boeing and McDonnell-Douglas are competing against Airbus for the Saudi contract, but Airbus intends to have Pratt & Whitney build the engines for its airplanes. The United States would be reluctant to gather information that might harm one American company in order to benefit another.

Second, Washington would need to consider how any intelligence would be made available to interested companies, if at all. Intelligence agencies would give information to policymakers, like the Commerce Department, not directly to industry. Sources and methods for clandestine information would have to be protected. The government could publicize "sanitized" information for the benefit of all. Or it could convey the information discreetly to the concerned executives. It could also say nothing at all to the industries but use the information in support of its own high-level advocacy for the "American" bid.

RECOGNIZING COMPETITIVE PROBLEMS

The U.S. government fights hard to help American firms export products. Yet recognizing foreign trade barriers or other competitive problems presents a different challenge. Other than in agriculture and a few other sectors, the United States does not pursue a systematic policy of government financial support and import protection for industries. American economic intelligence on problems in fair competition therefore tends to be reactive, responding to complaints from the private sector, and the use of intelligence is framed by the particular legal remedies available to injured businesses. Even where the U.S.

government has initiated Section 301 (of the Omnibus Trade Act of 1974) complaints of unfair trade practices, the action has usually been stimulated by grievances filed by the private sector, not from government sources.[10]

A thorough effort to discover hidden foreign subsidies or nontariff barriers to market access usually requires an examination not of a particular lost bid but of the structure and practices of the entire industry. Patterns of government behavior and nongovernmental obstacles to competitive entry become apparent only over time. The Commerce Department's industry analysts, focused on export promotion, do not regularly perform a strategic market openness analysis, and may lack the data or expertise to do such work even if they wanted to. There are some experts on particular industries scattered throughout government, but none of the agencies has systematically built up the comprehensive analytical expertise required. The institutions furthermore lack any incentive to make such analysis part of their mission unless private companies have already banded together to get the matter placed on the public agenda. Formal legal requirements are not enough: although Congress has required the State Department to collect comprehensive information about foreign government subsidies to business, there is no evidence that State maintains such a database.[11]

More typically, U.S. producers—say, of glass—might approach the U.S. government (if their stockholders are prepared to risk public discussion of their competitive difficulties) and complain that Japanese distributors will not buy their products. They, perhaps acting jointly as the Flat Glass Installers Association, could present evidence that the distributors are all effectively controlled by one or another of Japan's three glass producers. Some of this evidence might even be available from public sources in Japan. American officials, possibly in the Office of the U.S. Trade Representative, might then seek to confirm the private claims. The CIA, Commerce Department, or American diplomats in Tokyo could be asked what they think of the companies' assertions. The USTR might also call upon the highly regarded staff of the International Trade Commission, if the complaint fell within the legal mandate of that body.

If these agencies corroborated the assertions, maybe even from anecdotal evidence quickly collected, the U.S. government would have to decide whether the problem was important enough to take action. This process of corroboration and deliberation could take months (at which point the industry has presumably already been hurt), perhaps more than a year, especially if the government needed to develop its position on the problem without the benefit of any pre-existing opinion or intelligence of its own.[12] If the complaint were confirmed, then U.S. officials might raise glass in trade talks with the Japanese, using information supplied from industry and supplemented by government agencies. (American firms seldom have access to information unavailable to the U.S. government; they simply spend the money to compile available data into a useful form, even, as one industry representative put it, "repackaging the government's own information for the government.")

Reliance on industry-supplied information works only if affected industries have the will, organization, and resources to bring to bear. Only a tiny fraction of American companies have full-fledged intelligence offices within their corporate structures, and they tend to rely more on consultants to perform strategic market analysis. Government institutions, unlikely to have well-qualified experts who had already been working the stated problem for years before the complaint arrived, find themselves dependent on the aggrieved industry. On the other hand, the U.S. government cannot do full-scale analyses of restrictive market conditions for every U.S. industry. Yet a middle ground may be possible. The U.S. government could make a deliberate decision to build up its institutional capacity to provide highly qualified and independent advice about subsidies, pricing practices, and entry barriers in some selected industries.

TRADE AGREEMENTS

Once a problem has been recognized as suitable for government action, American negotiators will want background information pertinent to the issue, intelligence about the attitudes and options of their foreign counterparts, and an analysis of the impact of any likely dispute resolution. Then, after an agreement is concluded, government agencies will be expected to monitor compliance with it, even to "verify" compliance. These are the intelligence requirements whether negotiating a semiconductor trade agreement, a fisheries accord, or a Strategic Arms Reduction Treaty.

Although intelligence agencies have clearly mastered the art of meeting these requirements in the case of an arms control agreement—eventually developing a highly talented Arms Control Intelligence Support staff for this purpose—they do not generally get high marks for the quality of their support for trade negotiations. The intelligence community does provide serviceable background material for negotiations. As mentioned above, industry analysis is not one of its strengths, since it depends on whether the analysts at hand know the field and the issues. The Commerce Department or the CIA might happen to have an excellent expert on petroleum distribution, for instance, but might not be able to contribute much to an analysis of foreign industrial policies in steel. A more reliable asset of the CIA is its ability to add political insights. Biographical reports on foreign officials are valuable, as are portraits of the political economy of another system. In negotiations with the European Community over agriculture, senior officials needed information about infighting between the European Commission, the Council of Ministers, and the Council of Agricultural Ministers, or between Commission staff and the permanent representatives of the European Council; they also needed to grasp the vital byplay between the Commission's chairman and its directorates general handling external relations and agriculture, as well as the commissioners representing those policy briefs. Much of the background information is available from overt sources, though negotiators are sometimes vexed by what they consider the overclassification of material they hope to use in their talks. The challenge, as is so often the case, is to put together a tutorial that goes beyond banalities and says something useful about the dynamic of the negotiation.

Economic intelligence occasionally gives officials valuable information about the attitudes of their foreign counterparts in the talks. Officials place a tremendous importance on tactical intelligence of this kind, insight into the negotiating positions of the other side. Clandestine sources can yield just such insights. Several former trade negotiators preferred to see intelligence of this kind in raw form, convinced that they could do a better job of evaluating its significance than the analysts could. Whether this information actually affects the outcome of the negotiation is another question.

Such espionage against friendly governments also carries costs. Reportedly spurred by senior Clinton administration officials anxious to demonstrate more effort on economic intelligence, an espionage operation against the French government was launched to learn about its position in trade negotiations and counter France's own espionage against America. The operation failed. The French dramatized the failure and embarrassed the U.S. government. More successful efforts to use technical intelligence collection against Japanese trade negotiators were also disclosed, apparently by gloating or careless American officials, prompting a ritual and empty exchange of reproaches. Since such American efforts are readily justified by French and Japanese spying against the United States, such episodes raise two questions: First, are the intelligence benefits for America from such operations greater than the political and organizational costs of running them? Second, are there opportunities for the negotiation of reciprocal understandings to achieve mutual restraint so that all involved can concentrate their efforts against genuine enemies? American officials have not offered any public analysis of either issue.[13]

Intelligence agencies are considered weaker in their ability to analyze the effects of potential agreements. Again this problem stems from the variable quality of government information and expertise on particular industries. One veteran negotiator, former deputy trade representative Julius Katz, has commented that "most of the analytical reports I received were just not very good. At best they added little that was new or important." Katz added that when he reacted negatively to some, he was told "that those products were not intended for negotiators but for those lacking in expert knowledge of the subjects. My facetious retort was that the government could save itself a lot of money by subscribing to the *Financial Times* and the *Economist*."[14] The CIA gets somewhat better marks, however, from officials involved in trade issues in the Clinton administration.

Nor do intelligence agencies appear to have adapted fully to the growing burden of monitoring compliance with trade agreements. The 1992 Airbus accord, for example, contained detailed limits on the extent of foreign government subsidies in commercial aviation. But there is no evidence that either Congress or the executive branch has insisted on the systematic monitoring of compliance that would be customary if the agreement involved more traditional security interests of the United States. Government agencies might hope that embassy reporting can do the job of checking on compliance with the Airbus agreement, though the task transcends the writ of individual posts in Brussels, Bonn, or Paris. Or the government might hire a private consultant, such as Gelman Associates, to assess compliance for them. This may not be a satisfactory solution, however.

Some of the most well-publicized bilateral trade negotiations in recent years were those between the U.S. and Japan over semiconductors. In that case the private sector took primary responsibility for compiling and presenting intelligence about the problem. The U.S. negotiators relied heavily on an advisory group from industry to support their work. In 1985, frustrated with the results of bilateral discussions, the Semiconductor Industry Association filed a Section 301 petition and several antidumping cases, while the Commerce Department initiated another antidumping case. In 1986 Japan and the United States signed an agreement in exchange for dropping the 301 and antidumping cases.[15]

The agreement was designed to improve market access for foreign semiconductors in Japan and eliminate the dumping of Japanese chips in external markets. Japan agreed to provide significant amounts of information about industry costs in order to help determine whether its chips were being "dumped" in violation of the agreement. The U.S. trade negotiators then delegated the definition of noncompliant dumping to the Commerce Department, which devised a "foreign market value" methodology to measure appropriate pricing. Though discounted "forward pricing" to grab quick market share is common and sensible in the semiconductor industry, where the economies of scale are so important to reducing manufacturing costs and improving quality, there was no particular relationship between "foreign market value" and any economic theory that allowed for forward pricing.[16] One result was that, based on price data provided by U.S. businesses, the Japanese were quickly found to be "dumping" in violation of the Commerce criteria, especially in Asian markets where Japanese manufacturers were also competing against South Korean producers. This finding, as much as any other, led President Reagan in 1987 to impose sanctions on Japan for the first time in postwar history.

In the semiconductor case, U.S. intelligence agencies played a secondary role from start to finish. Industry alerted the government to the problem. The criteria for monitoring and determining compliance with the agreement was developed by the Commerce Department, a strong advocate within the government for action against Japan, and the data on prices were provided in large part by business. Industry representatives served on the verification advisory committee set up under the agreement. Major policy decisions by the president about U.S.-Japan relations were effectively driven by this process.[17]

Speaking on the value of intelligence to trade negotiators, Katz remarked that "intelligence support is a supplementary source of information and a check against the opinions and biases of officials. To be useful, it must be value-added." He concluded, "To be honest, if I had to grade the overall impact of intelligence on our trade policy and trade negotiations, the grade would be just above passing. Intelligence was helpful, but not critical to our operations."[18] Again, however, Clinton administration officials are inclined to be more positive in their recent appraisals of intelligence support.

TRADE SECRETS

There is no doubt that foreign governments conduct intelligence operations against American companies in order to steal proprietary trade secrets to benefit their own nations' firms.[19] The scale and depth of the threat of this foreign espionage is difficult to measure. The American Society of Industrial Security reported that in 1992 the thirty-two largest American companies lost data valued by them at $1.8 billion to theft. More than 70 percent of these cases, though, were not due to spying by foreigners, and more than half involved the defection of current or former employees.[20] The overall significance to the U.S. economy is quite small, though the impact on specific businesses could be catastrophic.[21]

Numbers may not give a complete picture because foreign intelligence services tend to target a relatively small number of companies at the edge of technological progress, in sectors like aerospace, biotechnology, nuclear energy, or telecommunications. Many methods are used. Documents are bought or stolen; foreign nationals are infiltrated to get inside information; Americans are hired as agents; foreign scientists are placed in research facilities; or front companies order illicit products and falsify end-user certificates. One Canadian report identifies Asia, followed by Western Europe, as the principal source of industrial or economic espionage against Canadian firms.[22] Director of Central Intelligence Robert Gates testified that nearly twenty governments have been involved in intelligence collection activities "that are detrimental to our economic interests at some level." Intelligence technologies are more widely available and, with economic opportunities depressed in the former Communist bloc,

Gates noted that "the reservoir of professionally trained intelligence mercenaries is growing."[23]

The U.S. intelligence community is committed to counterintelligence operations against such foreign operations, both directly and in lending assistance to American business. First the government must trace the activity back to its foreign government sponsor, often difficult since the primary actor may be a multinational business or trade organization. Second, Washington will want to find out what is being collected, the "shopping list." Here it is important to note that foreigners, like some American officials, are realizing that some of the greatest payoffs can be gained just from more effective processing of openly available material.

Third, U.S. intelligence agencies need to look at where the intelligence is actually being collected. Often foreign intelligence services prefer to work against American businessmen or companies when they are overseas, ideally in the foreign country itself where there are likely to be few legal repercussions if the spying is discovered. Fourth, the United States must consider how the information is being acquired. Services might try to elicit information unwittingly from American businesspeople, either through intermediaries or by technical means, bugging hotel rooms or monitoring a company's communications and computer system. Finally, U.S. counteragents can try to determine how countries disseminate the information they have gathered (usually through informal networks between officials and businesses).[24]

The CIA and FBI have primary responsibility for counterintelligence work. They can alert companies found to be targets of foreign intelligence collection. They also participate in an industrial briefing program to help companies develop better internal security procedures.[25] In 1992 the FBI brought Defense and Commerce Department experts into a reorganized counterintelligence division. "Unfortunately, since [that time] the FBI has virtually stripped the reconstituted counterintelligence division by reassigning half its personnel" to domestic criminal investigations.[26]

Legally, the government does not have powerful weapons to use against the industrial spies of foreign governments. Federal espionage laws require that the information being conveyed to the foreign government "relate to national defense" or be formally classified. The government must prove that information is being transmitted "to help a foreign nation or injure the United States."[27]

As mentioned in the introduction, some commentators, like former director of central intelligence Stansfield Turner, have argued that American intelligence agencies, like some of their foreign counterparts, should help companies with industrial espionage. While Turner was DCI, an interagency committee chaired by the general counsel of the Department of Commerce considered intelligence assistance to private firms. "The fact is that American firms do obtain information and judgments from CIA that are basically unclassified but not for attribution, through discussions with [Directorate of Intelligence] analysts and through the judicious disguising by State or Commerce officials of intelligence information in briefings of private firms."[28] The majority position was that such help could only be offered informally, through the policymaking departments rather than the spy agencies, and that no systematic program should be developed for this purpose.[29]

Nevertheless Senator Dennis DeConcini, the chairman of the Senate Select Committee on Intelligence, complained in August 1993 that "while this [government espionage for American companies] is a topic that has been debated at great length, we are not much further along than when we started in terms of having an overall policy. The Bush administration never came to grips with it, and, although the Clinton administration promised a review of the subject, we still have no overall policy guidance in this area."[30]

Yet there is no great pressure from American businesses to have the U.S. government help them ferret out their competitors' trade secrets. Testifying in that same August, a vice president of Boeing asked for help with countering foreign intelligence but stated flatly, "The Boeing Company is not dependent today, nor should we be in the future, on U.S. intelligence community efforts to acquire for us technological, marketing or economic information about our competitors." There were already enough market distortions, he added, and "we do not wish to introduce another whole category of potential disruptions to this tenuous international market structure."[31]

It is also hard to find evidence that businesses themselves are spending as much of their own resources as they possibly could in order to gather intelligence on competitors. There is some suspicion that, "to a large extent, some U.S. businesses are asking the government to do things that are entirely within these business's capabilities but not within their high priority needs or desires."[32] For their part, intelligence officers are not anxious to offer their services to business.

As one officer put it to the author, "I'm prepared to risk my life for my country. But I'm not ready to put my life on the line for GM."

Though the U.S. government can do things that would be unlawful for private businesses, Washington must also consider some legal issues. Domestic laws aside, one of the trade agreements signed in the Uruguay Round of multilateral trade negotiations dealt with protection of "trade-related intellectual property rights." This agreement, which represented a major goal for the United States in the Round, prohibits the theft of intellectual property, including trade secrets, and provides for the enforcement of these standards both within countries and at international borders, with specific provisions on injunctive relief and damages. Having fought so hard to get this accord, it would be extremely awkward for the U.S. government to be held liable for violating it.[33]

The United States would also encounter difficulty in determining which firms have no "American" connection and are thus safe and legitimate targets. The copious intelligence sharing that now takes place routinely with countries like Britain and Australia would need to be qualified and limited, despite the fact that neither of these countries is among the prime offenders in spying on the United States. There is some difficulty as well in disseminating the information impartially to all interested American companies without revealing sources and methods. The government must in addition be mindful of how the interests of other American citizens, in labor unions or consumer groups, for example, might be affected by the information it provides to businesses.

Perhaps hardest of all are the practical problems in setting an intelligence collection policy. Trade secrets can be very specific bits of information about an industrial process or design. Often the information only has value to a particular company for a particular operation. It is hard to imagine an intelligence mission that would not sweep up vast quantities of commercial information in the effort to find a single piece of useful data, a nugget that might not be spotted without potentially compromising involvement of private firms in the collection process itself. Finally, despite widespread knowledge about foreign espionage, many American businesses worry that their business relationships might be threatened if foreign counterparts became wary of systematic American technical intelligence efforts. Nor are many American companies ready to set a precedent that would legitimize even more ambitious foreign espionage efforts against them as retaliation for their government's activities.

The best answer for businesses, as well as for government agencies seeking to understand foreign practices in an industry, may be the persistent and methodical use of open sources. "Gray intelligence," legally available but perhaps not published or widely diffused, can be "extremely fruitful"[34] for a broad spectrum of consumers. "What should be kept in mind are the orders of magnitude: open information is at least ten times as abundant as grey information, and the latter in turn is at least ten times as abundant as secret or confidential information."[35] There appears to be enough scope for improvement in intelligence collection by legal means to put off, at least for the time being, pressures to engage the U.S. government in the conduct of industrial espionage.[36]

I Notes

Introduction

1. Stansfield Turner, "Intelligence for a New World Order," *Foreign Affairs* 70, no. 4 (Fall 1991): 150, 151.

2. Ibid., pp. 151–52 (emphasis added).

3. David L. Boren, "The Intelligence Community: How Crucial?" *Foreign Affairs* 71, no. 3 (Summer 1992): 52, 58.

4. Ibid., p. 58.

5. Remarks by Robert M. Gates to the Economic Club of Detroit, April 13, 1992; testimony of Gates before the Economic and Commercial Law Subcommittee, U.S. Congress, House, Judiciary Committee, 102d Cong., 2d sess., April 29, 1992.

6. Quotations are from Gates, remarks to the Economic Club of Detroit; the "twenty governments" figure is from Gates's testimony before the Economic and Commercial Law Subcommittee.

7. Quoted in Gerald F. Seib, "Business Secrets: Some Urge CIA to Go Further in Gathering Economic Intelligence," *Wall Street Journal*, August 4, 1992, p. A1.

8. U.S. Congress, Senate, *To Reorganize the United States Intelligence Community*, hearings before the Select Committee on Intelligence, S. 2198 and S. 421, 102d Cong., 2d sess., March 4, 1992, p. 248.

9. Bill Clinton, "A New Era of Peril and Promise," address before the diplomatic corps, Washington, D.C., January 18, 1993; Clinton, "American Leadership and Global Change," address at American University, February 26, 1993.

10. Michael Richards, "Clinton Administration Grapples with New CIA Role," *Christian Science Monitor*, March 22, 1993, p. 6.

11. R. James Woolsey, "The Future of Intelligence on the Global Frontier," address to the Executive Club of Chicago, November 19, 1993; see also Woolsey, opening statement to the Select Committee on Intelligence, U.S. Congress, Senate, 103d Cong., 2d sess., January 25, 1994.

12. For variations on this theme, see, for example, Jeffrey E. Garten, *A Cold Peace: America, Japan, Germany, and the Struggle for Supremacy* (New York: Times Books, 1992); Ira C. Magaziner and Robert B. Reich, *Minding America's Business: The Decline and Rise of the American Economy* (New York: Vintage Books, 1983); Laura D. Tyson, *Who's Bashing Whom: Trade Conflict in High-Technology Industries* (Washington, D.C.: Institute for International Economics, 1992); Lester Thurow, *Head to Head: The Coming Economic Battle among Japan, Europe, and America* (New York: William Morrow, 1992); Wayne Sandholtz et al., *The Highest Stakes: The Economic Foundations of the Next Security System* (New York: Oxford University Press, 1992); Edward N. Luttwak, *The Endangered American Dream: How to Stop the United States from Becoming a Third World Country and How to Win the Geo-Economic Struggle for Industrial Supremacy* (New York: Simon and Schuster, 1993); Samuel P. Huntington, "Why International Primacy Matters," *International Security* 17, no. 4 (Spring 1993). Garten became a top official in the Clinton administration's Commerce Department, Reich was named the administration's secretary of labor, Magaziner served as a senior White House staffer, and Tyson was chosen by Clinton as chairperson of the Council of Economic Advisers.

13. Paul Krugman, "Competitiveness: A Dangerous Obsession," *Foreign Affairs* 73, no. 2 (March/April 1994): 28, 30; see also Paul Krugman, *Peddling Prosperity: Economic Sense and Nonsense in the Age of Diminished Expectations* (New York: W. W. Norton, 1994).

14. U.S. Congress, *To Reorganize the United States Intelligence Community*, p. 198.

15. See Peter F. Cowhey and Jonathan D. Aronson, *Managing the World Economy: The Consequences of Corporate Alliances* (New York: Council on Foreign Relations Press, 1993); I. M. Destler, *American Trade Politics*, 2d ed. (Washington, D.C.: Institute for International Economics and The Twentieth Century Fund, 1992).

16. Ernest May has pointed out that the "virtual disappearance of the Soviet threat" was only one aspect of the new era. "A second change is the near disappearance of any comparable threat." See "Intelligence: Backing into the Future," *Foreign Affairs* 71, no. 3 (Summer 1992): 63, 64.

17. David L. Boren, address to the National Press Club, Washington, D.C., April 3, 1990.

18. Seib, "Business Secrets."

Chapter 1

1. Quotation provided from the Historical Intelligence Collection, Central Intelligence Agency, Langley, Virginia.

2. For the memoir of an intelligence officer studying the Japanese economy for the Board of Economic Warfare, see Shannon McCune, *Intelligence on the Economic Collapse of Japan in 1945* (Lanham, Md.: University Press of America, 1989).

3. Walter Laqueur, *A World of Secrets: The Uses and Limits of Intelligence* (New York: Basic Books, 1985), pp. 43–44.

4. Arthur B. Darling, *The Central Intelligence Agency: An Instrument of Government, to 1950* (University Park, Pa.: Pennsylvania State University Press, 1990), p. 35. This declassified history by the CIA's first historian was written in 1952–53.

5. Memorandum from Rear Admiral Sidney W. Souers to the National Intelligence Authority, "Progress Report on the Central Intelligence Group," June 7, 1946, pp. 5–6 (declassified); minutes of fourth meeting of the National Intelligence Authority, July 17, 1946, p. 1 (declassified). Both documents are reprinted in Michael Warner, ed., *CIA Cold War Records: The CIA Under Harry Truman* (Washington, D.C.: Central Intelligence Agency, 1994), pp. 41–52, 55–62.

6. National Security Council Intelligence Directive No. 1, "Duties and Responsibilites," December 12, 1947; National Security Council Intelligence Directive No. 3, "Coordination of Intelligence Production," January 13, 1948 (declassified).

7. Darling, *The Central Intelligence Agency*, p. 336.

8. National Security Council Intelligence Directive No. 15, "Coordination and Production of Foreign Economic Intelligence," June 13, 1951 (declassified).

9. Memorandum from Walter Bedell Smith to the National Security Council, "Report by the Director of Central Intelligence," April 23, 1952, pp. 1–2 (declassified), reprinted in Warner, *CIA Cold War Records*, pp. 457–58.

10. Ludwell Lee Montague, *General Walter Bedell Smith as Director of Central Intelligence: October 1950–February 1953* (University Park, Pa.: Pennsylvania State University Press, 1992), pp. 149–50. This recently declassified internal history was actually completed in 1971.

11. National Security Council Intelligence Directive No. 3, "Coordination of Intelligence Production," April 21, 1958 (declassified); see also Maurice Ernst, "Economic Intelligence in CIA," *Studies in Intelligence* 28, no. 4 (Winter 1984): 1, 3. (This is a declassified article from CIA's in-house journal.)

12. See William M. Leary, ed., *The Central Intelligence Agency: History and Documents* (Tuscaloosa, Ala.: University of Alabama Press, 1984), pp. 33–34

(a republishing of a historical work written by Anne Karalekas for the Church Committee in the 1970s); Montague, *General Walter Bedell Smith*, pp. 152–54.

13. Montague, *General Walter Bedell Smith*, pp. 151–52; Leary, *The Central Intelligence Agency*, p. 69. Millikan was succeeded by another effective and energetic head of ORR, a lawyer named Robert Amory, who in 1953 became the CIA's deputy director for intelligence.

14. Ernst, "Economic Intelligence in CIA," pp. 2–3.

15. Ibid., pp. 68–70. Robert McNamara was an appreciative and demanding consumer of the CIA's work, and he helped reduce Defense Department resistance to sharing its information. In 1965 CIA director McCone and Deputy Defense Secretary Cyrus Vance formally agreed that the CIA had primary responsibility for studies related to the cost and impact on resources of foreign military and space programs.

16. Ernst, "Economic Intelligence in CIA," pp. 4–5.

17. The State Department's former mandate to provide economic intelligence was revised to extend only to "countries of the Free World." The CIA's limited mandate for the "Sino-Soviet Bloc" was replaced by general authority to "produce economic, scientific, and technical intelligence." National Security Council Intelligence Directive No. 3, "Coordination of Intelligence Production," February 17, 1972 (declassified). See also Leary (Karalekas), *The Central Intelligence Agency*, p. 91. The State Department retained primary responsibility for overt collection of foreign economic information. National Security Council Intelligence Directive No. 2, "Coordination of Overt Collection Activities," February 17, 1972 (declassified).

18. See Ernst, "Economic Intelligence in CIA," p. 7; National Security Council Intelligence Directive No. 1, "Basic Duties and Responsibilities," February 17, 1972 (declassified).

19. "The Year of Economics," *Foreign Affairs* 52, no. 3 (April 1974).

20. United States Intelligence Board, "Key Intelligence Questions for FY 1976," quoted in William R. Johnson, "Clandestinity and Current Intelligence," *Studies in Intelligence* 20, no. 3 (Fall 1976): 15, 45 (declassified).

21. Ernst, "Economic Intelligence in CIA," p. 13.

22. Ibid., p. 16.

23. Edward A. Casey, Jr., "Annex C: State's Economic Role," in Report of the U.S. Department of State Management Task Force, *State 2000: A New Model for Managing Foreign Affairs* (Washington, D.C.: Department of State, 1992), p. 169.

24. U.S. Department of State Management Task Force, *State 2000*, pp. 38–39.

25. Casey, "Annex C: State's Economic Role," p. 164.

26. A less formal but highly important source of overseas "reporting" is provided by private U.S. citizens and organizations. The CIA's domestic contact unit, in its various forms, has played a leading role in systematically debriefing

Americans with important knowledge of foreign economic activities. "The domestic contact units have been highly responsive to the needs of economic intelligence analysts who in turn often took the trouble to provide very detailed guidance and requirements because the pay-off was evident and quick." Ernst, "Economic Intelligence in CIA," p. 16.

27. Johnson, "Clandestinity and Current Intelligence," p. 64.

28. Ibid., p. 56.

Chapter 2

1. Maurice Ernst, "Economic Intelligence in CIA," *Studies in Intelligence* 28, no. 4 (Winter 1984): 15 (declassified).

2. Ibid., pp. 15–16.

3. For a concise introduction, see Poul Hoest-Madsen, *Macroeconomic Accounts: An Overview*, IMF Pamphlet Series no. 29, International Monetary Fund, Washington, D.C., 1979.

4. As a public service, the CIA coordinates the preparation of country economic profiles made available to American businessmen, prospective investors, or interested academics. These unclassified profiles typically rely on reports produced by the nation in question itself and publications by international organizations. The Agency adds value by synthesizing this information with political and geographic material, using concise writing and good graphics aimed at a more general target audience. Recent profiles of Kazakhstan and Uzbekistan, for example, try to make the data more interesting by using comparable data for Turkey and Mexico as reference points. Another recent report, on Eastern Europe, cites no sources for its unclassified information and estimates. Central Intelligence Agency, "Eastern Europe: Reforms about to Pay Off," DI EUR 93-10013, August 1993 (originally prepared for a subcommittee of the Joint Economic Committee of Congress).

5. See, for example, the "Good Statistics Guide," *Economist*, September 7, 1991, p. 102.

6. See, for example, Jan van Tongeren, "Treatment of Exchange Rate Differentials in the National Accounts," in Vicente Galbis, ed., *The IMF's Statistical Systems in Context of Revision of the United Nations' A System of National Accounts* (Washington, D.C.: International Monetary Fund, 1991), pp. 63, 82–84 (using the example of Venezuela). See also Irving B. Kravis, Alan Heston, and Robert Summers, *World Product and Income: International Comparisons of Real Gross Product*, United Nations International Comparison Project (Baltimore: Johns Hopkins University Press, 1982).

7. See, for example, World Bank, *World Debt Tables 1993–94: External Finance for Developing Countries*, vol. 1 (Washington, D.C.: World Bank, 1993), pp. 153–62.

8. For a sample product, see *Russian Economic Reform: Crossing the Threshold of Structural Change*, World Bank Country Study, Washington, D.C., 1992.

9. Ibid., pp. 73–75.

10. Paul M. Kennedy, "Great Britain Before 1914," in Ernest R. May, ed., *Knowing One's Enemies: Intelligence Assessment before the Two World Wars* (Princeton, N.J.: Princeton University Press, 1986), pp. 180–81.

11. Ibid., p. 199. "Britain declared war in 1914 upon a country which supplied her with the greater part of her requirements for machine tools, ball bearings, magnetos, and optical and scientific equipment, not to mention the chemicals necessary for high explosives and drugs!"

12. Compare the discussion of Britain's Industrial Intelligence Centre with the description of British estimates of the Luftwaffe given by Donald Cameron Watt, "British Intelligence and the Coming of the Second World War in Europe," in May, *Knowing One's Enemies*, pp. 244–46, 255–60, 265, 268–69; see also Angelo Codevilla, "Comparative Historical Experience of Doctrine and Organization," in Roy Godson, ed., *Intelligence Requirements for the 1980s: Analysis and Estimates* (Washington, D.C.: National Strategy Information Center, 1980), pp. 20–22.

13. Williamson Murray, *The Change in the European Balance of Power, 1938–1939: The Path to Ruin* (Princeton, N.J.: Princeton University Press, 1984), pp. 257–58; see also pp. 160–61. The British were cautious about both the probable course of a war and the effectiveness of a naval blockade. French intelligence was better informed on German shortages, and their intelligence officials apparently realized that "if the Germans were prepared to exhaust their stockpiles of raw materials, their self-induced economic crisis would necessitate continued territorial expansion." Robert Young, "French Military Intelligence and Nazi Germany: 1938–1939," in May, *Knowing One's Enemies*, p. 291.

14. Michael Geyer, "National Socialist Germany: The Politics of Information," in May, *Knowing One's Enemies*, p. 316.

15. Quoted in "Sunshine and Shadow: The CIA and the Soviet Economy," Case C16-91-1096.0, Kennedy School of Government, Harvard University, 1991, p. 2. Unless otherwise cited, the following account of the CIA's work on the Soviet economy is drawn from the material compiled in this case study.

16. Testimony of George Kolt, director of the CIA's Office of Soviet Analysis, U.S. Congress, Joint Economic Committee, Global Economic and Technological Change, hearings of the Subcommittee on Technology and National Security, 102d Cong., 1st sess., May 16, 1991, p. 155; see also

Michael Alexeev and Lee Walker, eds., *Estimating the Size of the Soviet Economy: Summary of a Meeting* (Washington, D.C.: National Academy Press, 1991).

17. Central Intelligence Agency, "Domestic Stresses on the Soviet System," *National Intelligence Estimate*, NIE 11-18-85, November 1985, p. 19 (declassified). The CIA began to perceive a leveling off of Soviet defense spending in the early 1980s, though its claims were heavily caveated because of disagreements from other agencies during the Reagan administration. Nevertheless, in the summer of 1988, the Agency was projecting unilateral Soviet defense cuts six months before they were first announced by Mikhail Gorbachev. Central Intelligence Agency, "Soviet National Security Policy: Responses to the Changing Military and Economic Environment," intelligence memorandum, DI SOVA, June 1988 (declassified).

18. "CIA and the Fall of the Soviet Empire: The Politics of 'Getting It Right,'" Case C16-94-1251.0, Kennedy School of Government, Harvard University, 1994.

19. See testimony (originally in closed session) of Martin Petersen, deputy director of CIA's Office of East Asian Analysis, in U.S. Congress, Joint Economic Committee, Global Economic and Technological Change, hearings of the Subcommittee on Technology and National Security, 102d Cong., 1st sess., June 28, 1991, pp. 459–61, and enclosed CIA report, "The Chinese Economy in 1990 and 1991: Uncertain Recovery," Appendix A (on problems in GNP estimation).

20. Young, "French Military Intelligence and Nazi Germany," p. 291. Though Hitler was driven by a world vision that transcended these economic factors, the French argument accurately identified a motive, the quest for natural resources, that indeed formed an important part of Hitler's outlook.

21. Robert Graham, *Iran: The Illusion of Power* (New York: St. Martin's Press, 1979), pp. 77–103; Mohsen Milani, *The Makings of Iran's Islamic Revolution* (Boulder, Colo.: Westview Press, 1988), pp. 162–75; Barry Rubin, *Paved with Good Intentions: The United States and Iran* (New York: Penguin, 1984), pp. 154–72.

22. Jahangir Amuzegar, *The Dynamics of the Iranian Revolution: The Pahlavis' Triumph and Tragedy* (Binghamton: State University of New York Press, 1991), p. 191.

23. See Graham, *Iran: The Illusion of Power*, pp. 242–45; Homa Katouzian, *The Political Economy of Modern Iran: Despotism and Pseudo-Modernism* (New York: New York University Press, 1981), pp. 256–61, 334–35. Katouzian demonstrates that growth was overwhelmingly concentrated in services rather than new industry, indicating both maldistribution and waste in the government's investment policies.

24. See Jack A. Goldstone, *Revolution and Rebellion in the Early Moc* *World* (Berkeley, Calif.: University of California Press, 1991), pp. 472–7

also Ervand Abrahamian, "Structural Causes of the Iranian Revolution," in Jack A. Goldstone, ed., *Revolutions: Theoretical, Comparative, and Historical Studies*, 2d ed. (Fort Worth: Harcourt Brace, 1994), pp. 129–32; Jerrold D. Green, "Countermobilization in the Iranian Revolution," in Goldstone, *Revolutions*, p. 142 (emphasizing new rural migrants to urban areas as "foot-soldiers" of the revolution).

25. Central Intelligence Agency, Office of Economic Research, April 17, 1975, p. 5 (declassified); see also, for example, Central Intelligence Agency, "Economic Intelligence Weekly," ER EIW 75-19, May 14, 1975, pp. 4–6 (declassified).

26. U.S. Embassy to Iran, "End of Tour Report: The Outlook for Iran," Tehran A-170 (airgram), July 30, 1975, p. 1 (declassified), see also p. 9 for a more detailed illustration of the same ambiguity. For a similar line, see U.S. Embassy to Iran, "Iran's Modernizing Monarchy: A Political Assessment," Tehran 6776, July 1, 1976 (declassified).

27. Memorandum from Blee to Ambassador Little, "Part I, Reporting Assessment—FOCUS Iran," November 4, 1976, p. 4.

28. "Iran," transition briefing paper, Department of State, January 3, 1977. The paper's discussion of Iran's economy had the same confident tone.

29. William H. Sullivan, *Mission to Iran* (New York: W. W. Norton, 1981), pp. 30–31.

30. Ibid., pp. 68–69.

31. Anthony Parsons, *The Pride and the Fall: Iran 1974–1979* (London: Jonathan Cape, 1984), pp. 15, 45–46 (emphasis added).

32. See "The Fall of the Shah of Iran," Case C16-86-794.0, Kennedy School of Government, Harvard University, 1986, p. 9; see also Zachary Karabell, "'Inside the US Espionage Den': The US Embassy and the Fall of the Shah," *Intelligence and National Security* 8, no. 1 (January 1993): 44.

33. "Prelude to War: US Policy toward Iraq, 1988–1990," Case C16-94-1245.0, Kennedy School of Government, Harvard University, 1994. Unless otherwise cited, the following discussion of Iraq is drawn from this case study.

34. It is possible that any effort to rally the Gulf states behind a new strategy of confronting and containing Iraq would have failed. Perhaps it took Iraq's invasion to convince the Gulf states that they could actually be attacked by a brother Arab leader. Perhaps it took Operation Desert Storm to convince the Arab world that an American deterrent was possible or credible. Perhaps the invasion of Kuwait was even fortunate from a long-term perspective because it gave other states a chance to disable Iraq's weapons of mass destruction during and after the war. None of these points should prevent using this case to consider how the United States could have developed the best possi-
•le assessments of Iraq's economic dilemma and future plans.

5. David French, *British Economic and Strategic Planning, 1905–1915* •don: George Allen & Unwin, 1982), p. 28. The matter was studied

several times between 1908 and 1914, and Foreign Office diplomats, such as Sir Francis Oppenheimer, accurately concluded that Germany could overcome temporary shortages if it could rely on trade with neighboring neutral states. The Cabinet decided it would have to ration imports to the neutrals to regulate their ability to export surpluses to Germany, but likely American reaction was not considered, and the plans remained "riddled with elements of wishful thinking" (p. 30). Many of the strategic premises were based on mistaken analogies from the experience of the Napoleonic Wars.

36. See Alfred von Tirpitz, My Memoirs, vol. 2 (New York: Dodd, Mead & Co., 1919), pp. 137–53, 189–206; Ernest R. May, The World War and American Isolation, 1914–1917 (Cambridge, Mass.: Harvard University Press, 1959), pp. 113–75, 214–17, 228–31, 240–45, 404–15; John Terraine, Business in Great Waters: The U-Boat Wars, 1916–1945 (London: Leo Cooper, 1989), pp. 12–15.

37. It is possible to argue, from the available documents, that at the beginning of November 1956, before London had agreed to the UN cease-fire, Eisenhower was concentrating principally—though not exclusively—on political instruments (maneuvering in the UN, Soviet missile rattling, the postponement of Prime Minister Anthony Eden's visit to America) as the British cabinet was being swayed by Harold Macmillan's exaggerated report of imminent financial catastrophe. But the CIA's estimates spent little time judging British economic vulnerabilities. See generally Diane B. Kunz, The Economic Diplomacy of the Suez Crisis (Chapel Hill, N.C.: University of North Carolina Press, 1991), esp. pp. 131–33.

38. See "The Reagan Administration and the Soviet Pipeline Embargo," Case C16-91-1016.0, Kennedy School of Government, Harvard University, 1991.

39. Testimony of R. Richard Newcomb, director of Treasury's Office of Foreign Assets Control, U.S. Congress, House, Banking Committee, Economic Impact of the Persian Gulf Crisis, 101st Cong., 2d sess., November 27, 1990, pp. 56–61.

40. See, for example, Gary Clyde Hufbauer and Jeffrey J. Schott, Economic Sanctions in Support of Foreign Policy Goals (Washington, D.C.: Institute for International Economics, 1983).

41. Testimony of Gary Hufbauer, U.S. Congress, Senate, Foreign Relations Committee, U.S. Policy in the Persian Gulf, 101st Cong., 2d sess., December 4, 1990, p. 61. The same hearing includes the testimony of Schlesinger, Galbraith, McNamara, and Kipper; see also Graham Fuller's testimony, U.S. Congress, House, Foreign Affairs Committee, and Joint Economic Committee, The Persian Gulf Crisis, 101st Cong., 2d sess., December 11, 1990, pp. 440–43.

42. Testimony of William Webster, U.S. Congress, House, Armed Services Committee, Crisis in the Persian Gulf: Sanctions, Diplomacy and War, 101st Cong., 2d sess., December 5, 1990, p. 112–13.

43. See Wyland Leadbetter, Jr., and Stephen Bury, "Prelude to Desert Storm: The Politicization of Intelligence," *International Journal of Intelligence and Counterintelligence* 6, no. 1 (Spring 1993): 43, 46. The authors interviewed Webster and the analysts who had worked on his testimony. On the *New York Times* story, see Michael Wines, "Head of CIA Sees Iraqis Weakening in 3–9 Months," *New York Times*, December 6, 1990, p. A1. It is possible that Wines was misled by Webster's inadvertently dropping the word "fully" from the fourth conclusion in his prepared testimony. Compare George Lardner, Jr., "CIA Director: Sanctions Need Nine More Months," *Washington Post*, December 6, 1990, p. A43.

44. Testimony of William Webster, *Crisis in the Persian Gulf*, p. 115.

45. Leadbetter and Bury, "Prelude to Desert Storm," pp. 47, 50–51. As a reader of the intelligence community's assessments on this issue from August 1990 onward, I can attest to the consistency of the public statements with the judgments provided in classified estimates during the crisis. For the mistaken contrary allegation, see Sidney Blumenthal, "Whose Agents?" *New Republic*, February 11, 1991, p. 20.

46. Nor did they, much less the CIA, discuss the political implications of maintaining sanctions once it became clear that, to be truly effective, the sanctions would necessarily cause massive suffering among the innocent civilian population before they affected the privileged leadership and military elites. The vast majority of Iraqi civilian deaths attributed to the Gulf crisis were actually caused by sanctions, not by the Allied bombing. The humanitarian dilemma in maintaining sanctions also gained attention in the recent case of Haiti.

CHAPTER 3

1. Melvyn P. Leffler, *A Preponderance of Power: National Security, the Truman Administration, and the Cold War* (Stanford, Calif.: Stanford University Press, 1992), p. 64 (discussing the Potter-Hyndley report presented to Truman in June 1945). All of Truman's advisers agreed with the report's conclusions, and Truman promptly wrote to Churchill on the consequent need to restore production of German coal.

2. Richard Funkhouser, "Discussions with British on AIOC" (September 14, 1950), quoted in Ethan Kapstein, *The Insecure Alliance: Energy Crises and Western Politics Since 1944* (New York: Oxford University Press, 1990), p. 78.

3. See James A. Bill and William R. Louis, eds., *Musaddiq, Iranian Nationalism, and Oil* (Austin: University of Texas Press, 1988); Kermit Roosevelt, *Countercoup: The Struggle for the Control of Iran* (New York: McGraw-Hill, 1979).

4. See the report of Arthur Flemming, director of the Office of Defense Mobilization, and the responses of Eisenhower and John Foster Dulles in the memorandum of discussion, 292d Meeting of the National Security Council, August 9, 1956, in Department of State, *Foreign Relations of the United States* [hereafter *FRUS*], *1955–1957*, vol. 16, pp. 171–74. Though the CIA was supervising preparation of several special national intelligence estimates during the Suez crisis, these contain little information about world oil supplies. The CIA was not yet in the business of providing such information, and there is little evidence that the State Department was providing it instead. The Interior Department, of course, had little direct data of its own on oil production and refining in Saudi Arabia, Kuwait, Mexico, or Venezuela.

5. See, for example, the extensive and clear planning for use of American oil leverage evident in the memorandum of discussion, 303d Meeting of the National Security Council, November 8, 1956, in *FRUS*, *1955–1957*, vol. 16, pp. 1070–77. Intelligence to inform these judgments came from the Middle East Emergency Committee, a group of officials from oil companies engaged in foreign operations created by the Foreign Petroleum Supply Committee. This group in turn coordinated responses with emergency committees created by the OEEC (the predecessor to the OECD).

6. See Kapstein, *The Insecure Alliance*, p. 119. The Texas Railroad Commission was then headed by General Ernest Thompson.

7. Ibid., p. 144.

8. Central Intelligence Agency, "Impact on Western Europe and Japan of a Denial of Arab Oil," intelligence memorandum, RR IM 67–35, June 7, 1967 (declassified).

9. Central Intelligence Agency, "Supplement to Arab-Israeli Situation Report," intelligence memorandum, June 10, 1967 (declassified); see also Kapstein, *The Insecure Alliance*, pp. 144–47.

10. Remarks by Robert Gates to the Economic Club of Detroit, April 13, 1992. These analysts were concentrated in a new branch of the Office of Economic Research in the Directorate of Intelligence.

11. Maxwell Taylor, "The Legitimate Claims of National Security," *Foreign Affairs* 52, no. 3 (April 1974): 577, 593; Raymond Vernon, "An Interpretation," *Daedalus* 104, no.4 (Fall 1975): 1, 13.

12. Henry Kissinger, *Years of Upheaval* (Boston: Little, Brown and Company, 1982), p. 871.

13. Task Force Report, U.S. Cabinet Task Force on Oil Import Controls, quoted in Kapstein, *The Insecure Alliance*, pp. 156–57.

14. Joel Darmstadter and Hans H. Landsberg, "The Economic Background," *Daedelus* 104, no. 4 (Fall 1975): 15, 22–35.

15. Testimony of James Akins, former State Department oil expert and ambassador to Saudi Arabia, U.S. Congress, Joint Economic Committee

Multinational Oil Companies and OPEC, hearings of the Subcommittee on Energy, 94th Cong., 2d sess., June 1976, p. 173.

16. Quoted in Daniel Yergin, *The Prize: The Epic Quest for Oil, Money and Power* (New York: Simon and Schuster, 1991), p. 59. One of Nixon's first exposures to national security deliberations at the top was his participation in the NSC discussions about Iran in the first days of the new Eisenhower administration.

17. Kissinger, *Years of Upheaval*, p. 871.

18. On the varying reserve projections, see John M. Blair, *The Control of Oil* (New York: Pantheon, 1976), p. 11.

19. Morris A. Adelman, "Is the Oil Shortage Real?" *Foreign Policy*, no. 9 (Winter 1972–73): 69, 77 (emphasis in original). Adelman's views, concentrated on the distorting influence of the OPEC cartel, are often contrasted with another widely noted article by James Akins, who seemed to argue that the supply shortage was real. The "debate" between these two articles seems occasioned more by their sharply contrasting titles than by the substance of their arguments. See James Akins, "The Oil Crisis: This Time the Wolf Is Here," *Foreign Affairs* 51, no. 3 (April 1973): 462–90. This flawed perception of Akins's thesis was quite influential, and Akins himself encouraged the focus on absolute supply shortages in other public remarks. Yet in his article Akins argued that the supply shortage was only real outside of the cartel. Both he and Adelman shared a common desire to encourage government action to help the oil companies break the cartel's monopoly position.

20. Darmstadter and Landsberg, "The Economic Background," pp. 32–35; see also Joseph Kalt, *The Economics and Politics of Oil Price Regulation* (Cambridge, Mass.: MIT Press, 1981). Part of the reason for relaxing import controls was, oddly, a desire to make the United States more self-sufficient by hoarding the finite U.S. oil reserves in the ground. Aside from the failure to see that hoarding the oil strengthened the OPEC cartel and therefore aggravated the self-sufficiency problem, the companies had not built the production capacity to exploit this "stockpile" in a crisis.

21. Morris Adelman, U.S. Congress, House, Committee on Government Operations, *Alternatives to Dealings with OPEC*, hearings before Environment, Energy, and Natural Resources Subcommittee, 96th Cong., 1st sess., June 1979, pp. 208–9.

22. Kissinger, *Years of Upheaval*, pp. 873–74. Daniel Yergin has called particular attention to the problem of inadequate information. "In the midst of the cutbacks, there was great uncertainty about how much oil was available, combined with an inevitable tendency to exaggerate the loss. The confusion resulted from the contradictory and fragmentary nature of information and from the massive disruption of established supply channels, all overlaid by rabid and violent emotions." Yergin, *The Prize*, p. 614.

23. Quoted in Blair, *The Control of Oil*, p. 266. OPEC's cut in production, interestingly enough, had been preceded by record-high levels of production

during the months just before the crisis, so that world inventories and stockpiles were relatively high when the war began. After a sharp cut in October, production by OPEC countries (including its Arab members, led by Saudi Arabia) was climbing rapidly again by November, contrary to the cartel's public rhetoric at the time. See the tables in Central Intelligence Agency, Office of Economic Research, "International Oil Developments: Statistical Survey," November 13, 1975 (declassified). There is no evidence that the CIA was able to provide this vital, reassuring information at the time, however.

24. Adelman's celebrated article, published nearly a year before the crisis, commented: "The OPEC nations may wish to deny oil to some particular country. But if some or even most of them do so, the capacity of others will be available, and at most there will be a reshuffling of customers. Yet let us now assume that all OPEC nations unite to boycott one country. They must also prevent diversion of supplies of crude oil and products from other consuming countries to the victim. Yet nobody has suggested why the non-OPEC nations should join in this profitless persecution. Moreover, non-OPEC oil is large relative to a single consuming country's needs." Adelman, "Is the Oil Shortage Real?" pp. 100–101.

25. Maurice Ernst, "Economic Intelligence in CIA," *Studies in Intelligence* 28, no. 4 (Winter 1984): 7.

26. Ibid.

27. Central Intelligence Agency, *The International Energy Situation: Outlook to 1985* (Washington, D.C.: Government Printing Office, 1977).

28. Testimony of Maurice Ernst, U.S. Congress, House, *Intelligence on the World Energy Outlook and Its Policy Implications*, hearings before the Permanent Select Committee on Intelligence, 96th Cong., 1st sess., October 17, 1979, p. 4.

29. Ernst, "Economic Intelligence in CIA," p. 10.

30. "Faced with uncertainty, the immediate response of the Western allies to the Iranian shutdown was one of panic and a scramble for available supplies. . . . Two economists have neatly summed up the alliance experience during the Iranian revolution. 'In 1979,' they wrote, 'the industrialised countries of the OECD inflicted on themselves one of the most disastrous events in their economic history.' A small supply shortfall caused a 150 percent increase in oil prices, with severe economic implications for the countries of North and South alike." Kapstein, *The Insecure Alliance*, pp. 186, 191 (quoting Daniel Badger and Robert Belgrave).

31. Testimony of Maurice Ernst, *Intelligence on the World Energy Outlook*, p. 4.

32. In 1979 the Department of Energy's Energy Information Administration (EIA) prepared its own forecasts for energy supply, which were slightly more optimistic than the CIA's, seeing serious supply shortages as emerging by 1985 rather than by 1982. The CIA's methodology was to

analyze the production policies of each major producer on an individual basis, looking at geological, technical, and political factors. EIA did not make a country-by-country analysis but instead relied on econometric modeling that treated oil price as the major factor in determining supply over the long-term. After examining these estimates and receiving expert testimony on them and their methodologies (including from the Office of Technology Assessment), the Oversight Subcommittee of the House Permanent Select Committee on Intelligence (chaired by Les Aspin) commended CIA's forecast, found broad agreement with it, and praised the warning of an imminent oil shortage leading to sharp price increases. See Subcommittee Report, "Intelligence on the World Energy Future," in U.S. Congress, *Intelligence on the World Energy Outlook*, pp. 223–31.

33. Central Intelligence Agency, *Prospects for Soviet Oil Production* (Washington, D.C.: Government Printing Office, 1977).

34. Quoted in Walter Laqueur, *A World of Secrets: The Uses and Limits of Intelligence* (New York: Basic Books, 1985), p. 52.

35. Ernst, "Economic Intelligence in CIA," p. 10.

36. See Kapstein, *The Insecure Alliance*, pp. 198–99; Robert J. Lieber, "Oil and Power after the Gulf War," *International Security* 17, no. 1 (Summer 1992): 155, 163–66, 172, 174.

37. The Department of Energy's formal intelligence operation reportedly concentrates primarily on nuclear and proliferation-related topics, not on oil. Jeffrey Richelson, *The U.S. Intelligence Community*, 2d ed. (Cambridge, Mass.: Ballinger, 1989), pp. 133–34.

38. Kapstein, *The Insecure Alliance*, p. 181 (quoting Daniel Badger).

39. Lieber, "Oil and Power after the Gulf War," p. 159.

40. "There is no standard definition of a strategic material, but most definitions state that the material is necessary for producing military and essential civilian goods and services and that requirements may exceed domestic and foreign supplies in the event of supply disruptions." Raymond F. Mikesell, *Stockpiling Strategic Materials: An Evaluation of the National Program* (Washington, D.C.: American Enterprise Institute, 1986), p. 2.

41. For a relatively sophisticated analysis of nonfuel minerals (by a career intelligence officer), see Kenneth A. Kessel, *Strategic Minerals: U.S. Alternatives* (Washington, D.C.: National Defense University Press, 1990). He points out that "although some private studies, many press articles, and even congressional testimony often cite specific military or civilian vulnerabilities, these vulnerabilities . . . are often based on unrealistic assumptions or scenarios" (p. 75). For an exposition of the economic view that hardly any resource will ever be truly scarce, see Julian L. Simon, *The Ultimate Resource* (Princeton, N.J.: Princeton University Press, 1981). For more worried perspectives, see, for example, Marc D. Lax, *Selected Strategic Minerals: The Impending Crisis* (Lanham, Md.: University Press of America, 1991); Hanns

Maull, *Strategische Rohstoffe: Risiken fuer die wirtschaftliche Sicherheit des Westens* (Munich: Oldenbourg, 1988).

42. Compare, for example, Peter H. Gleick, "Water and Conflict: Fresh Water Resources and International Security," *International Security* 18, no. 1 (Summer 1993): 79–112; Thomas F. Homer-Dixon, "On the Threshold: Environmental Changes as Causes of Acute Conflict," *International Security* 16, no. 2 (Fall 1991): 76–116; and Raymond Vernon, *Two Hungry Giants: The United States and Japan in the Quest for Oil and Ores* (Cambridge, Mass.: Harvard University Press, 1983).

43. Gleick, "Water and Conflict," pp. 98–99. Further, he states, "in many regions of the world, water resource data are limited or unreliable, making the quantification of these indices [measuring comparative supply, demand, hydroelectric use, pumping of ground water, and hydrologic conditions] difficult. . . . most data on water use do not differentiate between water withdrawn and water *consumed*. Better data on water consumption are needed" (notes 52, 54). On the methodological problems that have arisen in forecasting demand for water, see also Organization for Economic Cooperation and Development, Environment Directorate, "Water Demand Forecasting in OECD Countries," *OECD Environment Monographs* no. 7, Paris, 1987.

44. Report of the Council on Environmental Quality and the Department of State, *The Global 2000 Report to the President: Entering the Twenty-first Century*, vol. 1 (New York: Penguin Books, 1980), p. 461.

45. Ibid., p. 464.

46. Ibid., pp. 461–78.

47. Ibid., pp. 479–80, 481.

Chapter 4

1. Remarks by William Webster to the Los Angeles World Affairs Council, September 19, 1989.

2. Anne Y. Kester and Panel on International Capital Transactions of the National Research Council, *Following the Money: U.S. Finance in the Global Economy*, Summary (Washington, D.C.: National Academy Press, 1995), p. 2; see also Lois Stekler, "Adequacy of International Transactions and Position Data for Policy Coordination," *NBER Working Paper* no. 2844, National Bureau for Economic Research, Washington, D.C., 1989.

3. See Anne Y. Kester, ed., *Behind the Numbers: U.S. Trade in the World Economy* (Washington, D.C.: National Academy Press, 1992), pp. 170–71, citing Lois Stekler, "The Statistical Discrepancy in the U.S. International Transactions Accounts: Sources and Suggested Remedies," *International Finance Discussio* Papers no. 401, Board of Governors of the Federal Reserve System, 1991.

4. Kester, et al., *Following the Money*, p. 4. Though the Treasury requires persons taking more than $10,000 in currency out of the country to file a Currency and Monetary Investment Report with the Customs Service, compliance with this requirement is low and enforcement is relatively weak, largely due to resource constraints. See, for example, United States General Accounting Office, *Money Laundering: U.S. Efforts to Fight It Are Threatened by Currency Smuggling*, GAO/GGD-94-73, 1994. See also Associated Press, "California Being Enriched by Underground and Illegal Money," *New York Times*, April 10, 1994, p. 17.

5. Much of the underreporting is in portfolio transactions, the area where international capital flows are growing fastest. One indication of the size of reporting discrepancies is found in comparing data from the Treasury International Capital (TIC) system with that compiled by the Bank for International Settlements (BIS). TIC maintains data on the foreign bank and nonbank claims and liabilities of U.S. nonbanks. BIS compiles data on the U.S. nonbank claims and liabilities of foreign banks. In theory, the BIS number should be significantly lower, since it excludes American nonbank claims and liabilities of foreign nonbanks, while the TIC base would include such transactions. But between 1986 and 1989 TIC flow data averaged $20–25 billion *less* per year than data from the BIS; Kester, et al, *Following the Money*. Evidently U.S. nonbanks are not reporting very thoroughly to the TIC. Subsequent estimates made by the Commerce Department, the Federal Reserve Bank of New York, and the Treasury point to underreporting of onshore and offshore capital transactions by both foreigners and Americans apparently amounting to well in excess of $170 billion between January 1992 and May 1993. If American bank deposits overseas were underestimated by such large amounts, then multibillion-dollar underestimates entered the balance of payments totals for U.S. interest earnings from abroad. Lois Stekler, "Accuracy of U.S. Data on International Capital Flows," Board of Governors of the Federal Reserve System, February 1990; see also Lois Stekler and Guy V. G. Stevens, "The Adequacy of U.S. Direct Investment Data," in Peter Hooper and J. David Richardson, eds., *International Economic Transactions: Issues in Measurement and Empirical Research* (Chicago: University of Chicago Press, 1991); Michael Ulan and William Dewald, "The U.S. Net International Investment Position: Misstated and Misunderstood," in James A. Dorn and William A. Niskanen, eds., *Dollars, Deficits, and Trade* (Norwell, Mass.: Kluwer Academic Publishers, 1989).

6. Kester, et al., *Following the Money*. There are few, if any, good estimates on the scale of these complex networks of interdependence or of how they might distort the otherwise predictable effects of government policy moves, though it is commonly assumed that markets have become more sensitive and volatile.

7. Ibid. To give a sense of scale, U.S. statistics show that in 1992 foreign-s sold or purchased $5.3 trillion in U.S. securities, while Americans sold

or purchased only $1.3 trillion in foreign securities. Yet the statistics also report that U.S. residents earned $16.5 billion more on their investments abroad than foreigners earned on their total investments in the United States.

8. The IMF's 1993 *Balance of Payments Statistics Yearbook* indicates that recorded capital inflows exceeded outflows by an average of $120 billion every year between 1989 and 1992. In theory the two numbers should match (unless all the money is coming from nonreporting countries like North Korea, which seems unlikely).

9. Kester, et al., *Following the Money* presents the NRC panel's conclusions. It is a sequel to the NRC's earlier work focusing largely on trade data, Kester, *Behind the Numbers.*

10. Defenders of the Bonn summit approach attribute the subsequent upsurge in inflation to unforeseen developments such as the sharp rise in oil prices after the Iranian revolution. But even to such defenders, the episode highlights the uncertainties about available information. "While this criticism of the Bonn summit agreement can be dismissed, it raises a more general question. Is the future so unpredictable that discretionary policy actions such as those agreed in 1978 will often backfire?" Robert Solomon, background paper in *Partners in Prosperity: The Report of the Twentieth Century Fund Task Force on the International Coordination of National Economic Policies* (New York: Priority Press Publications, 1991), p. 56.

11. Quoted in "What the Market Will Bear: The CIA and the International Debt Crisis," Case C16-91-1032.0, Kennedy School of Government, Harvard University, 1991. Subsequent discussions of the LDC debt episode are drawn from the information compiled in this case study.

12. This portion of the paper relies on the selection of government documents obtained by the Senate Banking Committee and released in declassified form on June 29, 1995. A memo from Rudiger Dornbusch to the Federal Reserve Board of New York, "Stabilization, Reform, and No-Growth" (May 1994) summarizes the pessimists' argument. But staff of the New York Fed had already accepted most of Dornbusch's premises some time earlier.

13. For example, memo from OASIA, "Background and Talking Points: Macroeconomic Developments," May 1, 1994; Memo, Lawrence Summers to Lloyd Bentsen, "Briefing for Your Meeting with U.S. Ambassador to Mexico James Jones," Department of the Treasury, May 2, 1994; Memo, Jeffrey Shafer to Lawrence Summers, "Dinner with Mexican Finance Officials," Department of the Treasury, May 6, 1994.

14. Memo, Piggott to Bennett, "The Mexican Peso," Federal Reserve Bank of New York, June 3, 1994.

15. Memo, Siegman to Alan Greenspan and Alan Blinder, "The Implied Probability of a Peso Devaluation," Federal Reserve Board, August 19, 1994. Lawrence Summers later acknowledged that, "Contrary to much that has been said, figures on Mexican *tesobono* debt were freely, immediately and

publicly available throughout 1994. And while foreign exchange reserves figures were provided irregularly, contemporaneous market reports contained quite accurate estimates." Lawrence Summers, "Summers on Mexico: Ten Lessons to Learn," *Economist*, December 23, 1995, pp. 46, 47.

16. Letter from Senators Arlen Specter and J. Robert Kerrey to Senators Alfonse D'Amato and Paul Sarbanes, U.S. Congress, Senate, Select Committee on Intelligence, SSCI #95-1327, March 29, 1995.

17. Council on Foreign Relations Task Force, *Lessons of the Mexican Peso Crisis* (New York: Council on Foreign Relations Press, 1996), p. 27. Unfortunately, this report contains little information about U.S. policymaking before or during the Mexico crisis.

18. For fairly typical examples of the staff-level analysis in Treasury, see memo, Lissakers to Jeffrey Shafer, "Mexican Update," Department of the Treasury, August 31, 1994; memo, Geithner to Lloyd Bentsen, "Briefing for Your Luncheon with Dr. Aspe," Department of the Treasury, October 27, 1994; Jeffrey Shafer to Lloyd Bentsen, "Bank of Mexico Intervenes to Support a Weakening Peso," Department of the Treasury, November 18, 1994.

19. Memo Siegman to Alan Greenspan, "Background Material for October 20 Visit by President-elect Zedillo's Adviser Luis Tellez," Federal Reserve Bank, October 19, 1994.

20. Memo, Lawrence Summers to Lloyd Bentsen, "Statement on Mexico," Department of the Treasury, November 21, 1994.

21. Memo, Geithner to Lawrence Summers and Jeffrey Shafer, "Mexico: Planning for the Next Stage," Department of the Treasury, December 5, 1994. The memo refers to a "September options paper" that may have been connected to a brief options memo Summers presented to Bentsen on September 27. Critical portions of that memo were not declassified, but it appears to refer to plans to talk to the Mexicans without a major U.S. policy development effort.

22. Department of the Treasury, "Bi-Weekly Report on Mexico," December 21, 1994.

23. Lawrence Summers to Robert Rubin, "Mexican Devaluation," Department of the Treasury December 21, 1994.

24. Memo, Lissaker to Jeffrey Shafer, "More on Mexican Commercial Banks," Department of the Treasury, January 6, 1995.

25. President Bill Clinton, "Remarks on Loan Guarantees for Mexico," White House, January 18, 1995.

26. Lawrence Summers, "Our Mexican Challenge," remarks at Georgetown University Law Center, Washington, D.C., February 20, 1995 (draft and version prepared for delivery, both in documents released by Senate Banking Committee, with speech misdated as delivered on January 20).

27. Debbie Galant, "Why Wall Street Missed Mexico," *Institutional Investor*, May 1995, pp. 73, 74.

28. Address by Michel Camdessus, managing director of the International Monetary Fund, at the UN World Summit for Social Development, Copenhagen, March 7, 1995.

29. See Barry Eichengreen and Albert Fishlow, *Contending with Capital Flows: What Is Different about the 1990s?* (New York: Council on Foreign Relations Press, 1996) pp. 39–40; Council on Foreign Relations Task Force, *Lessons on the Mexican Peso Crisis*, pp. 31–32.

30. Note the emphasis on the surveillance task of "national finance ministries" in Summers, "Summers on Mexico," p. 47. Aspects of the Summers recommendations are strikingly similar to Eichengreen and Fishlow, *Contending with Capital Flows*, but he does not echo their suggestions for new capital controls.

31. Both Fed and Treasury staff did reportedly analyze the prospect of reducing the trade deficit through devaluation, reaching pessimistic conclusions. Yoichi Funabashi, *Managing the Dollar: From the Plaza to the Louvre*, 2d ed. (Washington, D.C.: Institute for International Economics, 1989), pp. 33–34, 39. Certainly any estimate would have concluded that the J-curve would not begin its upward swing (showing a reduction in the trade deficit) for a number of months, probably for more than a year. Therefore, one can only infer that the political perception of improved terms of trade by Congress was the real object. It was to create this political effect that the Plaza accord was followed, a day later, by a major trade policy initiative. Politics also explains why the Plaza accord communiqué is full of promises of macroeconomic policy changes to change the terms of trade, when in fact the design of the accord relied almost exclusively on exchange rate intervention to drive down the dollar. In judging congressional perceptions, Baker and Darman had little need for intelligence estimates from government agencies. Many other, more technical issues would have required some specialist information and judgment. But on at least one of these, the impact of exchange rate intervention and the effects of unsterilized versus sterilized interventions, no particular analysis appears to have influenced U.S. policymakers, except that they dismissed the pessimistic conclusions about intervention associated with the 1983 G-7 study known as the Jurgensen report. See also the succinct discussion of this point in Nigel Lawson, *The View from No. 11: Memoirs of a Tory Radical* (London: Bantam Press, 1992), pp. 801–2.

32. Testimony of Richard Kerr, acting director of central intelligence, U.S. Congress, Senate, Foreign Relations Committee, *The BCCI Affair*, hearings of the Subcommittee on Terrorism, Part 3, 102d Cong., 1st sess., October 25, 1991, pp. 572–73.

33. Ibid., p. 575.

34. See ibid., pp. 582–90; U.S. Congress, Senate, Select Committee on Intelligence, *Nomination of Robert M. Gates to Be Director of Central Intelligence,* Exec. Rept. 102–19, 102d Cong., 1st sess., October 24, 1991, pp. 188–90.

35. U.S. Congress, Senate, Select Committee on Intelligence, *The Intelligence Community's Involvement in the Banca Nazionale del Lavoro (BNL) Affair*, staff report, 103d Cong., 1st sess., February 1993, pp. 13–14, 55–57. The CIA did know that a British machine tool manufacturer, Matrix Churchill, had been acquired by an Iraqi-controlled front company and had also established a subsidiary company in Ohio. The CIA and DIA recognized that Matrix Churchill was part of Iraq's arms procurement network and reported this information to officials.

36. Ibid., p. 16.

37. Ibid., p. 17. The Justice Department was debating BNL-Rome's culpability during early 1990. Its Atlanta attorneys insisted that Rome did not know, citing extensive efforts in Atlanta to conceal the illegal activities and their own inability to provide any proof of authorization from Rome for the Iraqi loans. Justice was still uneasy, however, and took testimony from BNL-Rome officials in January 1991. As a result of the testimony, "Main Justice finally relented and agreed (not without continued misgivings) to an indictment which did not include BNL employees outside Atlanta," (p. 22).

38. Ibid., p. 36.

39. Ibid., pp. 37–50.

CHAPTER 5

1. Aaron L. Friedberg, *The Weary Titan: Britain and the Experience of Relative Decline, 1895–1905* (Princeton, N.J.: Princeton University Press, 1988), p. 44; emphasis in original. See generally pp. 40–45.

2. Ibid., p. 284.

3. See, for example, the presentation of competing recommendations in *The Free Trade Debate: Reports of the Twentieth Century Fund Task Force on the Future of American Trade Policy* (New York: Priority Press Publications, 1989).

4. Anne Y. Kester, ed., *Behind the Numbers: U.S. Trade in the World Economy* (Washington, D.C.: National Academy Press, 1992), pp. 6, 7, 94. The Panel on Foreign Trade Statistics of the NRC's Committee on National Statistics was chaired by Robert E. Baldwin.

5. Ibid., pp. 15, 25–26.

6. Trade Promotion Coordinating Committee, "Implementation of the National Export Strategy," Year-end Report to the President, Washington, D.C., December 31, 1993, p. 6.

7. Ibid., p. 12.

8. Trade Promotion Coordinating Committee, "Toward a National Export ᵎgy," Report to the U.S. Congress, Washington, D.C., September 1993, p. 17.

9. Gerald F. Seib, "Business Secrets: Some Urge CIA to Go Further in Gathering Economic Intelligence," *Wall Street Journal*, August 4, 1992, p. A7.

10. The United States also tends to encourage rather than prevent foreign acquisition of domestic assets. Occasionally, however, intelligence does alert policymakers to foreign investments that cause concern. In 1992 the U.S. government was advised of a pending acquisition of the missile division of the LTV Corporation by a French firm, Thomson/CSF. CIA and DIA reports about aggressive, clandestine French efforts to acquire foreign technology helped kill the deal. Washington was able to encourage a successful American bid for the target company.

11. Such a requirement for comprehensive data can be contrasted with the general, narrative list of foreign trade barriers compiled from embassy reporting and Washington agencies by the Office of the U.S. Trade Representative. See *1993 National Trade Estimate on Foreign Trade Barriers* (Washington, D.C.: Office of the United States Trade Representative, 1993). The American embassy in Tokyo, under Ambassador Michael Armacost, was, however, highly regarded by some for the wide ranging analytical work it has done on Japanese industrial organization in connection with the Bush administration's Structural Impediments Initiative.

12. In 1982, Houdaille Industries filed a complaint (legally flawed) about Japanese government subsidy and protection for its machine tool industry. The Commerce Department formally recommended import quotas nearly two years after the original complaint was filed, and two more years passed before the White House finally decided to seek voluntary restraint agreements. In the meantime about a quarter of the U.S. machine tool industry went out of business. See Clyde V. Prestowitz, Jr., *Trading Places: How We Allowed Japan to Take the Lead* (New York: Basic Books, 1988), pp. 213–29.

13. On the 1995 French and Japanese episodes, see Tim Weiner, "C.I.A. Confirms Blunders During Economic Spying on France," *New York Times*, March 13, 1996, p. A10; David E. Sanger and Tim Weiner, "Emerging Role for the C.I.A.: Economic Spy," *New York Times*, October 15, 1995, p. A1; David E. Sanger, "When Spies Look Out for the Almighty Buck," *New York Times*, October 22, 1995, p. E4.

14. Prepared remarks by Julius Katz, "Foreign Economic Policy and Intelligence," Intelligence Fellows Program at Wye Center, Maryland, August 17, 1993, pp. 16–17.

15. See David B. Yoffie and Laura D'Andrea Tyson, "Semiconductors: From Manipulated to Managed Trade," in Yoffie, ed., *Global Trade and Competition* (Cambridge, Mass.: Harvard Business School Press, forthcoming); Laura D. Tyson, *Who's Bashing Whom? Trade Conflict in High-Technology Industries* (Washington, D.C.: Institute for International Economics, 1992), pp. 85–154;

"The Semiconductor Industry Association and the Trade Dispute with Japan (A)," Case 9-387-105, Harvard Business School, revised March 1991, pp. 1–9; Timothy J. C. O'Shea, "The U.S.-Japan Semiconductor Problem," Pew Case Study in International Affairs no. 139, Graduate School of Public and International Affairs, University of Pittsburgh, 1988.

16. See "The Semiconductor Industry Association," pp. 9–11; Andrew Dick, "Learning by Doing and Dumping in the Semiconductor Industry," *Journal of Law and Economics* 34 (April 1991): 133–57.

17. U.S. efforts since 1987, including the 1991 U.S.-Japan Semiconductor Agreement, have focused more on market access than on dumping. See Semiconductor Industry Association, "Obtaining Access to the Japanese Market: Interim Report on the U.S.-Japan Semiconductor Agreement," Washington, D.C., May 1993. This change in emphasis may both result from the difficulty of judging given prices as amounting to dumping and also because of divergent viewpoints within the industry, since several American firms benefited from the pricing of Japanese products.

18. Katz, "Foreign Economic Policy and Intelligence," pp. 13–14.

19. A survey of the problem is Peter Schweizer, *Friendly Spies: How America's Allies Are Using Economic Espionage to Steal Our Secrets* (New York: Atlantic Monthly Press, 1993). For an astute analysis of the foreign espionage threat, see Kay Oliver, "Analyzing Economic Espionage," *Studies in Intelligence* 36 (Spring 1992): 23–27 (declassified). For some recent accounts of foreign espionage against American industry, often defense contractors, see Bill Gertz, "Allies' Spying in U.S. Reported," *Washington Times*, February 22, 1996, p. 9; John Mintz, "CIA: French Targeted Secrets of U.S. Firms," *Washington Post*, April 27, 1993, p. C1.

20. Figures cited in statement of Mark Lowenthal, Congressional Research Service, U.S. Congress, Senate, hearings before the Select Committee on Intelligence, 103d Cong., 1st sess., August 3, 1993, pp. 4–5.

21. For a solid survey of issues in industrial espionage from the business perspective, see Richard Eells and Peter Nehemkis, *Corporate Intelligence and Espionage: A Blueprint for Executive Decision Making* (New York: Free Press, 1984).

22. Samuel B. Porteous, "Economic Espionage: New Target for CSIS [Canadian Security Intelligence Service]," *Canadian Business Review* (Ottawa), Winter 1993.

23. Testimony of Robert M. Gates before the Economic and Commercial Law Subcommittee, U.S. Congress, House, Judiciary Committee, 102d Cong., 2d sess., April 29, 1992. See also Leonard Fuld, *Monitoring the Competition* (New York: Wiley, 1988); Hans Porter, *Nichts bleibt geheim: eine Reise in die Welt der Industriespionage* (Bad Oldesloe, West Germany: Kroeg, 1988); John J. McGonagle, *Outsmarting the Competition* (New York: McGraw-Hill, 1993).

24. This list of counterintelligence questions is drawn from the Gates testimony before the Economic and Commercial Law Subcommittee.

25. See also Michael Saunders, *Protecting Your Business Secrets* (New York: Nichols, 1985).

26. William T. Warner, "Economic Espionage: A Bad Idea," *National Law Journal*, April 12, 1993, pp. 13, 14.

27. See 18 U.S.C. sections 791–794, 798.

28. Maurice Ernst, "Economic Intelligence in CIA," *Studies in Intelligence* 28, no. 4 (Winter 1984): 21.

29. On the range of views, see Schweizer, *Friendly Spies*, pp. 290–300; Warner, "Economic Espionage," p. 13; Marvin Ott, "Limits on Spying," *Washington Post*, August 11, 1993, p. A19.

30. Opening statement of Senator Dennis De Concini, U.S. Congress, Senate, Hearings before the Select Committee on Intelligence, 103d Cong., 1st sess., August 5, 1993.

31. Prepared statement of John Hayden, U.S. Congress, Senate, Hearings before the Select Committee on Intelligence, 103d Cong., 1st sess., August 5, 1993. Another veteran of international business, Thomas Faught, also testified that "I see no value in the US government engaging in clandestine industrial or economic intelligence activities, although I believe the government well could have a role in protecting American industry from foreign intelligence collection." Prepared statement of Thomas Faught, U.S. Congress, Senate, Hearings before the Select Committee on Intelligence, 103d Cong., 1st sess., August 5, 1993.

32. Statement of Mark Lowenthal, U.S. Congress, Senate, Hearings before the Select Committee on Intelligence, 103d Cong., 1st sess., August 3, 1993.

33. A standard definition of a trade secret under common law is "any formula, pattern, device or compilation of information which is used in one's business, and which gives him an opportunity to obtain an advantage over competitors who do not know or use it. . . . The subject matter of a trade secret must be secret. Matters of public knowledge or of general knowledge in an industry cannot be appropriated by one as his secret." Restatement (First) of Torts, section 757, comment b (1939).

34. The quote is from an illustration of the technique to "show how a whole landscape of information" can be developed on the Japanese electronics industry. Jon Sigurdson and Patricia Nelson, "Intelligence Gathering and Japan: The Elusive Role of Grey Intelligence," *International Journal of Intelligence and Counterintelligence* 5, no. 1 (1991): 17–34.

35. Nicolas Jequier and Stevan Dedijer, "Information, Knowledge and Intelligence: A General Overview," in Dedijer and Jequier, eds., *Intelligence for Economic Development: An Inquiry into the Role of the Knowledge Industry* (Oxford: Berg, 1987), pp. 19–20.

36. Though the Brown-Rudman commission on the future of American intelligence misunderstood the nature of economic intelligence and did not consider the subject in depth, it did examine this question of industrial espionage. Its conclusions mirror those offered here. Report of the Commission on the Roles and Capabilities of the United States Intelligence Community, *Preparing for the 21st Century: An Appraisal of U.S. Intelligence* (Washington, D.C.: Government Printing Office, 1996), pp. 23–24.

❙ INDEX

I About the Authors

Allan E. Goodman is academic dean of the School of Foreign Service at Georgetown University. He served as presidential briefing coordinator for the director of central intelligence during the Carter administration and is coauthor (with Bruce D. Berkowitz) of *Strategic Intelligence for American National Security* (Princeton University Press).

Gregory F. Treverton is director of the International Security and Defense Policy Center, RAND Corporation. He has served the director of central intelligence as vice chair of the National Intelligence Council and he has been senior fellow and director of the Europe-America Project and the Project on America's Task in a Changed World for the Council on Foreign Relations. He is the author of many books and articles on intelligence, security, and American foreign policy.

Philip Zelikow is associate professor of public policy, John F. Kennedy School of Government, Harvard University. A former diplomat, he has served as director for European security affairs on the staff of the National Security Council. He is the coauthor (with Condoleezza Rice) of *Germany Unified and Europe Transformed: A Study in Statecraft* (Harvard University Press).